HITLER'S MIRACLE WEAPONS

HITLER'S MIRACLE WEAPONS

Secret Nuclear Weapons of the Third Reich and their Carrier Systems Volume 1: The Luftwaffe and Kriegsmarine

Friedrich Georg

HELION & COMPANY LTD

Helion & Company Limited
Unit 8 Amherst Business Centre
Budbrooke Road
Warwick
CV34 5WE
England
Tel. 01926 499619
Email: info@helion.co.uk
Website: www.helion.co.uk
X (formerly Twitter): @Helionbooks
Facebook: @HelionBooks
Visit our blog at https://helionbooks.wordpress.com/

Published by Helion & Company 2003. This new edition 2024
Originally published as *Hitlers Siegeswaffen Band 1: Luftwaffe und Marine* by AMUN-Verlag in co-operation with Heinrich-Jung-Verlagsgesellschaft mbH, Germany, 2000

Designed and typeset by Carnegie Publishing Ltd, Lancaster, Lancashire
Cover designed by Paul Hewitt, Battlefield Design (www.battlefield-design.co.uk)

ISBN 978-1-804517-26-0

British Library Cataloguing-in-Publication Data.
A catalogue record for this book is available from the British Library.

For details of other military history titles published by Helion & Company Limited, contact the above address, or visit our website: http://www.helion.co.uk

We always welcome receiving book proposals from prospective authors.

Contents

Acknowledgements

This book could never have been written without the unstinting support of a large number of people. I need therefore to give my sincere thanks to those who are not individually mentioned here, as well as to those who are.

I should like to give special thanks to my publisher, Herr Thomas Mehner, for his help and advice while I was working on the book. A most important contribution to the success of this work was made by Herr Igor Shestakov. His drawings enabled us to picture, for the first time, many of the projects of the period.

I should like to thank Herr Manfred Griehl (Koblenz), Mr Richard Lewis Mendes (USA), Herr Kristian Knaack (Bonn), Mr Henry Stevens (USA), and Frau Gerolf (Deutsches Museum in Munich), for the help they gave me. A outstanding contribution was made by my secretary, Uschi. From my countless dictation sessions, and scraps of paper bearing corrections, she was able to conjure up a text that made sense.

Extra special thanks, and also an apology, go to my wife and my three children, for the patience and support which they mustered during the years I was working on this book.

Foreword

When in 1988 I published two books about secret terrestrial technologies, I had no idea what the consequences would be. The discussions, set in motion by the author Harald Fäth, caused a sensation. His book, *1945 - Thuringia's Manhattan Project,* concerned possible production of nuclear weapons, and long distance rockets, in the area Jonastal, a troop exercise area in Ohrdruf, Thuringia. Until now the book has been distributed only in German-speaking areas. However, over the course of time, information arrived from all parts of the world. It confirmed the author's hypothesis that essential elements of the history of high technology, in the Third Reich, had been concealed from the general public.

Remarkably, no criticism was to be heard from the camp of the official historians. Instead, from some representatives of that camp, more confirmatory information was received. However, it is true, they requested that no names be mentioned. The doubts, that something is not right about the official presentation of this history of technology, are daily growing more powerful.

In the meantime, for instance, throughout the world researchers are convinced that elements of knowledge concerning German miracle weapons are being concealed from the public. Thus, official bodies continue to insist that during the 1940s the Third Reich, although it led the field in theoretical nuclear physics, had not tackled the project of applying the theory militarily, and had left the field to the Americans. Moreover Hitler, they said, had not understood the potential of such a weapon and had preferred conventional projects.

Goethe once said that you had to preach the truth 'every day anew', in order to combat the errors and lies widespread among the masses. That wise statement also applies to the subject of German nuclear and miracle weapons. What seems incomprehensible to me is the fact that all those who, up to now, have re-written the history of the atomic bomb, have also neglected to carry out basic research. Much that was written, it seems to me, was filled with errors, half-truths and even lies.

For example, did those authors not know of the reports immediately after the end of the armed confrontation in the European theatre of war? Reports were published in broadsheet American east coast newspapers, such as the *New York Times.* Were those authors not aware of the admission, by the American Department of Defense and its subordinate authorities, that the Third Reich was working on an extremely advanced atomic bomb project? Those reports were never denied.

For a brief moment, in the euphoria of victory, the Allies had lifted a tiny corner of the veil of secrecy concerning German miracle weapons, only to let it fall again a little later, when the Cold War against the Soviet Union began. Suddenly, people realised that what had been found in Germany represented a considerable strategic advantage over the Russians. As a result, the subject came under the rubric of national security, and was taboo regarding any further disclosures.

If there was such a far-advanced programme of atomic weapons research in the Third Reich, logically there must also have been locations, personnel and all the unusual things that go along with them. In fact, that was the case. There were indications of all those. To date, it is unclear which procedures were used by German physicists in their attempts to obtain the basic material for making the atomic bomb. However, it appears it must have been a simpler procedure than that used by the Americans. Within the Manhattan project vast quantities of personnel, money and time were used. Moreover, it is clear that what the German nuclear physicists repeatedly presented to the public could only have been the tip of the iceberg.

Significantly, there were many German-speaking nuclear experts, among whom some must have been considerably more successful than only those who were named. In that connection, something known to few, is that during the 1950s Peron, the Argentinian head of state, wanted, by means of such a project, to provide the economy of his country with atomic energy and thus make it competitive. It is said that he employed 2,000 German-speaking nuclear experts. That is not the only extraordinary fact.

Another question is why the German *Luftwaffe,* towards the end of the war, was making feverish efforts to revive the project for the long-range 'America bomber'. Amazingly, that was done in the face of Allied air supremacy, and the continuing bombardment of German cities by Anglo-American aircraft. However, Göring thought it a possibility and also viewed it as a propaganda plus.

It is precisely that question which the author, Friedrich Georg, pursues in this book. Over the course of 12 years he has gathered together a collection of remarkable material. The first volume is now to be made available to the public. The information will, I am sure, cause even the most determined sceptic to think again. For example, the *Oberkommando der Luftwaffe* (OKL) requested that long-range bombers should be designed for carrying bomb weights which, until now, have never been able to be verified, i.e. 4 tonnes. It seems impossible to keep such information secret. Is the relevant information, for understandable reasons, being kept secret even to this day? Or, towards the end of the war, had the Third Reich's *Luftwaffe* leadership simply 'lost their minds'?

I have already said that the indications are growing that significant facts relating to the history of technology are being concealed. A lot of material remains under lock and key in Allied archives. In the case of the material in some archives, the period during which access is prohibited has even been extended. But why should that be so? Do those who are responsible consider that we, the people of the information age, are incapable of dealing with the truth? Or must the documents be kept back, in order to support what one might call a possible system of lies. The fact is that a true reappraisal of history is only possible when the last secret document in Allied archives has been declassified, and is available for historical research. History cannot be built on half-truths.

At this point I add my own point of view. Recently, in my opinion, there have been the first tentative attempts, by representatives of the official side, to use polemical methods to undermine the arguments put forward by some authors. This is, by the way, a favourite procedure if you yourself cannot bring any factual counter-argument against a theory. For instance, in all seriousness, it is being maintained that certain information was only being disseminated to force the responsible authorities to react. In this connection too there is also talk of 'profiteering'.

To me, all this is sheer polemics intended to conceal the real heart of the matter, and to evade the interest of the general public. In the first place, authors are concerned to find out the truth, which should be the most precious possession of every civilised person. It may be that such high aspirations are foreign to many responsible officials. In view of allegations of corruption, and scandals, regarding donations to political parties here in Germany, that would not be surprising in my opinion. In the search for the truth, the possibility that occasional errors can enter into chains of argument cannot be excluded, particularly in view of the difficult situation relating to sources. But, in any event, this should be a reason for discussions relevant to the issue, not for unqualified attacks.

Moreover, care should be taken. If it should turn out that the truth is different from that which has been revealed to date, it would shed very significant light on the knowledge and analytical capabilities of the 'experts'. It would show what 'expert' knowledge is worth. In many cases, 'expert' knowledge is based on hearsay and was never subjected to scrutiny by those involved. In the history of technology of recent decades, there are simply too many contradictions that have yet to be explained. It is a legitimate right to be able to subject them to scrutiny.

Friedrich Georg's book brings a further accumulation of information, from many sources, that shows there were not only one but several German nuclear weapons, and their carrier systems. The information, here presented to the public will, for some, be 'hard to swallow'. But this is only the beginning of a developing process. The author and German publishers are not responsible for the fact that there are contradictions in history, and in the history of technology. We are not responsible for the Allied system of secrecy. We are not responsible for the evasions and inaccuracies that lead every serious minded person to reflect and to query. Responsibility for such things belongs, exclusively, to those people who have deliberately misled the general public that now may feel it has been manipulated. However, year on year, more accurate information becomes available.

Thomas Mehner (German publisher of Friedrich Georg's book)

Introduction

'He who controls the past, programmes the future'.
Valentin Falin

'I refused to use a weapon which could have destroyed the whole of civilization'. Those words were spoken by Hermann Göring when he was arrested by the Allies on 7 May 1945.[1] To his American guards this statement remained so completely incomprehensible that they passed it on to posterity. What can he have meant by it? Was it here that the first outlines of a terrible secret were already beginning to emerge? Hermann Göring, as former Supreme Commander of the *Luftwaffe* and Head of the Third Reich's 'Reich Advisory Council on Research', was kept very closely informed of all secret weapons development programmes.[2]

This book is the result of 12 years' work. The idea for it came about by chance, in the context of my interest in scale-models of planes. The special group of enthusiasts to which I belong has, for a long time, been involved in a project for the converting of standard plastic model kits. In converting them we create particular individual models, mainly of military aircraft, which must still be based on reality. For that purpose I began to study military literature.

In one book, I came across a piece of information that aroused my curiosity. In 1945, Allied troops in Prague were said to have captured a Heinkel He 177 that was equipped to drop nuclear weapons. Of course, I was aware how strange the information was, because official historians still insist that Germany had given up nuclear research for military purposes after 1942. Thus, no German nuclear weapons could exist. So of course I had to investigate the obvious contradiction. There were, in fact, verifiable photographs of the converted aircraft.

Those remarkable circumstances started my activities as a researcher, and finally led me on to the trail of Hitler's 'miracle' weapons. My research not only brought to light the strange circumstances concerning German nuclear research, but also revealed the carriers of the so-called miracle weapons. However, as the years passed, I made many new friends among those who were also working on the subject. They made available to me valuable information and material without which this present work would never have been possible.

When I began my researches I could never have imagined what I was to find. What was particularly remarkable in the process, was that I scarcely ever came across any contradictory data. On the contrary, suddenly it seemed like a jigsaw puzzle when all the various pieces begin to fit together. The subject of miracle weapons went far beyond atomic bombs. Intercontinental aircraft, multi-stage rockets, and the forerunners of present day nuclear submarines were investigated, as much as were weapons of an entirely new type of construction. Even today scarcely anything is known of the latter. Such weapons systems are discussed in this volume and, in due course, following volumes. After long research, there is now so much material available that it is possible to show a definitive picture of development at that time.

It may be, because of difficulty with the material, that many inexactitudes or mistakes have crept in. Whether this book represents a fanciful interpretation of chance events, or whether, staying with the idea of the puzzle, it succeeds in assembling the many separate pieces into a conclusive picture, is left for each reader to decide. Therefore the discussion is open.

As of now, it seems to me that any writing on historical subjects is mostly done for three reasons. These are firstly, history 'as accusation', secondly history 'as a quarrel with history', and thirdly history 'as justification'. Certainly, in relation to World War II, there are already in existence far too many books, in my opinion, that use history principally to accuse and/or to justify. This book belongs to none of the three categories. The purpose of my book is to awaken the curiosity of the reader, so that each can ask, what was the true course of historical events? If this book can perhaps lead some of its readers to begin their own personal research, on the subject of miracle weapons, then my work has served its purpose.

From a present-day perspective, and in the knowledge of a great deal of detailed information, it seems to me that mankind can think itself lucky that those weapons never came to be used. According to the information that I have amassed, in 1945/46 modern civilisation escaped, by a hair's breadth, a first nuclear exchange between Germany, America and Japan. If that exchange had taken place, the consequences for all involved would have been unimaginable.

As I said at the beginning, all this started with my research into a particular variant of the Heinkel He 177. Since then I have discovered enough details to be able to begin the conversion of my scale-model. But to be able to complete it, down to the last detail, I still need a little more information. Perhaps one of the readers of my book can help me?

PART I

Pre-history and Development

Search for Evidence

Before David Irving's remarkable work, *Der Traum von der deutschen Atombombe* (The Dream of the German Atomic Bomb), was published in 1967, it was not even clear whether there had ever been a German nuclear research programme during World War II. The reason was that because of the thoroughness with which the Allied military intelligence, and other intelligence services, worked in the post-war period, almost every trace of evidence that such a programme could ever have existed was wiped out.[3]

Although so much time has now passed since the end of World War II, it seems that it is still not clear what happened in many decisive areas. But there are people who continue to try to prop up the 'edifice of lies' which was erected at the time. An example of that is the part played, in influencing the whole course of the war, by cracking the German and Japanese secret codes, i.e. Magic/ULTRA.[4] For how long was the general public misled on that subject, I wonder?

This is even truer for the history of Germany's nuclear weapons, which, according to official opinion, should not have existed. The official line is that German scientists and technicians had never worked on such weapons, and that Hitler had not understood the strategic significance of A-weapons. New information, 'curiosities', and hard facts, *ad absurdum*, lead those assertions.

Considering the nature of the case it is understandable, with regard to the actual nuclear research programme of the Third Reich, that many things are still unknown. But there is the justified hope, that one day even those blank areas will be filled in.

Miracle Weapons - Fact or Fiction?

Adolf Hitler never made any secret of the fact that he would bring World War II to an end by using a 'miracle' weapon. He always insisted however, that Germany had not been sufficiently prepared for the early outbreak of a war.

On 19 September 1939, immediately after his 'satisfactory' conclusion of the Polish campaign, Hitler gave a speech in the Danzig Guild Hall before members of the NSDAP. He was already threatening to use new kinds of weapons to bring the war to a victorious end. 'The moment could very quickly be coming', he said, 'when we could use a weapon which would prevent us ever being attacked again'. From that time onwards, Germany's belief in victorious miracle weapons, animated the resistance at the front and at home, right to the bitter end. But the war passed without such miracle weapons having ever been used. During the post-war period, therefore, the subject of miracle weapons was dismissed as 'lies, to encourage people to hold on'. The dominant belief in miracle weapons, widespread in large sections of the German people until the end of the war, is regarded even now as an example of Goebbels' skill at propaganda.

But were there really no such things as miracle weapons? Today there are many books on the subject of German secret weapons that scarcely broach the subject of miracle weapons. The subject seems to be deliberately ignored, suppressed, falsified and made into a taboo. A reappraisal of the material would have revealed surprising connections, not to mention the effects on 'official history', and on our understanding of high technology. But, however strong the lies and cover-ups may be, in the long run the truth cannot be suppressed. The fact is that World War II was also a war of high technology. The Allies tried everything they could to get hold of the knowledge of German specialists.

There are sceptics who doubt the official history of miracle weapons that has prevailed until now, and assert that they must have existed. The insistence is always made that those 'unknown' weapons systems would quite certainly have been used if they had actually existed. In addition, the post-war statements are produced of the responsible German personnel, such as Wernher von Braun and Albert Speer. In fact the two of them were active at the very front line of secret weapons development. Their statements are repeated when proof is necessary to refute the arguments of the critics. Thus, von Braun was suddenly only an 'advocate of peaceful space travel', and was only 'thinking of future interplanetary flights', while Speer confirms that 'within his area of armaments there was nothing', and certainly 'nothing like miracle weapons', otherwise he would have 'known about it'.

But that argument overlooks the fact that all those people, because of their previous prominent position in the Third Reich, had a lot to lose in the post-war period. Why risk your neck by talking, if keeping quiet about certain information might at least guarantee that you survive? So can it be held against them if they, like many others at the time, only told of things which suited them, or the victorious Powers, and denied the rest in a conspiracy of silence?

For decades, nobody was interested in pointing out the lies and contradictions. Thus, after the atom bomb was dropped on Hiroshima in August 1945, interned German nuclear scientists at Farm Hall in England, drew up a joint memorandum in which, they declared they had never worked on an atomic bomb. But even then the scientists Dr Bagge and Dr Korsching at first refused to have anything to do with the memorandum. They said that it was a political document and was 'not appropriate'.[5] But even today that 'political document' is an important piece of evidence.

As early as 1951, Henry Pickers' important seminal work, *Hitler's Table Talk*, was first published. It could have been realised then that many things in the previously published 'history' of Hitler's miracle weapons could not have been true.[6] Nevertheless, it was to take until the 1990s for discussion to get going properly. It was in the territories of the former GDR, in Czechoslovakia and in Poland that important elements of Hitler's miracle weapons programme had been built. Then suddenly, in the 1990s it was possible to publish everything that had previously been hushed up for decades.

With this book, the author hopes to be able to contribute, in a small way, to setting straight the historical truth that has been taught to date. In this connection there is much that is still dubious or imprecise, and needing further research. But clearly, much that has been told to us for many decades would appear to be false.

In view of the former dictatorship in the Third Reich, and of Germany's defeat in World War II and the ensuing Cold War, even if that approach had a measure of justification in the eyes of many, now, surely, the moment has come to reveal the truth. The 'trick', practised by officials in positions of power, of waiting to publish the truth until the last eyewitnesses of events are dead, cannot work. Far too many documents, photographs, and items of documentary evidence, that have already been saved, turn the hitherto accepted truth on its head. Therefore the old view of the world can no longer be maintained.

Unfortunately, towards the end of World War II, many irreplaceable documents were lost or deliberately destroyed. But it is clear that the crucial evidence is still in the archives of the victorious Powers. In this connection, we only need recall Max von Laue's 'atomic confessions', to which access is denied until 2017. What Speer is alleged to have said about Kammler is also still secret. The extensive collection of files, relating to both of those, is securely locked up in secret British vaults. Therefore the appeal goes out to the former Allies that they should make all the material available for research.

Start and 'Abandonment' of Nuclear Weapons Programme

All the main belligerent countries in World War II, even including neutral states such as Holland were, at that stage in the armed conflict, involved in carrying out research on nuclear weapons. But when World War II broke out in September 1939, Germany was the only one of the world powers to have a military department. Under Dr Diebner, it was concerned exclusively with studying the military implications of nuclear fission.[7]

As early as 1941 a meeting of the *Heereswaffenamt* (HWA) took place. A study of reliable reports, from agents in the USA, had shown that in the USA, in the area of nuclear physics, work was intensifying. (See section in Part III 'What did Hitler know about the Manhattan Project?') Reputable scientists raised the 'various' possibilities for producing a propellant, or an explosive, by means of nuclear fission. To investigate further, the HWA decided to enlarge the experimental station in the KWI (Kaiser Wilhelm Institut) in Berlin-Dahlem. Similar experimental institutes in Gottow (HWA) and Miersdorf near Berlin (*Reichspost* Research Institute: RPF) were enlarged for the same purpose. In a number of agreements it was decided to use an *Uranbrenner*,[8] as a means of arriving at an atomic bomb.[9] How far collaboration progressed in that connection, between the HWA and the RPF, and a SS atomic bomb project, which it is highly likely was carried out in the Prague area (Skoda), and later in Thuringia, has still to be researched.

Today, in the official version of history, 6 June 1942 is repeatedly given as the date on which Germany finally gave up striving to create an atomic bomb.[10] Afterwards, it is said, Germany was wholly concerned with achieving such 'noble' goals as the use of nuclear energy. Reich Armaments Minister Speer, the nuclear physicist Heisenberg, and *Generalfeldmarschall* Milch all agree, in their post-war memoirs, in giving that date as the one when the programme ceased. But there are no official papers with the corresponding 'Führer orders'. There are no orders to cease the programme, nor even file notes concerning the

Map of the known German nuclear research establishments (according to David Irving, *Der Traum der deutschen Atombombe*). From a present-day perspective, this picture appears incomplete, because some important places directly connected with German nuclear physics are missing: Ohrdruf (near Stadtilm, Thuringia), Melk and Bornholm.

discontinuation of the nuclear weapons research. Remarkably, until now, almost no-one has critically questioned those circumstances.

Without specifying an exact date, Speer states in his memoirs that in the autumn of 1942 he had another discussion with the nuclear experts. When they informed him that no decisive results could be expected sooner than 'within three or four years', that 'we discontinued the atomic bomb project'. According to reports which all agreed, had they not already discontinued the project in June.

Hitler, the Supreme Commander, certainly saw things very differently. At the end of September 1942, he informed *Generalfeldmarschall* Erwin Rommel about the new weapons. Hitler said that such weapons would soon 'relieve his position' in North Africa. Hitler also told him about a secret new explosive that had such explosive power that it would 'throw a man from his horse at a distance of over two kilometres'. That was nothing other than a reference to the atomic bomb.

We are also led to believe that the Germans, at that time leading the world in the field of nuclear research, remained from summer 1942 right up to the end of the war at practically the same level of knowledge. We are told that in the three years after 1942 they had only made as many discoveries as they could have made in as many months.[11] As a world power, Germany had everything needed to produce an atomic bomb. Those opportunities were recognised and acted upon. The nuclear project of the Third Reich had enough capable scientists, the greatest uranium reserves in the world at that time, heavy water, and of course the interest of the German leadership.

In any event, right in the middle of the war, and in full knowledge that the Allies were striving to produce nuclear weapons, would they have been able simply to give up the nuclear weapons project in that way, even if they had wanted to? In my opinion, definitely not.

Even in published history the Germans were the first to achieve positive neutron production, with their Leipzig kiln L 4. Unfortunately, on 23 June 1942, a nuclear accident occurred on that project, although at that time Germany's atomic bomb programme had, allegedly, already been discontinued. Nevertheless, a statement made by Professor Döpel, who was involved in the experiment, slipped through the post-war censorship. In his statement, Döpel had said after the accident, that 'hundreds more would be killed to achieve this last goal, the atomic bomb'.[12] Those prophetic words would never have been said, if there were no German nuclear weapons programme after June 1942. But shockingly, they were then to come true in 1944/45.

In actual fact, until the end of the war, there were several nuclear weapons programmes within the Third Reich. They were partly in competition and partly linked. Spread across almost the entire area under its control, they even included islands such as Bornholm. Even on Fuerteventura, in the Canary Islands, the rumour stubbornly persists to this day, that work had been carried out on Germany's nuclear weapons and rockets on the Jandia peninsula.

A large number of German firms, under the overall direction of Siemens, AEG and IG Farben, were involved in those programmes. The State side of the operation comprised the Reich Research Council, the German *Reichspost* Research Institute, the Army (HWA) and the SS (Technical Department). It is still not clear to what extent elements of the *Wehrmacht*, the *Luftwaffe* and the *Kriegsmarine* were involved in developing nuclear weapons, beyond involvement with carrier systems.

The story of power and intrigue within the competing research groups and institutions of the Third Reich must be dealt with in a separate publication (see tables on the following pages).

The objection could now be raised, given that all the above were true, that a correspondingly high 'level of urgency' would have been ordered for the nuclear weapons programme. Normally that would also have been the case. But there were proven cases of projects to which no official 'urgency' could be assigned, because of secrecy, but which had a greater degree of urgency than all other programmes. With a degree of probability verging on certainty, that would have been the case with the atomic bomb.

What sort of miracle weapons were completed? How were they completed? How was it planned to use them? Developments went in various directions, and were unnecessarily prolonged because of petty jealousies among the competing teams. Treachery and sabotage also played a considerable part.

Irrespective of what Speer, Heisenberg and Milch may have stated in the post war period, it is precisely from 1942 that weapons, of 'that kind', were demanded by Hitler and Himmler. The war situation was growing more and more unfavourable. It had become clear to Hitler in the winter of 1941 that the war could no longer be won by conventional methods. When it was nearly too late, and the strategic situation of the Third Reich had already drastically deteriorated, the miracle weapons seemed to move within reach.

Tables showing decentralisation of German military nuclear research

The three main nuclear research groups in the Third Reich (1944/45)*

The official uranium project

Group leader	Heisenberg	Diebner, Harteck
Location	Berlin	Gottow, Stadtilm/ Ohrdruf
Military aims of research	Atomic propulsion system for U-boats	Uranium bomb Isotope bomb Hydrogen bomb

The RPF (Reichspost Research Institute) nuclear project

Group leader	Houtermans	von Ardenne
Location	Berlin/Lichterfelde	
Military aims of research	Isotope bomb	Uranium bomb
	Atomic propulsion system for U-boats Atomic rocket propulsion system	

The SS nuclear project

Group leader	Seuffert (?)	Stetter, ?	?	?
Location	Ohrdruf, Hirschberg	Bad Sachsa, Vienna, Innsbruck	Prague	Melk
Military aims of research	Uranium bomb	Plutonium bomb	Atomic aircraft propulsion system ?	Atomic aircraft propulsion system Uranium bomb Plutonium bomb

*Important ancillary research groups in the Third Reich**

Group leader	?	Zippermayer	Haxel	Daellenbach	Grothe
Location	Schloss Sigmaringen	Lofer (Tyrol)	Dänisch-Nienhof (Kiel)	Bissingen	Celle
Military purpose	Radioactive gases	Special carbon-based explosives with nuclear isotopes	Hydrogen bomb	Production of plutonium	Isotope bomb Uranium bomb

* Note: These tables represent the current state of knowledge as at August 2000 and were created on the basis of available information. It is to be assumed that cross-connections existed between the individual research teams, for instance between Heisenberg - Houtermans, Diebner - Seuffert, Harteck - Grothe, Heisenberg - Daellenbach.

This outline only names the better-known locations and does not exclude the possibility of there having been other important research groups. The following locations are listed as examples of such research institutes or production centres little known to the general public: Tegernsee, Leipzig (Taucha), Lehesten, Porta Westfalica, Roggendorf, Peenemünde/Bornholm, the Leitha mountains and the Carinthia area.

Breakthrough in Summer 1944

After tenacious research in the two years after the summer of 1942, a decisive breakthrough was finally made towards the middle of 1944. For that reason, in June 1944, Heinrich Himmler announced to a conference of top NSDAP party leaders that great progress had been made in the area of 'new kinds' of explosives.[13] Had Germany's atomic bomb already been fully developed from July 1944? Certainly a number of corroborative statements,[14] obtained through contemporary research and information, agree in pointing to that date.

According to the statements, two groups of scientists working under Dr Ingenieur Seuffert (SS) and Dr Diebner (*Wehrmacht*) succeeded in producing the prototype of an 'A-weapon' in a Thuringian experimental installation for technical nuclear experimentation. The 'master plumber', Gerhard Rundnagel, worked in the nuclear experimental laboratory in Stadtilm.

At a hearing in the 1970s, held by the former State Security Service of the German Democratic Republic, Rundnagel gave an account of conversations. He had had them at the beginning of July 1944, with the scientist Dr Rehbein, who also worked at the laboratory. According to him, Dr Rehbein said that 'within a few days you will hear a decisive announcement upon which the fate of the war depends'. Then, on 20 July 1944, the assassination attempt on Hitler took place. When Rundnagel asked Dr Rehbein whether it was this that he had meant, Rehbein only laughed and said, 'now it will not be used. The war is lost'. In other conversations, Dr Rehbein told Herr Rundnagel that what was being developed there had greater explosive force than anything he could even imagine, as a former military engineer. With one single bomb, he said, you could annihilate all life within a radius of 20 kilometres, even if there were a hundred thousand people. When the incredulous Rundnagel continued with his questions, Dr Rehbein only said, smiling, that the entire bomb was only a few decimetres long, but weighed about eight kilograms. When Rundnagel asked whether he could see 'the thing', Dr Rehbein just waved him aside, because that could have cost both of them their lives.

What is interesting, in this connection, is Rundnagel's statement that the Stadtilm experimental institute 'had not been completely built at that time'. It had not yet been working to its fullest extent, and everything the scientists had done there, he said, did not really 'look like work'. That would also seem to indicate that the real work on the nuclear weapon was not carried out in Stadtilm itself, but in *Object Burg*, which was first mentioned by H. Fäth. *Object Burg* consisted of several installations in the area of the Ohrdruf/Crawinkel troop exercise area. Unlimited resources were available, and approved, for the work carried out there in the experimental nuclear factory, if a reliable source is to be believed.[15]

There was a direct connection between *Object Burg* in Ohrdruf, and Diebner's laboratory in Stadtilm, although the nature of the connection is not quite clear. In the nuclear centre experiments were also carried out by other Berlin research groups, e.g. HWA, SS, KWI and the *Reichspost* Research Institute. Even Japanese scientists worked there. Whether the Stetter group, later very successful in Innsbruck, worked for a time in Ohrdruf is not known, but it is possible.

Of course, Adolf Hitler learned of the progress that had been achieved in developing the German nuclear weapon. On 5 August 1944, during a conversation with *Feldmarschall* Keitel, Foreign Minister Ribbentrop, and the Romanian Marshal Antonescu, Hitler spoke covertly about atomic bombs.[16] He pointed, as Himmler had done before him in June, to the recent German work on new explosives, 'development of which had been brought up to the experimental stage'. He added that, in his opinion, 'the qualitative leap from explosives currently in use, to these new types of explosive substances, was greater than the leap from black gunpowder to the explosive substances in use at the beginning of the war'.

The difficulties were the same with all new weapons, Hitler explained. He said he had ordered that no weapon should be used, if counter-measures against it had not already been developed in Germany. For this reason, he said, a new, recently developed mine had not yet been used. Germany, he said, had a total of four secret weapons. The V-1, i.e. the flying bomb, and the V-2, i.e. the rocket, were only two of them. Another of those weapons, he said, had such a powerful effect that within a radius of 3-4 kilometres from the impact point, all human life would be annihilated.

An interesting thing about those remarks, which Hitler made on 5 August 1944, is firstly that he mentioned the V-2 rocket before it was used, and secondly that the two other, future secret weapons, were not described in more detail. While he indicated that the destructive radius of one weapon was 3-4 kilometres, nothing was said about the other, the fourth weapon. Two generations of post-war researchers have tried to ascribe the designations, V-3 and V-4, to appropriate weapons development programmes. They indicated that confusion prevailed about designations. For example, V-3 was the designation not only for the high-pressure pump, HDP, but also for a long distance rocket. In fact that can only be the A9/A10, the so-called 'America rocket'. There is simply not enough basic information to be able to be more precise.

Moreover, that statement of Hitler's contains the most direct description of the effect of a nuclear weapon, up to that time. Hitler probably took the risk of mentioning the weapon only under extraordinary circumstances. Marshal Antonescu was, at that time, heading a Romanian delegation to Berlin. Their mission was to find out to what extent the German Reich could provide additional help to the Romanian army which was struggling vainly against the Red Army. But in August 1944, in view of the fact that Army Group Centre had been shattered on the Eastern Front, and that France threatened to be lost to the Anglo-Americans, Hitler could not promise any additional material support for Antonescu. Simply mentioning the completed A-weapons, however, did not have its intended effect on the morale of the Romanian delegation. Shortly after Antonescu returned to Bucharest, a *coup d'état* took place in Romania. As a result, the country changed sides, from the Axis to the Soviet Union. This was a further catastrophe on the Eastern Front, almost as bad as that of Stalingrad.

Thus, in the summer of 1944, the attempt by the political leadership of the Third Reich, to use the completion of the atomic bomb as a political weapon, was unsuccessful. Perhaps they should have taken the Romanian delegation to one of the development locations and let them see for themselves the new miracle weapon.

After Germany's A-weapon was finally completed, the next step was to make preparations for its production, testing and military deployment. This required time, above all else. It was, of course, necessary to enter into completely new territory in technological and military terms. The setbacks and disasters, on the fighting fronts, thus raised the question as to whether Germany might not collapse before its miracle weapons could be used.

What is remarkable in that connection, is the sudden speed and energy with which work was carried out, from summer 1944, on various carrier systems. Of course that was not surprising. The new weapons would have been little use without transport systems.

Hitler's Hope for a Second 'Seven Years War'

In July 1944, the breakthrough in developing the miracle weapons occurred in the period of the terrible disasters on the Eastern and Western Fronts. There had also been the assassination attempt on 20 July. At the time, Hitler is supposed to have said that those were 'the worst days of my life!'

But by the middle of September 1944 fresh hope sprang up among the leadership of the Third Reich. Both in the East and in the West they had temporarily managed to stop the gigantic masses of enemy material and troops before they could overflow the German borders. There were German bridgeheads on the French Atlantic coast, on the Channel Islands, Crete, and Courland. The vain hope was that the bridgeheads could be the future springboards for counter-attacks. The OKW, i.e. the *Oberkommando der Wehrmacht,* wanted to hold the Carpathian line on which German and Hungarian troops were deployed. It was even planned to re-occupy Belgium and Romania.

Germany's military industry was working at unprecedented capacity. The production of superior conventional weapons was under way. There was also the chance, so it seemed, to complete the miracle weapons. But could the German forces hold out long enough, or was it not the case that there had already been too many German losses?

The Allied demand for the unconditional surrender of the Axis powers left no alternative, but to carry on fighting. Thus the hope sprang up for a second Seven Years' War. It was said that history would soon repeat itself. Hitler believed, as had been the case with Frederick the Great, he would only have to hold out, and put up resistance, until he was saved by the break-up of the enemy alliance. That Hitler's hope was not without foundation is something that has been discovered, in recent times, by Russian authors. In actual fact, they were able to document that from 1944 there were such splits in the apparently monolithic bloc of the Allies. The deployment of miracle weapons would then be the catalyst to change the course of the war. It was a matter of gaining time until this happened.

PART II

Miracle Weapons Systems

Hitler's Miracle Weapons: Offensive or Defensive?

They were called 'miracle' weapons because they were the 'weapons of the last hope' of the Third Reich, for a favourable turn in the course of the war. By a surprise use of their devastating power, Germany's 'victory' was supposed to be still possible in 1944/45, even if at the time there were only a few weapons available. Superior technology was their watchword.

Among those weapons were, in the first instance, nuclear weapons and so-called radiological 'dirty charges'. In addition, work was also continuing at the same time on other miracle weapons whose details are still unknown today. To use them successfully the miracle weapons would have to be divided into offensive and also defensive components.

The defensive component, used with all urgency, could have shown the Allies that Germany was still able to carry out devastating strikes against their countries, for which there were no counter measures. Planned targets for such attacks were, principally, London and New York. Since 1942 New York had been Hitler's long-term target but, at the time, that was still unattainable. London was to stand in as an attainable alternative target. Interestingly there are indications, only a short time before the end of the war, that at the same time Moscow was also a planned target for an attack by miracle weapons.

The miracle weapons were principally to have a political effect and, 'victoriously', to force the end of the war. In the Third Reich it seems that those responsible believed that the enterprise could more easily be carried out by attacks on the capital cities of the 'decadent' West. Today, in that connection, it appears incomprehensible that in December 1944, Hitler turned down an acceptable offer of peace from Stalin. In taking that decision, had he been influenced by the delusion that he could still achieve 'everything' by using his miracle weapons?

For transporting radiological or nuclear airborne weapons, bombers, rockets, aircraft and even the use of underwater mines had been suggested. There are indications that the German Reich carried out work on all those alternatives for transport. From 1944 even intercontinental distances were no longer thought to be an obstacle.

At the same time, the war in Europe would need to have been brought to an end by defensive miracle weapons, in order to stabilise the fronts where there was no current fighting. In doing that, it was intended to make clear to the enemy the foolishness of any further attack. In addition to radiological and nuclear bombs, rockets, aircraft and long-range artillery were also considered suitable for similar blocking measures. For those plans too there is evidence which must be taken seriously.

Of course, in that connection the question is raised as to whether German troops would ever have been able to occupy the irradiated areas. The planned deployment of such defensive weapons must also have presented a great threat to the civilian population. Those disadvantages still apply today, in connection with the deployment of tactical nuclear weapons. Nevertheless, during the Cold War, the planners in both East and West did not let that stop them from making firm plans to use such weapons, in a possible European theatre of war.

SECTION 1
Miracle Weapons of the *Luftwaffe*

It seems as if, in the main, the German *Luftwaffe* was surprised when the atomic bomb, developed in all secrecy, became available in the summer of 1944. In order to use the new weapons, there then arose the paradoxical situation that suitable carrier aircraft would first have to be created. However, until the summer of 1944, little preparatory work had been done in that area by the *Luftwaffe* leadership. There was also the fact that even then the aircraft designers charged with the responsibility for developing weapons carriers, apart from details of weight, knew nothing of the appearance, the functions and the use of the miracle weapons that they were supposed to accommodate.

In that respect, it is surprising that neither Adolf Hitler, nor Hermann Göring, who had been informed from the beginning about the development of the miracle weapons, had acted earlier and made appropriate arrangements to knock the *Luftwaffe* planning into shape. One of the main reasons for that may have been the extreme secrecy that surrounded the development of their nuclear weapons. Secrecy was necessary, in view of the proven level of treachery that prevailed in the Third Reich. Treachery was to be encountered, even in the highest levels of the leadership. Because of previous experience, not least in connection with Peenemünde and Rjukan, it could have resulted in immediate destructive strikes by the Allies, and once again have thrown into question everything that had been achieved. Despite all that, what was achieved, in the short time that still remained, was indeed remarkable.

A: Miracle Weapons Carrier Aircraft

1) Conventional Intercontinental Bomber for Miracle Weapons 1944/45: Nuclear Target America

Messerschmitt Me 264: the Flying 'Mock-up'?

How can it be explained that, in the summer of 1944, Germany possessed no *Amerikabomber*, although the prototype of such an aircraft had already been flying for several years? The history goes back to November 1937 when, on his only visit to the BFW aircraft works in Augsburg, Hitler was shown the 'mock-up' of the Bf 165. It was a project for a four-engined long-range bomber, the predecessor of the Messerschmitt Me 264 that was designed later in the war. Willy Messerschmitt, the designer, specified for the 'mock-up' aircraft a range of 6,000 kilometres with a 1,000 kilogram bomb load and a speed of 600 kilometres per hour. At the time, the gentlemen from the Reich Air Ministry (RLM) were completely surprised by the 'mock-up', while Hitler showed great interest. But he demanded that the aircraft would have to be faster in order to be able to escape from fighter aircraft.

Therefore, it can be seen that he was well able to evaluate the possibilities for deploying such an aircraft. The fact that this incident became public knowledge at all is thanks to the published memoirs of Hitler's Adjutant, Nicolaus von Below. It is true that what became of the project for the Bf 165 has never been made known.[17]

From the outbreak of the war in 1939, a small design group was engaged in developing long-range aircraft that would be deployed at great distances across the Atlantic and in the direction of America. The initiative had come from *Generalluftzeugmeister* Ernst Udet, as the *Luftwaffe* command staff had indicated no wishes, nor any requirements, in that development. The specification issued to industry, inviting tenders for the aircraft, had specified a minimum range of 12,000 kilometres. That was the distance from Brest, still unoccupied at that time, to New York and back. The technical requirements, taking into account the necessary reserves, produced the need for a final range requirement of 15,000 kilometres. The aircraft was to be able to carry a load of 3- to 5-tonne bombs, together with normal armament and equipment.[18] Therefore, it can be seen that from the beginning, insufficient preparation was made for the long-range aircraft project. Under the pressure of the battle of the Atlantic, and the increasing tensions with America, only in 1940 was the project pursued more urgently.

Although the Reich Air Ministry had ordered the Messerschmitt factory to work exclusively on fighter aircraft, sporadic development work had already taken place on Atlantic Project 1061. From 20 December 1940 the work was carried forward with greater impetus by Willy

Messerschmitt. He also received a commission to develop six prototype P 1061 aircraft, which were given the designation Messerschmitt Me 264. It was said that if the aircraft proved to be successful, a further order would be issued for 24 aircraft to carry out 'disruptive attacks against the United States of America'.

Equipped with four Jumo 211 J-1 engines, the Messerschmitt Me 264 V-1 (RE + EN) took its first flight on 23 December 1942. From the outset its qualities and performance in flight were outstanding. The Me 264 had an aerodynamic fuselage of circular cross-section. The crew area was a cockpit with all-round visibility. Attached to that was the bomb bay, with a passageway over it which contained a galley, rest area and equipment area. The aft crew area consisted of the weapons and equipment area. The tail unit, with its two disc-shaped fins, was at a slight V-angle in the Me 264 V-1 and V-2. From the V-3 onwards, the aircraft had a straight horizontal tail unit that improved the field of fire for the B-2 position. The complete undercarriage consisted of a retractable main undercarriage, and a retractable nose undercarriage.

The large individual wheels were intended to make it possible for the aircraft to land safely on poorly constructed airfields. For take-off with a full load, each main wheel unit had an additional wheel that was jettisoned after take-off. During flight trials the wingspan of the Me 264 V-1 was increased from 38.9m to 43m and the poorly-performing Jumo J-1s were replaced by four, more powerful, BMW 801 D/Gs.

In the wing tanks the aircraft had a fuel capacity of 26,400 litres. Another 13,000 litres could be carried in six additional external fuel tanks. In September 1944 heavy fuel tanks were designed, weighing 5,100 kilograms, which would have extended the range even further. Rockets, with a total of 6,000 kp thrust, were planned to assist take off when the aircraft was heavily loaded, or for short take-off runs. With optimal fuel loading, and by keeping to a precisely calculated flight plan, the maximum range of the Me 264 was still 15,800 kilometres.

The second prototype, the Me 264 V-2, in addition to its extended wings, was to have over 1,000 kilograms of armour plating for its vital parts. Although it had no defensive armament, it was already capable of carrying a bomb load. But this machine was destroyed in an air raid before its first flight. The Technical Office decided to commission as a priority, construction of the Me 264. It was to be ready for action at the front at the beginning of 1944.

Messerschmitt's original proposal envisaged an aircraft that was to carry 1,800 kilograms of bombs to New York. The attack would have to be carried out from high altitude, in order to avoid being caught by enemy fighters. For that reason all defensive armament was dispensed with, in order to reduce to a minimum air resistance and weight. The Me 264 would have matched those requirements. The whole design of the Messerschmitt Me 264 was directed towards saving weight and improving performance.

But the specifications were later modified. By then, an aircraft was required that would carry a small bomb load of 1,000 kilograms, to the Eastern coast of the USA, and then return to a European base. Alternatively, it would have to carry a heavy bomb load of 4,000 to 5,000 kilograms on a one-way flight. After dropping its bombs on the target, it would ditch in the sea, along the coast, beside a German U-boat, so that the crew could be picked up.

Ideas for mid-air refuelling were also developed. A second aircraft would fly with the actual *Amerikabomber*, for 3,000 kilometres, and then deliver fuel. The craft would then have enough fuel to take it its full range. The procedure for mid-air refuelling had already been successfully tested with the Ju 290. However, the plan was dismissed by Jeschonnek, at that time Chief of the General Staff of the *Luftwaffe*, on the grounds that it could not be carried out under wartime conditions.

Even before the flight of the first prototype, on 27 April 1942, there were great plans for the new aircraft. Reconnaissance missions were to be carried out far into Siberia, to the Gulf of Aden and to other targets in West and Central Africa. Not only New York and New Jersey were to be within range of the Me 264; attacks were also planned on targets in Ohio, Pennsylvania and even Indiana. In addition, there were plans to station some Me 264s on Japanese island bases to the north-east of the Philippines. From there they would fly reconnaissance missions to Australia, India and even far into the Pacific region. At the same time, an improved version of the Me 264 was under development. It was to receive the powerful Juno 222 engines with the G M 1 injection system.

But nothing was to come of any of those plans. Even before the flight of the first prototype, the so-called 'Messerschmitt effect' came into operation, i.e. one delay followed another. The delays were caused by a shortage of design and construction capacity. Attempts by the Messerschmitt factory to assign elements of the development to firms like Fokker, Dornier, Zeppelin and Weser also failed to significantly improve the situation. There, too, capacity was overloaded. Thus, the conversion of the Me 264 V-1, to the more powerful BMW 801 power units, itself took 8 months, from 11 August 1943 to 15 April 1944.

Personal rivalries between Hermann Göring, Erhard Milch and Willy Messerschmitt, also delayed the production of the new type. The question was repeatedly asked whether Messerschmitt's data were not too optimistic, and whether the whole thing was anything other than a flying 'mock-up'.

Göring had hoped for great things from the deployment of a long-range bomber. Disappointed, in March 1943 he said: 'I can remember - it's exactly one year ago - that an aircraft was shown to me in Augsburg, for which there was nothing to do but give the order for mass-production to begin. The aircraft was supposed to fly to the East Coast of America and back, from the Azores to the American West Coast, and it was also supposed to carry a load of bombs. That is what they told me in all seriousness. At that time I was still in a confident mood, so that I at least half believed it was possible'.

In May 1943 a telegram from the RLM reached Willy Messerschmitt, telling him that work on the Me 264 was to be discontinued. But, on 8 June 1943, Adolf Hitler promised his further support for the production of the Me 264. At the same time, however, he changed his earlier decision to bomb the cities on the East Coast of the USA, because the 'few aircraft' which would be able to reach there would only provoke the population to further resistance. Evidently, this shows that the development of the miracle weapons was in crisis at that time. On the basis of that intervention by Hitler, *Generalfeldmarschall* Milch, the next day, ordered the construction of three Me 264 prototypes 'for the purposes of study'.

On 14 October 1943 Messerschmitt stated, that although the flight trials with the V-1 had not yet been concluded, he had produced the parts for the first five prototypes. But he said that there would be a shortage of space and production capacity in which to assemble them. In order to provide space for the production of the Me 410, all Me 264 machine parts and moulds were removed from the Augsburg firm, and stored in Gersthofen.

Then, on top of the construction problem, there came the shortage of production capacity in the Messerschmitt factory. It was working at full capacity in building the Me 109, 110, 410 and 262 fighters. A short review indicated that the Weser factory too was not in a position to bring the Me 264 to production status, nor to build the first models. Previously, consideration had been given to getting the French SNCASCO factory, and the Blohm & Voss, Focke-Wulf and Siebel factories, to build the first 28 aircraft of the type Me 264. But all those firms were already working at full capacity.

On 18 July 1944, after all the unnecessary to-ing and fro-ing, for years on end, the Me 264 programme suffered a decisive blow. On that day, in an air-raid on Memmingen, the Me 264 V-1, together with the parts of the V 3 and V 4 and also 80% of the stored Me 264, production installations were destroyed.

Shortly before, in June 1944, the construction of some very long-range bombers had been once more discussed with Adolf Hitler. Messerschmitt had offered his Me 264 with additional turbojet engines. He promised that he would be able to build three or four aircraft in an accelerated operation without fixture construction. Hitler was enthusiastic at the thought and said: 'At long last we should be drawing decisive tough consequences from the thought of building focus points of resistance. If we know this way is the only right way to proceed, making revolutionary innovations, and not blundering about, then I am inclined to say that you should really get down to work on the Me 264. This Me 264 shows us possibilities of absolutely revolutionary significance in its combination of conventional piston engines and turbo jets. In view of its load-bearing capacity, and its penetrative long range, it seems ideally suited to carry out everything we want, and to do it in relatively small numbers, too'.[19]

The KdE, i.e. the *Luftwaffe* Testing Station Command, considered the Me 264 to be unusable, because of excessive area loading, complications with the take-off, excessively long take-off runs, and poor armament. However, on 26 July 1944, *Sonderkommando* Nebel was set up for the testing and production of Me 264 prototypes. In a meeting of 5 August 1944, Hitler assigned particular importance to accelerating the production of the aircraft.

Leading the *Sonderkommando, Kapitän* Nebel from the Rechlin testing station, was already extremely familiar with the prototype through having made many flights in the Me 264 V-1 at Memmingen, and he knew all about the details of its production. His *Sonderkommando* was one of the most remarkable units in the *Luftwaffe*. What the entire German aircraft industry had not managed to do in five years' development, his military unit was then to achieve. They would create a combat-ready America bomber for carrying miracle weapons.

The situation that *Sonderkommando* Nebel found in the air-raid of the 18 July, was that 80% of the production installations and many completed structural parts of the Me 264 had been destroyed. It was not expected that they could be replaced before February 1945. But the requirement for so-called 'very long range reconnaissance aircraft', must have been pressing enough for the *Sonderkommando* then to manufacture some individual models of the Me 264, from structural parts taken from storage. Certainly the parts themselves must have been available. But they were only partly suitable for assembly because, in many places, they had to be finished and reinforced, to take account of experience with the prototype V-1.

In spite of an extensive search, however, the structural parts could not be found anywhere. Had they already been destroyed in the earlier air raids or had they been prematurely scrapped? Was carelessness or sabotage at work? In any event, a report at the end of 1944 declared that the structural parts were no longer available. That therefore, was the end of the Me 264, and all the hopes that went with it.

What consequences can be drawn from all this? With our knowledge today, it must be quite clear that the individual prototype models of the Me 264, which *Sonderkommando* Nebel had to produce by hand, would have been completely unsuitable for Atlantic reconnaissance. For regular reconnaissance over the Atlantic, with its 'difficult climate', the great demands made on the aircraft would have required constant maintenance, supplies of replacement parts, and for replacement aircraft to be available. In the case of the individual Me 264 aircraft, each of which would have been a sort of one-off, that would have been impossible to achieve. Therefore, in that connection, the requirement could only have been for individual aircraft, for special tasks, with extreme range. Also striking is the haste with which, after years of delay, Me 264s were suddenly supposed to be produced. In the case of the Me 264, the problem involved versions that were, at the end of the war, also being planned as courier aircraft with extreme range. They could only have been intended as carrier aircraft for miracle weapons.

Apart from that, developments did not pass by the Me 264. The aircraft, which in 1942 was a technological miracle, was in 1944 known only as a transitional prototype until the new jet bomber became available. It was also known to the General Quartermaster of the *Luftwaffe*. Not three weeks after the order was issued for *Sonderkommando* Nebel to be set up, he suggested that work on the Me 264 should finally be discontinued, and instead, work should begin on developing a new aircraft. That programme later produced the *Amerikabomber* Horten Ho XVIII. But it was no longer possible to make up lost time from previous years.

Paradoxically the Me 264, together with the Messerschmitt Me 262 jet fighter, had already been in development since 1939. If priorities had been properly set, the Me 264 could have given the Third Reich a weapon that might have turned the fortunes of the war. However, both chances were thrown away.

Transatlantic Improvisations: Parasite Bombers, *Anhängerflugzeuge* and 'One-way' Bombers

In the desperate situation of summer 1944, after years of neglect, the former plan of flying retaliatory attacks against America with all available means was revived once again. Suddenly, it seemed that there would be something very important which could be taken to America. The plan, which was probably first revived in July 1944, was for a large aircraft to carry a small bomber most of the way across the Atlantic and afterwards to turn back, while the bomber itself flew on to the target, bombed New York and finally ditched in the Atlantic. The crew was to be picked up by a U-boat.

That plan was dropped on 21 August 1944. It is the subject of a short entry of that date in the diary of *General* Kreipe, the *Luftwaffe* chief of staff: 'Short entry concerning attack against New York with long range bomber. *Kriegsmarine* can no longer provide U-boat for supply and pick up. Abandon operation'. One last discussion took place with Admiral Bricke of the *Kriegsmarine*. It lasted until 5pm. During the night Kreipe once again spoke by telephone to Meisel, the Chief of Naval Staff, concerning the America operation.

For the first time a similar plan cropped up, in Volume 14 of *Feldmarschall* Milch's discussions as *Luftzeugmeister*. In May and June 1942 he spoke several times of the possibility of bombing New York and San Francisco. The difficulty was always that it was not possible to transport a bomb any larger than one tonne. That discussion took place shortly before the meeting on the 4 June 1942 in the Harnack Haus, when *Feldmarschall* Milch asked Professor Heisenberg how large an atomic bomb would need to be to destroy an entire city.

Was that by chance? What was behind it?

As early as the beginning of 1944 a test flight was probably undertaken, in the Ju 390 V-2, almost as far as New York. That reconnaissance flight could well have been a test flight to examine the possibility of carrying out later bombing raids on New York. At the time, only the Ju 290, He 177, or the Ju 390 V-2, would have been suitable as transport aircraft for a small bomber.

The use of 'parasite' aircraft had already been considered for all three types. As a parasite aircraft in the stricter sense, the Messerschmitt Me 328 would have been suitable. The Messerschmitt Me 328 B was a light high-speed bomber intended for daylight attacks on strongly defended targets. Of wooden construction, it was intended to be used for attacks at low-level, below radar cover. It was to carry a bomb load of 1,000 kilograms, up to a maximum of 1,400 kilograms, over a range of 800 kilometres. It too, as had been planned in the previous project from 1942, the required payload of 1,000 kilograms is mentioned, which corresponds to the weight of the 'radiological', 1 tonne bomb.

If what was required was to transport a small uranium bomb of about 250kg, as was available from 1944, the range could have been extended. By inserting an intermediate spacer, it was planned to extend the fuselage of all models of the Me 328, in order to extend the aircraft's range. It was planned to carry the Me 328 as an on-board bomber on long-range missions, and to release it before the target was reached. The on-board bombers deployed in that way would afterwards, if possible, look for a landing site close to a waiting U-boat.

The planned power units were two 3,600mm-long thruster tubes originating from the V-1. Later, the tubes, each weighing 138kg, were to be replaced by four smaller tubes of about half the power. They were to be fixed to the fuselage, in order to reduce the severe wing vibrations caused by the larger tubes, which had had very adverse effects on the aircraft's flight characteristics. It was those poor flight characteristics, as well as the very uncertain chance of the pilot returning alive, which were the main reasons why, apart from three trial prototypes, only seven more of the aircraft were produced.[20]

It is not yet clear what was meant by the designation *'Anhängerflugzeug'*. Under that procedure, a larger carrier aircraft was to carry a smaller aircraft with its engine switched off, over as great a distance as possible, to maximise range. Only after reaching a point that brought the smaller aircraft within range of the target, was the smaller aircraft's engine to be started and the aircraft released.

Similarly, it is not yet known which smaller bomber was to be carried across the Atlantic, in that way, and then begin its one-way flight. It may have been the Me 410. There is evidence that the *Anhängerflugzeug* principle was used, in action, by the German *Luftwaffe*. Thus in spring 1944, Heinkel He 111s, using that system, carried agents in Messerschmitt Bf 108 courier aircraft across the Mediterranean into the Sahara. Once arrived in the operational area, the Bf 108s were released, in flight, and flew on into the interior of Africa.

Another possibility of exploiting the *Anhänger* principle was in towing 'winged' fuel tanks, in order to increase range. Again there is evidence that the *Luftwaffe* carried out work on that procedure. They used converted fuel tanks, BV 40 gliders, and V-1 shells fitted with wheels.

The question was, which of the procedures was to be used in 1944, for the transatlantic operations. In the post war description of the Junkers Ju 390, there is an indication that from spring 1944 'necessary lessons were to be learnt from releasing such a team of aircraft over the Atlantic'. But, remarkably, the name of the team originally mentioned in the documents had become indecipherable when it was published. That was another unanswered question.

At the same time, consideration was also given to using individual aircraft, of the increased performance type Heinkel He 177 A-7, for kamikaze-type individual attacks against America. It is thought that only five individual models of that superior version of the He 177 were produced, by conversion of A-5 aircraft. Of those, one model was captured by the Allies at the end of the war, without the seven aircraft ever having been previously used in action. In the case of the He 177 A-7, consideration had also been given in planning, to the possibility of the aircraft ditching in the Atlantic, and the crew being picked up at a point close to the enemy coast.

The sudden urgency for creating such a transatlantic bomber is remarkable. All three methods of attack, i.e. parasite bombers, *Anhängerflugzeuge*, and one-way bombers, would only have made it possible to carry small numbers of individual bombs to America. In any case, little could have been achieved with such small numbers of bombs, except that dropping a few bombs would have increased the American population's fear of the 'German peril'. In fact, the effect would have been totally counter-productive. But how would things have looked if, instead of dropping, with considerable difficulty, a few conventional 1,000 kilogram bombs, something completely different was planned. The British historian, David Irving, himself tending to be cautious in this connection, in his reference work 'The Dream of the German Atomic Bomb', makes a connection with German nuclear weapons plans.[21]

In order to ensure the survival of the crew, Adolf Hitler forbade such kamikaze-type, transatlantic, 'one way operations' against the USA.[22] Apart from that, the end of such improvised efforts, for the rapid creation of an 'America bomber', coincided with great changes in German air armament.

Junkers Ju 390: the 'Phantom Aircraft'

With the Junkers Ju 390 we are dealing with a piston-engined long-range aircraft which, even today, is linked to an unsolved mystery. An entry, dated 9 February 1945, in the flying log of *Flugkapitän* Joachim Eisermann, shows two flights in the Ju 390V-2. One lasted 50 minutes in Rechlin itself. The other lasted 22 minutes, from Rechlin, with a subsequent landing at Lärz, an airfield also belonging to the testing station. Registration markings, as is unfortunately often the case in Rechlin flying logs, are not shown. According to *Oberleutnant* Eisermann, the aircraft remained in Lärz. Afterwards all trace of it was lost. A month later, when members of FAGr. 5 were at Rechlin and Lärz for some time, there was still nothing to be seen of the aircraft. It had gone. Even today no-one knows precisely what happened to the aircraft. No date can be found for its destruction, nor was it captured by the Allies.

The affair became even more mysterious. At his hearing before the British, on 26 September 1945, Professor Heinrich Hertel, chief designer and technical director of the Junkers Aircraft and Motor Works, stated that the Ju 390 V-2 had neither been completed nor had it been flown. The same thing was said by the aircraft's captain, Pancherz. As project pilot, he would have been responsible for carrying out the test flight. It appeared that they had a secret to hide.

As early as 1942, the Junkers factory was involved in a competition in which the *Technische Amt* (GL/C) had invited designs for a long-range bomber. It was to be able to strike targets in the USA, principally New York. Participating in that competition were Heinkel with the He 274 and 277, Messerschmitt with the Me 264, and Tank with the Ta 400 and Projects 0310224.30 and 0310225. The invitation to tender was for a long-range, reconnaissance, transport and guided-missile carrier aircraft. It had to have a range of 12,000 kilometres.[23]

Under the direction of *Diplom-Ingenieur* Heinz Kraft, the Junkers design office in Prague began work on a six-engined version of the Junkers Ju 290 C. The fuselage and wings were to be considerably enlarged by the insertion of fuselage and wing spacing pieces, using the block construction system. Since that solution required the smallest expenditure, in terms of production facilities and equipment, Junkers was commissioned to build two prototype aircraft.[24]

However, on 10 October 1942, the level of urgency for the programme was reduced from S to DI. Since, in constructing that aircraft type, it was possible for the most part to use components from the Ju 290, and even the Ju 90, the first flight of the Ju 390, with the markings G H + UK, took place as early as 21 October 1943. Because of its good flight characteristics, it was planned to go into mass-production.[25] In May 1944 a review was instituted at Junkers, as to how the weight of the Ju 390 could be reduced, in order to further increase the flight range of 8,500 kilometres which had then been achieved.

The reason was that for political reasons the required range had been increased to 11,000 kilometres, with a payload of 8 tonnes. It was intended to achieve the revised level of performance, with a take-off weight of 80.5 tonnes, by removing 5 tonnes of equipment and armament. In the winter of 1944/45, Hermann Göring also stipulated the same range requirement for the '*Amerika* jet bomber'. Now, it is an open secret that that jet aircraft was intended to carry a 'radiological' or nuclear weapon to New York. Thus, in the light of such 'political reasons', mentioned in May 1944, in actual fact, what was planned with the Ju 390, must have involved carrying a similar miracle weapon. But, of course, the writer of the post-war report would not, or could not, express it in that way.

Earlier, in November 1943, the Führer's personal pilot, *Flugkapitän* Hans Baur, ordered a model of the Ju 390 for the Government flight. (F.d.F.)[26] The aircraft was to serve in the flight to replace, or to complement, the Focke-Wulf 'Condor' which had been used until then. There may have been a desire, at the highest level, to undertake courier flights in that aircraft, to Germany's ally Japan. Perhaps there was already a plan to use it as an aircraft in which to escape. Considering that the borders of the area under German control at that time, had already shrunk considerably, the long range, provided by the Ju 390, would not have been necessary.

The further history of the Junkers Ju 390 is full of uncertainties and contradictions. Because of the excellent test results in the flight trials of the Ju 390 V-1, it was decided to shorten the period of the trials and not to build any more V- and O-types. Instead, consideration would be given to the improvised Junkers 390 V-1, as the prototype for the series. But a report of October 1943 contradicted that fact. It stated that, in March 1944, six experimental aircraft V-2 to V-7, and 20 mass-produced aircraft (as A-1) were to be built. It was also planned to complete the V-2, and begin its flight trials at the end of September 1944. Six weeks later the V-3 was to be completed. The V-3 had the definitive bomber fuselage of the A-1 series. However, on 20 June 1944, the entire Ju 390 programme was axed, by order of Hermann Göring.

Present day research indicates that of the Junkers Ju 390 only the aircraft V-1 and V-2 were completed. Further components for other Ju 390 aircraft may also have existed. It is true that it is not yet certain when work on the V-2 was completed. As early as 19 October 1943, a document from Dessau reported trim and weight trials, in Prague, on the Ju 390 V-2. The V-2 was distinct from the lighter J U 390 V-1.[27] As further proof that the type existed, documents in the Junkers factory, dated 6 October 1944, relating to construction on licence clearly indicate components which do not belong to the Ju 390 V-1.

There is also a photograph, about which arguments are still ongoing amongst experts, showing details that clearly differ from the Ju 390 V-1. The photograph shows a Ju 390 with (retouched) registration markings 'RC + DA'. Clearly differing from the V-1, the forward fuselage of 'RC + DA', from the wing edge to the nose, is about 1.5m longer and the aircraft has a different vertical tail construction. The altered components correspond exactly with those, in the autumn of 1944 documents, relating to construction on licence. It is probable that the Ju 390 V-2 was originally completed as a large transport and not as a bomber. Also, on the photographs of parts of the Ju 390 V-2 no parts of the fuselage can be seen with any armaments. In contrast to this, the licence documents, intended for Japan, show a bomber version with armaments. Reports from October 1944 described firing tests, on a Ju 390, which could only have been on the V-2 version.

To date there is no explanation for such contradictions. On the German side, until construction was discontinued, there were acrimonious arguments about the armament of the future Ju 390. A great deal of work was carried out on test mountings and variations of armament. It even resulted in the Henschel factory delivering to Prague a specially prepared telescopic visor (*Fevi*) with a rate action calculator for the Ju 390. Perhaps the Ju 390 V-2 large transport was to be converted into an armed version.

On the basis of the previous extended experiments, and construction of mock-up versions, it is conceivable that a complete conversion of the fuselage could have been carried out. It may have produced a bomber version. But there is no photographic evidence. One of the most likely possibilities would be the installation of so-called keyhole mountings, with a limited radius of movement. Similar gun mountings, intended to accommodate 3cm MK 108 cannon, were delivered for the Ju 390. In the summer of 1944 they could also have been installed, without too much difficulty in conversion, into the available V-2 transporter fuselage. It is probable that the licence documents, intended for the Japanese, represented the definitive bomber fuselage of the A-1 series. Possibly they could no longer be implemented in the V-2.

Perhaps the Ju 390 V-2 was completed earlier than has hitherto been thought possible. The documents we have, to date, that speak of completion within the period September/October 1944, may in fact have been superseded by others. If that were the case, then the test flight from Mont-de-Marsan (France), almost as far as New York, would have been possible. Mentioned in British secret reports from August 1944, that flight could have taken place at the beginning of 1944. The flight may have achieved the 8,500 kilometre range that is mentioned in the documents of the firm. According to British accounts, photographs were brought back which were said to have shown the American coast, 20 miles away. It could be proved if the photographs were made available.

The purpose of such an operation can only have been to test the feasibility of a flight to attack New York. After a successful test run they could then have tried the real operation, perhaps with the Ju 390 or another type. There must in that connection have also been another attempt to improve the range over the Atlantic. During the lifetime of the Ju 390, mention is made of 'experiments involving *Anhängerflugzeuge* with regard to the release of the (...)-*Anhänger* over the Atlantic'. Unfortunately this (...)-concept was made indecipherable, possibly deliberately, in the post-war documentation. Therefore we do not know what failed operation the papers were describing.

It seems there are mysterious reasons for the denial of the existence of the Ju 390 V-2. It seems clear what became of the Ju 390 V-1. There was no question of using, in action, an aircraft that was only assembled in a makeshift manner. So further trials were carried out on it in Prague. Finally, it was flown to Dessau by Captain Pancherz, on 15 November 1944. There it remained, without propellers, in a disposal area, until the end of the war. The burnt-out remains of the aircraft, which was set on fire by the Germans shortly before the area was taken by the Allies, were later subjected to a detailed evaluation by the Americans.

Since there are no indications of the Ju 390 V-2 having been destroyed or captured at the end of the war, there are several possibilities as to its fate. It was perhaps to have been used for a secret mission, which failed. Perhaps it was to have served as an escape vehicle for top-level Nazis. The aircraft may have been intended for delivery to Germany's ally, Japan.

In support of the possibility of a secret special mission, it should be said that the Ju 390 V-2 would have been a long-range combat aircraft fully capable of being deployed in action. That in October 1944 the V-2 was in Rerik, in the Baltic, to test its weapons installations, tends to support that possibility. The long-range bomber would have been capable, at a maximum speed of 472 km/h, and a maximum ceiling of 8,900m, of carrying a bomb load of 4,400kg, i.e. the weight of the Hiroshima bomb, as far as New York. As already mentioned, the V-2 is said to have made a solo test flight almost as far as New York. Perhaps it was intended, in March 1945, to send the Ju 390 V-2 from Norway to New York, carrying an atomic bomb. That would have been technically possible. Moreover, there are press reports[28] in existence that have never been retracted, that at the end of the war, long-range bombers were standing by, near Oslo, for an attack on the USA. The intention to carry out an atomic bomb attack on the USA, whatever the reasons for it not having taken place, would be a possible reason for covering-up the existence of the Ju 390 V-2 in the post-war period.

The second possibility that the Ju 390 V-2 served as an escape vehicle, for important high-level Nazis, would have been just as awkward. One only needs to think of the possibility that SS *Obergruppenführer* Dr Kammler, with the help of that aircraft, could have got out of Bohemia and Moravia just before the end of the war. It is known that many legends and contradictions are connected with the 'alleged' death of *Obergruppenführer* Dr Kammler. The fact that such a powerful Third Reich insider, until now believed to be dead, could have escaped to a distant country, with many secret personal documents, would itself have been sufficient reason to cover up the existence of the aircraft. It is true that we know that Dr Kammler was afraid of flying. Therefore, he perhaps preferred another means of escape.

The third, and most likely possibility is, that the Ju 390 V-2 was transferred to Japan. The Japanese Army was extremely interested in the Ju 390, because with that aircraft they could attack the West Coast of the USA from Japan. Japanese designs for that kind of aircraft were still at the project stage. There is a collection of documents, relating to construction on licence, dating from August 1944. They prove that at that time Junkers, certainly with the approval of, or even commissioned by the RLM, had been working to assemble the documents in question for the Ju 390 to be constructed, on licence, in Japan. Indeed, in February 1945, all the documents were ready, but it is said that it was no longer possible to send them to Japan. However, according to the Kammler researcher Tom Agoston, on 28 March 1945, a *Luftwaffe* test pilot flew a six-engined, long-range Ju 390 bomber, non-stop over the Polar route, to Japan. Considering the situation at the time, the aircraft in question could only have been the Ju 390 V-2.

On that mission, the aircraft flew, from Norway, in a Great Circle to Manchu-Kuo. From the Bardufoss airfield in northern Norway the route led first to the Bering Strait. Then it went across the Northern Ocean, over the eastern part of the Kamchatka peninsula to the island of Pamuschiro, in the Japanese area of control. From there it went over Manchuria to Tokyo. During the flight in the northern polar region, astro-navigation was said to have been used because of the expected failure of the compass.

Aboard the aircraft, according to Agoston, were important replacement parts, microfilms, and also key personnel. *Generalmajor* Fritz Morzik, who as a former general in air transport must have known of it, wrote in an official US Air Force post-war study, that the Ju 390 was used for courier flights to Japan. But the American publisher hastened to add that no additional information could be found concerning Ju 390 flights to Tokyo.

Technically, the Ju 390 would have been capable of such an aviation success. The weather stations in the Arctic that would have been necessary were already in position. In addition to many automatic weather stations that were transported, by U-boats, to their various locations, from Labrador to Greenland, the Meteorological

Unit at Haudegen was working from Spitzbergen, from September 1944. The station was particularly active, from the end of the polar nights, in March 1945. From its base in Norway, it received the request as to whether the Haudegen personnel could remain in Spitzbergen until the autumn of 1946, instead of autumn 1945, as originally planned. They were told that if that was the case it was planned to send two aircraft with supplies and reinforcements. But those aircraft never arrived. It is interesting, from a military history point of view, that there was evidently an intention on the part of Germany, to carry on the war from Norway. Station Haudegen only surrendered on 4 September 1945. It was the last known unit of the German *Wehrmacht* to do so.

Until now, in Japanese documents, there is nothing to confirm the polar flight of the Ju 390 V-2. There are no other indications about where the aircraft ended up. There are publications only of intercepts of Japanese radio messages, concerning a planned Ju 290 flight to Japan in May 1945. Perhaps radio messages concerning the transfer of the Ju 390 have been suppressed. It seems that on 21 March 1945 there was a radio report from the Japanese Naval Air Service attache in Germany. In it he made reference to a plan for a co-ordinated, rapid transport operation, by air and sea, to Japan. It was to take place within three weeks.

Subsequently, the weapons and documents designated for sea transport, together with personnel assigned to Japan, put to sea in U 234 on 25 March 1945. The air route, by the Ju 390 V-2, was planned as part of the combined transport operation on 28 March 1945. In that case it would have to be assumed that the Ju 390, in the meantime fitted with armament, played a part, like the U 234, in the planned transfer to Japan of elements of German nuclear weapons material. The U 234, as a result of the war coming to an end, was never able to reach its original destination. However, the Ju 390 would have arrived with its cargo in the Japanese area of control in March 1945.

Now comes the controversial question of the bilateral transfer of secrets between the Axis Powers, Germany and Japan. America and the Soviet Union had begun to transport away captured German V-weapons, and to hire the experts who had developed that technology. But long before that, top-secret information, concerning rockets, modern aircraft, industry, science and other military secrets was regularly being passed on to Japan. Of course, London and Washington had no knowledge of that happening. Even fissile uranium-235 was sent out of Germany to its Japanese Axis partner.[29] The whole extent of that secret transfer has remained, until now, as unclear as the exchange of patents between the two countries. The whole subject would require a separate book.

The exchange principally took place by means of U-boat traffic between the two countries. But, because the Allies had cracked the secret code, many of the transport U-boats were lost on the way. Many mysteries could be solved, by salvaging those sunken U-boats. The wide spectrum of German technological know-how, passed on to Japan, astonished the Allied technology experts as they were evaluating the countless captured documents. To take just one example, Japanese factories were found which were already producing parts of the German *Bachem Natter* secret weapon.

However, as already mentioned, there is still a great deal in both countries which remains unknown. Between the time of the Japanese surrender, and the occupation of Japan by Allied troops, there was enough time for Japanese experts to be able to hide, or destroy, the relevant material. Perhaps the Ju 390 V-2 also fell victim to the process. Perhaps the Japanese were still planning to carry out an attack with that aircraft, carrying an F-Go weapon, against cities on the west coast of America. Today it is known that there was a well-advanced Japanese nuclear weapons programme, i.e. the 'F-Go'. Thus, in August 1945, the Japanese were able to carry out a nuclear test explosion in Korea.[30]

Until it is possible to find out the exact truth about the transfer of technology between Germany and Japan, the fate of the Ju 390 will still need to be considered as that of a 'ghost' plane.

The end of the conventional German Bomber Fleet

From February 1944, at the latest, the Allies were increasingly in command of the air over the Reich area. They were able to hit German war industry and, above all, German fuel supplies. Thus it became increasingly more complicated to ensure sufficient supplies of fuel, for the available medium and heavy bombers. The few bombers that now and then were able to take off in the west of the Reich, were not able to get through in the face of the Allied air superiority. That fact emerged particularly during the Normandy invasion, when the German night bombers and torpedo aircraft, so carefully hoarded, were decimated within a very short time. In view of that situation, Hitler also changed his strategical view. On 26 June 1944, Hitler ordered the *Luftwaffe* command staff 'to shift the emphasis of the air war over to defence. It was necessary', he said, 'to build fighters, and still more fighters, otherwise we must risk the loss of an operational *Luftwaffe*'.

For that reason, on 28 June 1944, *Reichsmarschall* Göring ordered all production of bomber and torpedo aircraft. All training related to those aircraft was also stopped. The production of many types of aircraft was axed. On 23 September 1944, Hitler gave his agreement to the 'Programme for Concentrating Air Defences', previously agreed between Göring and Speer. The halt in production hit even the brand new four-engined Junkers Ju 287 jet bomber, which had made its first flight on 8 August 1944.

Hauptdienstleiter Karl-Otto Saur, who later succeeded Armaments Minister Albert Speer, summed up the situation on the occasion of a speech to the fighter staff. He was certain, he said, that in the next three or four months, the hardest stretch of the war would be overcome with 'the greatest means of assistance', and with the least effort. Then there would be a possibility of finally overcoming the crushing superiority of the enemy.[31]

The interpretation placed upon those measures, by military historians in the past, was always that they represented a belated shift, from the offensive to the defensive. Then, all hope was focused on the new jet and rocket-powered fighters. But there is also an entirely different possibility that, until now, has been studiously overlooked. There was recourse to offensive weapons of the newest kind. It is true that, as a result of the war, they would have been produced in only small quantities. However, they could cause a decisive about-turn in a war that was soon to be lost. But for that to happen, enough time had to be gained to allow them to be used. That was what the desperate defensive measures were meant to achieve.

In the second half of 1944, when Hermann Göring learned that Germany would soon have the atomic bomb, he and the highest levels of the Reich Air Ministry began, once again, to prepare for strategic aerial warfare of a unique kind. In that situation, in August 1944, the *Reichsmarschall* called a meeting in Dessau. He told the leading representatives of industry, and the RLM, to build jet-powered large bombers, and then invited bids to tender. The intention was to develop a jet-powered long-range bomber that, with a range of 9,000 kilometres and a 4-tonne bomb, would be able to fly to the USA. Strikingly, the 4-tonne bomb load was also specified as the required payload in other late projects. For example, the Junkers Ju 287, the Ju 390 A, that was built under licence by the Japanese, and the 'Singer' bomber which was to be used in the Antipodes. Even on the other side of the world, in Japan, Germany's ally, the last long-range bombers such as the Nakajima G8N-1 'Renzan', were designed for a 4-tonne bomb load.

However, even today the official opinion is still that there could have been no actual German and Japanese 4-tonne bombs, despite the fact that an entire class of bomber aircraft was designed for precisely that payload.

2) The new '4-Tonne' Bomber Programme from Summer 1944

Junkers Ju 488

In December 1943, the Junkers factory proposed to the RLM the design of a new superior 4-engined long-range bomber to succeed the He 177. It would require only a minimum of new machinery and moulds. Essentially, the Ju 488 was to be assembled from already existing Junkers aircraft. Thus, from the Ju 388, came the complete forward section of the fuselage and pressurised cabin, the wings and the wooden flooring of the bomb bay to hold the bomb load. From the Ju 188 came the fuselage mid- and stern sections, and from the Ju 288 C, the tail section with tail-plane. The only new elements needed for that collection of existing components were a new fuselage midsection, and part of the wings to hold the four engines. Once the project was accepted by the RLM, work began on the first two experimental prototypes, the V 401 and the V 402, at the Latécoère works in Toulouse. The V 401 was to have a maximum speed of 690km/h and a maximum range of 3,142km with a bomb load of 2,000kg. It was not planned to fix any armament.

In view of the ominous development of the invasion battle, in July 1944, orders were given to transfer the prototypes, already largely completed, by rail to Bernburg. But they never arrived. The V 401 was irreparably damaged on the way, by sabotage. The V 402 fuselage was found by the Allies, at the end of August 1944, still loaded on railway wagons. Evidently, in the chaos of the retreat, it was no longer possible to transport it back to the rear in time.

A contributory factor may have been the fact that, in the meantime, the Ju 488 programme had been completely reconfigured, and a new, larger aircraft was planned. Of that model, called the Ju 488 A, four prototypes were ordered. A complete redesign was carried out on the fuselage. It was planned as a welded steel tube construction, with a sheet metal covering for the forward and mid-section of the fuselage, and a fabric covering for the rear. The new fuselage design was to enable the bomb load to be increased to about 5,000 kilograms at a speed of 690 km/h, the same as the original design. In place of the originally planned BMW 801 engines, the redeveloped Ju 488 was to be fitted with the 24-cylinder liquid-cooled Jumo 222, with 2,500hp take-off power. Remote-controlled gun positions (FDL) for the middle and rear sections of the fuselage were planned, with two 20-millimetre MG 151/20s in the mid-section, and two 13-millimetre MG 131s to the rear. The operational ceiling was to be around 11,500 metres.

Despite abandoning the V 401 and V 402, and calling a complete halt to all German bomber construction programmes, with the exception of the Ar 234, work continued on the Ju 488 V 403 and V 406. But at the end of November, the Ju 488 programme was also stopped by the RLM. All completed components were scrapped, despite the fact that the construction of the aircraft was already well advanced.

In January 1945 the documents for construction of the Ju 488 on licence, were released to Japan, but due to the war no construction on licence took place.[32] Almost automatically that raises the question of why, in the summer of 1944, the Ju 488 programme was reconfigured. It was done in such a way that the original advantages, of using already existing aircraft parts from other models, were lost. But why was the reconfigured programme to be continued, even after the halt to bomber construction in July 1944?

One explanation could quite simply be the need for urgent transport of heavy individual payloads, such as for example, atomic bombs over great distances. Only with the modified fuselage would the Ju 488 have been able to carry such a payload. In comparison with the already available normal Heinkel He 177, the new design would have made it possible to achieve a speed almost 200 kilometres faster, and also add greatly improved performance parameters. It is true, that with a completion date only in the middle of 1945, Heinkel would have to have reckoned with the Ju 488-A being ready for active service.

Then, in comparison with the Junkers Ju 287, and also the Horten Ho XVIII, the aircraft would already have been out of date. Additionally, it must be said that, in the autumn of 1944, hundreds of the Heinkel He 177 heavy bombers, the reliability of which had been considerably improved in the meantime, were parked uselessly on many airfields. Those aircraft would also have been suitable for conversion into nuclear weapons carriers. After appropriate modifications, they would have been capable of improving their performance to such an extent, that the difference between them, and the planned Ju 488, was negligible.

The Ju 488 was also in competition with the Henschel Hs 130, another 4-tonne bomber. Nothing further will be said at this point concerning the Henschel aircraft, because the RLM preferred the Ju 488 as a high altitude bomber. But in a following volume we shall return to the Hs 130, because, at the end of 1944, it was planned as a carrier for a large Henschel rocket-assisted flying bomb (204).

Heinkel He 177: the 'atomic *Reichsfeuerzeug*' from Prague

In expert circles, discussions have quietly gone on for years about the fact that the Heinkel He 177 was withdrawn from service, in summer/autumn of 1944, because of shortage of fuel. However, an interesting, albeit incomplete model of that type of aircraft was modified in Prague, planned to carry the German atomic bomb. In the meantime, it has been possible to discover many details, including photographs, concerning that aircraft.

Possibly the first prototype aircraft of an 'atomic bomber', was the Heinkel He 177 A-5 V-38. It was produced by

The inglorious end of Germany's atomic bomber: the Heinkel He 177 V-38 (KM + TB) was captured in an incomplete state on 8 May 1945 at Prague Rusin (Photograph: Griehl collection).

Post-war view of the He 177 V-38 atomic bomber version. Clearly visible is the damage resulting from the US air raid of 25 April 1945 (Photograph: Griehl collection).

May 1945: Scrap collection area at Prague Rusin. In the foreground another atomic bomber aircraft conversion of the type He 177 (ND + … ?) (Photograph: Griehl collection).

the Arado works in Brandenburg. The aircraft, with the markings KM + TB, was officially mentioned for the first time, on 27 April 1944, as an experimental carrier. It served as a prototype aircraft for testing the FuG 200 and 216 radar equipment and was fitted with a new A-position, with two MG 131s. The aircraft was delivered to the Werneuchen testing station. After that all official traces of it are lost until it was captured, in a damaged condition, on 8 May 1945 in Prague Rusin. Whether at that point it was still under the command of the KdE, i.e. Test Station Command, is unknown.

In some Polish documentation an excellent description

Close-up view of the enlarged bomb bay of the He 177 V-38 to take a German nuclear weapon (Photograph: Griehl collection)

is given of the He 177 V-38, before conversion began. Until now, no official documents or plans have been released concerning that conversion. However, on the basis of the photographs that are available, it is possible to say a lot about the highlights of the Prague 'atomic' Heinkel. Final clarification of all the specifications of that version must be left to a future date. The available photographic material, from May 1945, indicates the following modifications to the aircraft:

Bomb bay: The bomb bay was modified to take a large central individual payload, with modifications appearing to be restricted to the forward two-thirds of the bay. To one side there appears to be part of the retaining device for the planned bomb. Unfortunately, the main mechanism for suspending the bomb cannot be discerned on the photographs. The bomb doors are missing on all photographs. Either they had not yet been fitted or they were to be left off altogether.

Rear cabin: The planned modifications principally extended to the rear part of the cabin. It remained incomplete, possibly to install an observation position, or to improve accessibility from the cockpit to the bomb bay. Armament had been removed from the A2 and C positions. The oxygen installation may have been dismantled.

New windows: Provision of a camera window had been made on the right, above the bomb bay, and new windows put in behind the cockpit.

Armament: Removal of the B 1- (FDL B 131/2A), B 2- (MG 151 I), and also the A 2- (MG 151/20) and C-positions (MG 81 Z). Retention of the A 1- (MG 81 I) and rear gun positions (MG 151/20 I or MK 108 I 'keyhole mounting').

Interestingly, modifications 1 to 4 above, match remarkably exactly the conversion measures carried out by the Americans, on the atomic bomb version of the Boeing B-29.[33]

Nose cabin: In a central position there was a fairly large aperture like a keyhole. Then, the purpose of it was thought most likely to be for mounting a large antenna for measurements, similar to the He 177 A-7. But, the most recent knowledge, indicates that it was more likely to be a position for installing a new kind of 'keyhole gun mounting' for a MK 108, with a limited radius of movement. In 1945, the firm of Rheinmetall-Borsig was intensifying its work on the so-called MK 108 'keyhole mounting'. On the basis of the available photographic material, it seems that more progress had been made than previously thought.[34] During the final phase of the war, the short 3 cm MK 108 machine-gun was intended, from then on, to serve as the on-board armament for the many varied bomber projects. The reasons were the light weight of the weapon, and the devastating effect of a single direct hit that was sufficient to shoot down a single-engined fighter aircraft. But, until then, it was not known how it was intended to mount the MK 108 as a defensive weapon.[35]

Engines and wings: The outer wings and engines were dismantled on the prototype and had not been refitted by the end of the war. Therefore, in the absence of all the documents, it remains unclear as to what the final planned appearance of the aircraft would have been. By itself, the fact that the engines had been dismantled, does not indicate that extensive modifications were to be undertaken. At the end of the war, in many photographs showing He 177 aircraft, it can be seen that the engines had been dismantled. The reason may be that the Daimler-Benz engines of the Heinkel heavy bombers, grounded since the summer of 1944, had been

Close-up view of the He 177 (ND + ... ?) with clear signs of fighting (Photograph: Griehl collection).

dismantled to save maintenance work. The engines were kept in such a way that they could be quickly reinstalled, as required. In that way, by February 1945, 200 He 177s had been retained. Another possibility, if more speculative, is that instead of the usual DB 610 engines, two new DB 613s were to be fitted. The change promised dramatically to improve the performance of the aircraft. Certainly, the installation of the engines, which had already been successfully tested on a He 177, would have required measures to reinforce the tail-plane control surfaces and the tail wheel. Whether such measures were carried out cannot be decided on the basis of the available photographs. The fact that the outer wings are missing raises the question as to whether, instead of the standard A-5 wing tips, extended outer wings were to be used as on the He 177 A-7. They markedly improved the range and flight characteristics. The special nature of the V-38 suggests that it could well be probable that the extended outer wings were to be fitted.

Paint scheme: The existing paint scheme of the aircraft seems to have been largely removed. At the end of the war, through its subsidiary BASF, the IG Farben factory is said to have been working in a secret underground factory, in Ohrdruf, on the development of a special paint with radar-absorbing qualities.[36] Such paint could have been used in this instance. Current 'stealth' technology also seems to have had German parentage. (see chapter on the Ho XVIII)

If the question is asked, as to what conclusions can be drawn from all those planned measures, it is clear that one of the central elements was the modification in the area of the bomb-bay of the He 177 V-38. As is well known, the He 177 A-5 version was originally intended to carry exterior payloads. For example, the HS 293 or Fritz-X, and even the largest known *Luftwaffe* bombs, such as the 3,600 kilogram bomb, could be carried by that version, on special exterior carriers, without any problems. It also raises the question, as to what the special payload looked like that was to be carried by the aircraft. In the context of the secrecy policy at the time, it was perfectly normal practice that the relevant aircraft firms were not informed which special weapons their aircraft were to carry. However, post-war reports indicate that the aircraft was to drop a parachute bomb with a sensational explosive effect, from a height of 7,000 metres.[37] The reason for the massive conversion measures to the fuselage, by reducing the armament, may have been to achieve a significant increase in speed and range.

At the end of June 1944, the heavy nose-gun position and the armed B-2 gun turret were removed. Thus the speed of the lighter weight Heinkel, He 177, could be increased to a maximum of 569 km/h. A range of 7,000 kilometres was possible when the armament was reduced to one MG 131 Z in the B1 and rear gun positions, and one MG 131 1 in the C-position. As is now known, the armament of the He 177 V-38 was even more radically reduced. In the area of the former B-2 position, and in the tightly riveted wing tank, additional fuel could be accommodated. By further reducing the armament, and dispensing with the oxygen installation, it was expected that an airborne weight of about 40,000 kilograms, and a range between 7,500 and 8,000 kilometres would be achieved. Such technical performance data already very closely resemble the required range profile for the 'America bomber'.

The incomplete H E 177 V-38 conversion was set on fire in the heavy American air raids on Prague, and on the Skoda works on 25 April 1945. One wonders if that attack,

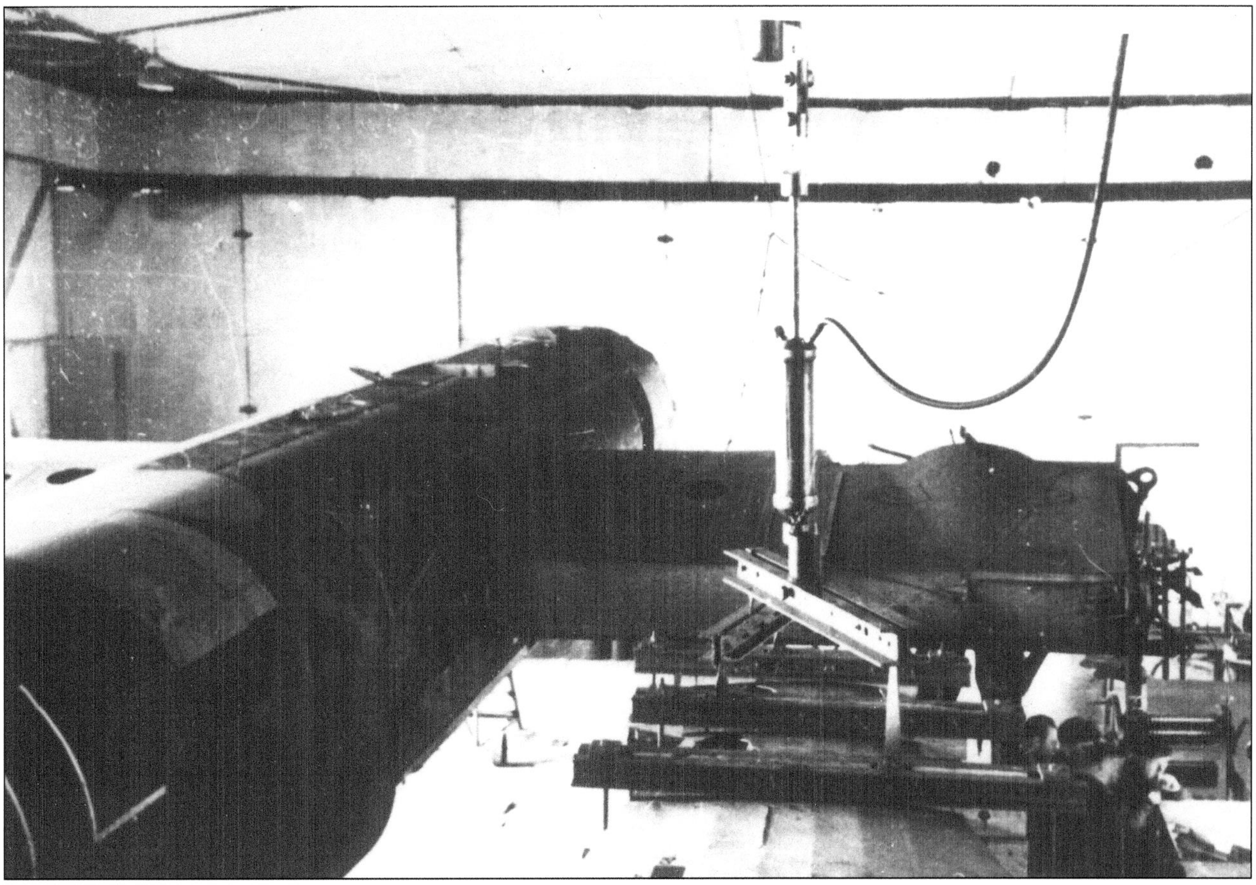

The Letov works in Prague (1945): a third Heinkel He 177 (... + NB) in the same process of conversion as the V-38. In the picture can be seen the roof of the bomb bay being subjected to a loading pressure test.

so shortly before the end of the war, on the previously untouched Skoda works in Prague and Pilsen, was intended to destroy, right under the noses of the Russians, the secret weapons that they had intended to capture. Only a short time before, the Potsdamer-Auer uranium/thorium works were comprehensively bombed by the American 8th Air Force on 12 April 1945, 'quite by chance', shortly before the Russians captured them.

The V-38, effectively in scrap form, was captured and photographed by the Allies at the end of the war.[38] There are, however, indications and photographic evidence that, in addition to the Heinkel He 177 V-38, another two machines were being similarly modified in Prague.[39]

However, the aircraft markings on the two He 177 aircraft are only partly known. (... + TD) and (ND + ...) A photograph of the first aircraft has already been published many times with an incorrect caption. But it clearly shows the same stage of construction, and the same conversion measures, as appear on the V-38. How far advanced the development of this aircraft was, at the end of the war, is unknown. What became of it is also completely uncertain. In the case of the third aircraft with the markings (ND + ...), the available photographic material indicates that the conversion measures had only reached a very early stage. The torso of its fuselage appears to have suffered heavy damage by machine-gun fire in the bitter final battles for the Prague Rusin airfield.

All those facts give the impression that the debatable Heinkel conversions were not to develop a single prototype only, but at least a planned small production series. Contradicting that is the fact that the Armaments Ministry on 8 July 1944 ordered all production, and further development of the He 177, to be halted under pain of penalty. If the conversions were not an original project of the Heinkel aircraft works, one wonders for whom the Prague Letov works and Lufthansa were working, at the time. Perhaps the SS had something to do with it, via the Skoda-Kammler complex. It is known that as early as 1944 the SS were trying to bring under their own control the production of the He 177, in the great Junkers factory in Oranienburg.[40]

The question has to be asked as to where the plans and documents for the 'atomic' Heinkel have been kept until now. Unfortunately, that is unknown. Interestingly, at the end of the war, in the same aircraft park in Prague, parts of the fuselage of a Ju 290 A and Ju 290 B were found. Perhaps there were also plans to convert those aircraft in the same way, to carry a 'miracle weapon'.

Addendum: When the conversion of the He 177 V-38 to an atomic bomber was under way, in the Letov works in Prague, one of the engineers involved in the project remarked: 'If we succeed in this we will conquer the world'.

However, in August 1944, work on the He 177 V-38, and its sister aircraft, which were also being modified, is supposed to have been stopped. The reasons, insofar as this information is correct, can only be surmised. Possibly it was the result of the same delays that also occurred at that time in Stadtilm/Ohrdruf. The 'atomic *Reichsfeuerzeuge*', however, were not scrapped but remained in a preserved state in Prague. That would also explain the removal of the engines seen on the photographs. On 25 April 1945, all the aircraft were said to have been seriously damaged in an American air raid. Whether, in the meantime, the conversion work had been resumed is something which still needs to be clarified. (J. R. Smith, Anthony Kay, *German Aircraft of World War II*, pages 286-287, Putnam, 1972)

Junkers Ju 287 V-3: the Stopgap

In March 1945, not only was the decision made to put the 'America bomber' into production, but also two further heavy bomber projects were, even then, tackled by the RLM. Thus, on 17 March 1945, it was decided to mass-produce the four-engined Junkers heavy jet-bomber, Ju 287, which had been axed in August 1944. The official version was that the jet bomber had to meet the Führer's requirement for a means of 'attacking long-distance shipping targets'.[41] The aircraft was to have a maximum speed of 885 kilometres per hour, at a height of 7,000 metres, and a range of 2,000 kilometres. Like the Hortens, it would carry a 4-tonne bomb. It was not possible to install the planned Heinkel-Hirth turbines, because of delays in development. So once again recourse had to be made to the BMW 109/003 turbine engines. They were to be mounted in one group of three, under each wing. That aircraft type carried the designation Ju 287 V-3 and by then was supposed to be ready for action.

By the end of the war, as a result of the previous halt in development, no other prototype could be produced, apart from the experimental aircraft Ju 287, a 'block construction aircraft' made from the parts of several different aircraft types. Instead, there was a full-scale mock-up with all fittings and specifications. But the construction was already planned for mass-production and completely finished. Secretly, the Junkers works had made in advance all preparations for a smooth prototype and mass-production run. Thus, all semi-finished products, forgings and stampings, and also the parts and equipment to be fitted were ready in sufficient quantities to be able to begin mass production. Despite the difficulties, due to moving individual production units, and production of individual components in many smaller outsourced factories, at the end of the war, completed components were already available for several aircraft. Since they had been moved to various locations, the individual components were scattered across the whole area of Saxony and Thuringia. Then, after the end of the war, prototypes were captured by the Soviets, completed by them, and taken for testing in the Soviet Union. A mysterious composite project of the Ju 287, with a Me 262 as an escort aircraft, remained on the drawing board.[42]

All that raises the question today, as to why such an expensive project was, even then, resumed in March 1945. The necessary material, the fuel and the production capacity could only have been bought at the expense of axing other aircraft types. From a resultant small production run of the Ju 287 aircraft, no shattering success could be expected in the war situation at that time. Also, the stated official purpose, of attacking shipping, does not seem to be important and credible enough for such forcible measures, and a changeover in production. All that was already known to the planners in the Third Reich. Now, one is forced to the conclusion that the Ju 287 aircraft were not created for conventional bombs, but to carry weapons, the dropping of which would decide the course of the war. That explanation would also make such measures comprehensible from a present day viewpoint. It is no coincidence, that the Junkers works used a Heinkel He 177 as a test carrier for the bomb bay, and the dropping equipment of the Ju 287.[43] Perhaps those were the same modifications that were also carried out on the Heinkel aircraft in Prague. (see this chapter)

The Ju 287 was a suitable transport aircraft with which to drop the new 4-tonne bomb on targets in Europe, even in daylight. Because of the extensive preparatory work by the Junkers factory on that aircraft type, the possible risks in development could only be small, so that rapid results could be expected. The Ju 287 V-3, the third prototype, could already be fully armed and consequently even ready for action. The aircraft was under construction at the end of the war.

The question arises of what would have happened if, in the summer of 1944, the RLM had had more foresight, and had not interrupted the development of the Ju 287. One possible explanation is that, at the time the Ju 287 was halted, it could not be foreseen that the miracle weapons would be ready to be used. Or, less flattering to the planners, perhaps the people responsible for discontinuing the programme knew nothing of the planned development of those weapons. The fact that the Junkers factory, despite official orders to stop work, continued working on the Ju 287 project suggests a greater likelihood that at Junkers and in the RLM there were individuals who knew that the miracle weapons were being developed. But, in the end, there was no time.

Horten Ho XVIII: the jet-powered '*Amerikabomber*' and its German competitors

It has been known for years that in 1944/45 there were many German designs, for jet-powered intercontinental bombers, among many different firms. However, such developments were long regarded as the results of wild fantasies on the part of designers, and no significance at all was attributed to them. The Allies too, in their evaluations after the war, only attributed significance to the actual jet fighter developments, i.e. Me 262, He 162, Ar 234 and Ta 183. But information concerning the intercontinental bombers was 'suppressed' from public knowledge. Only in 1989 did it finally become known[44] that those bomber projects represented a regular large-scale programme within the German aviation industry. They were based on a commission, from the RLM, to create an aircraft for the 'visit to America'. The project came into existence in the middle of 1944 and, even in March 1945, led to a large commission for such an aircraft. From the standpoint of 1989 it is understandable why the author of the source,[45] at the end of his report, 'gently shook his head', at how it was still possible to become involved with such projects, at a time when 'the Russians are reaching the Oder at Frankfurt'.

If one considers the results of the latest research, what was happening at that time appears to be logical and understandable. The winning design, the Horten Ho XVIII, if the war had lasted longer, would perhaps have had the wherewithal to become one of the best known aircraft in the history of the world. But what was the background?

Reichsmarschall Hermann Göring, from June 1942, had been chairman of the secret *Forschungsrat über Nuklearphysik als Waffe* (Research Committee on the Use of Nuclear Physics as a Weapon). In the middle of 1944, he was informed that Germany would soon have the atomic bomb.[46] That was something that he also told to the American officers, at his interrogations in the post-war period.

One of the possibilities for striking New York with that bomb was to develop a so-called 'America bomber'. In autumn 1944, two aircraft design conferences were held on the subject. Invitations to the conferences were sent to most of the leading aircraft firms in the German Reich, including Messerschmitt, Focke-Wulf, Blohm und Voss, Junkers, Arado and Heinkel, but not to the Horten Brothers. The aim was to design an aircraft that could carry a 4,000 kilogram bomb, at high speed, to the target over a distance of 9,000 kilometres. Then, without refuelling, the aircraft was to be able to return to the base from which it took off. To disguise the true intentions, besides carrying out strategic aerial warfare against the USA and the Soviet Union, there was talk of planned attacks on convoys.[47]

The Blohm und Voss designs, the B.V. 188 and those of Arado, the E 555, from the beginning, had only an outside chance. Heinkel, it appeared, did not turn up with any long-range bomber developments of that kind. Thus, as a result of the first conference, Göring commissioned the Junkers and Messerschmitt works to design and build long-range bomber prototypes. In response, Junkers designed a long-range version of their own Ju 287 jet bomber, work on which had been halted in August 1944. Messerschmitt developed from the high-speed fighter project H G III the four-engined Me P 1007.

During the preparatory work, it is true that it was already evident that both firms would not be able to produce the specified range requirements. The repeated failure of the aircraft developers was finally officially established at one of the conferences held by the DVL, under the direction of Professor Dr Bock. The early jet engines were real 'gas-guzzlers'! The intercontinental bomber project was then discussed between Hitler and Göring on New Year's Day 1945 and Göring optimistically promised his sceptical Führer that this long-range bomber would soon be developed.[48]

In the meantime, the RLM had even demanded a range of 11,000 kilometres. The brothers Reinhardt and Walter Horten were not invited to the second design conference. In November 1944 they were informed by *Oberst* Siegfried Knemeyer of the failure of the *crème de la crème* of the German aviation industry.[49] During the Christmas holidays the Horten brothers, in response to Knemeyer's request for them to present a project of their own, worked non-stop. They produced the draft design for their intercontinental bomber, called Horten XVIII A. Ten different variations of that aircraft were developed. Each one was to use a different number of the already existing jet engines. For example, four or six Heinkel-Hirth He SO 11 jet engines, eight BMW 003 A or eight Junkers-Jumo 004 B jet engines. The version that Horten preferred was to use six Jumo 004 B jets which were to be fixed to the fuselage, as in the Horton Ho IX. The all-wing aircraft was to take off on a take-off cradle, assisted by rockets, and land on a kind of skid. The Horten XVIII A would have been almost entirely made of wood. It would be glued together with a special carbon-based adhesive.[50] As a result the gigantic all-wing aircraft would be largely invisible to radar apparatus. Therefore, in 1945, a 'Stealth' bomber was envisaged.

In the meantime the Messerschmitt engineers improved their Me P 1107 design. On 31 January 1945, they presented to the head of the Armaments Staff, Karl-Otto Saur, documents relating to an improved version of the long-range bomber project, then called Me P 1108. In addition, Messerschmitt's data allowed the possibility, by use of appropriate armaments, of deploying the Me P 1108 as a fighter, fighter-bomber, or escort aircraft. Messerschmitt intended to submit the completed design of the Me P 1108 within eight weeks. When the Messerschmitt design was presented to Hitler, probably as the result of vigorous lobbying by Willy Messerschmitt, Hitler was wildly enthusiastic. Albert Speer writes that he had never seen Hitler so excited as he was then, as he imagined New York collapsing in a sea of flames. Hitler saw the skyscrapers transformed into gigantic torches. He saw them collapsing, and blazing up against the night sky in the reflection of the burning city. Hitler therefore commissioned Saur to proceed immediately with the development of the Messerschmitt Me P 1108 design. But that commission was never carried out.

Meanwhile, the Junkers engineers had also improved their designs using the new six-engined E F 131, and the all-wing project E F 130.

From 20 to 23 February 1945, another conference took place in Dessau, at which *Reichsmarschall* Hermann Göring was again present. The designs were assessed by two special commissions, *Flugzellenbau* and *Kampfflugzeuge.* The following are known to have been members of the commission: *Diplom-Ingenieur* Ludwig Bölkow (Messerschmitt), *Diplom-Ingenieur* Gropler (Junkers), Major Walter Horten, Dr Reimar Horten, *Oberstabsingenieur* Kohl (Director of Production), *Flugzeugbaumeister* Rüdiger Kosin (Arado), Prof. Dr Quick (DVL) and *Flugbaumeister* Egon Scheibe (OKL). While the Messerschmitt project produced the highest speed, the Junkers and Messerschmitt projects proved inferior to the Horten designs with regard to range and bomb loads. Moreover the simple steel tube, wood and fabric construction, especially in the light of the war situation at the time, similarly recommended the Horten project. A few days later the Horten brothers were ordered to go to *Reichsmarschall* Göring, who then commissioned the brothers to build their aircraft in partnership with Junkers. Thus Reimar and Walter Horten met the Junkers engineers, who had also invited colleagues from Messerschmitt to the meeting. Finally, it seemed as if the Horten brothers' design was to be built by a committee of the German aviation industry.

But, to the horror of the Horten brothers, the committee wanted to put a large tail fin on the rear fuselage of the Horten XVIII A. The resultant design was designated as the Junkers E F 140. At the same time, the committee was already considering a post-war use of their E F 140 as a civilian aircraft. They wanted to present the joint design to the RLM, and recommended that it should be produced in the underground factories, based in the Harz mountains.

Reimar Horten was very unhappy with the 'committee bomber', and began to reconfigure his Horten XVIII A design. It resulted in the Horten XVIII B. Again it was to be an all-wing bomber, whose three-man crew would be accommodated in a bubble cabin on the wing tip. Reimar Horten wanted to use four Heinkel-Hirth He S 011 jet engines for the aircraft, each providing 1,200 kilograms of thrust, which would be fitted in nacelles under the wings. The nacelle arrangement was required by the DVL for reasons of safety. That configuration of engines resulted in a weight saving of about a tonne. It made it possible to attach two, riveted, fixed undercarriage legs on the under-side of the wing, instead of an arrangement for landing on a skid, as in the case of the Horten Ho IX.

Each of the undercarriage components was to consist of four individual tyres in a tandem arrangement. During flight, in order to reduce drag, they would be covered with flaps. Horten believed that the use of a fixed undercarriage would save another tonne in weight, compared with using a retractable undercarriage. Thus, the aircraft was to have a speed of 850 km/h, a service ceiling of 16,000 metres and an overall flight time of 27 hours. Although defensive armament was regarded as unnecessary, Horten suggested that two MK 108 30mm cannon could be fitted directly below the cockpit. The Horten XVIII would have been an early form of a 'Stealth' bomber, quite similar to the present-day Northrop B-2. Contributing to that would have been its shape, which gave little echo on radar, its wooden construction, and the radar-absorbent special paint produced by IG Farben.

The special paint went under the codename *Schornsteinfeger,* i.e. chimney sweep.[51] It consisted of a bituminous paint that was strongly permeated with carbon. The thickness of the paint had to be applied in precise relation to the frequency of the enemy radar. In that way, the incoming radar signal was absorbed within the dielectric material, and the energy of its echo was reduced. The use of *Schornsteinfeger* was not only restricted to aircraft, but was also used as a protective paint for ships, e.g. S-boats or U-boat snorkels, and camouflaged objects on land. Another form of anti-radar defence was a material, like a honeycomb, that was stuck on the outer skin in mats. The special paints were produced in Ohrdruf/Crawinkel.[52] To the radar installations of the late 1940s, the Horten would have been practically 'invisible', in contrast to the present-day Northrop B-2. In addition it displayed superior flight characteristics.

From bomb proof, bunkered hangars such as those at Kahla or Mühldorf, the Horten could have flown in a single attack, at a height of 16,000 metres, without refuelling, to its target in the United States. There, guided by radar, it could drop its 4-tonne atomic bomb by parachute, and then return directly to its original base, or to another landing area specially provided for the purpose.

The Horten brothers called on Hermann Göring with their Horten XVIII B design, and on 23 March 1945, were commissioned to build it. At the same time, Messerschmitt and Junkers, by order of the RLM, had to halt their work on their long-range bombers. Horten was ordered to meet Karl-Otto Saur, the successor to Albert Speer, in order to find suitable locations for producing the new heavy bomber.

Saur wanted the work on the Horten to be carried out in two bombproof hangars in the vicinity of Kahla, code named *Lachs,* i.e. salmon. Saur told Horten that the two newly built hangers would have 5.6 metre thick concrete roofs, and would be completely bomb proof. In addition, two extra-long manoeuvring areas were being constructed, so that test flights could be carried out with the Horten aircraft in Kahla. Horten had already visited the production areas of the Junkers works, in the Harz Mountains, near to Hilbingerrode and Blankenburg. He was to be assigned 2,000 workers and to begin work immediately. Göring and the Armaments Ministry expected that the Horten XVIII B would be completed by late summer 1945. Saur's response to Horten's objections was simply: 'Well, along with the Horten, we'll produce the Me 262 and Jumo 004 B jet engines there too, and you can be in charge of the whole show'.[53]

A week later, on 1 April 1945, according to RLM documents, work began on the construction of the Horten XVIII B in the underground installations in Kahla. But, by the afternoon of the 12 April 1945, American troops had already occupied the works. Although it is known that production of the Me 262 was already under way there, until now no clear statement has been found concerning what the Americans actually discovered, and took away with them.[54]

Since then there have been indications that, possibly, at least one Horten XVIII had already been completed. That would suggest that construction began even earlier. The place where the aircraft was constructed is unknown, but the Ohrdruf/Crawinkel area is suggested in that connection. An American secret report actually confirmed the existence of secret underground aircraft hangars and workshops, to the south west of Ohrdruf. They are most likely to have involved aircraft of the A-version, which had been designed from January 1945. Horten had already shown, in their Ho IX jet fighter, that they had ways and means of building aircraft, even while circumventing the directly responsible officials in the RLM. In the absence of definitive evidence, however, those indications must be regarded with a necessary degree of reservation.

The significance attributed by the Allies to the work at Kahla is demonstrated by the fact that the Supreme Commander of the American Air Force in Europe, Air Force General Carl Spaatz, visited the installation. He may have been interested only in the German achievements underground and the production there of the Me 262. It is possible that he went there on account of the 'America bomber' project, to evaluate the danger it posed to the USA. In any event, it is known that, directly after he was taken prisoner in May 1945, Hermann Göring had a two-day interrogation by General Spaatz. Goring told him of the planned intercontinental bomber projects and, as the most recent knowledge indicates, also about Germany's atomic bombs.

It was only some years after the war that the Horten brothers discovered the true nature of the bomb load planned for their 'America bomber'. Not even during the five months in which they were working on their bomber project, did Knemeyer or Göring tell the Hortens that it was to involve an atomic bomb. However, the fact that they did not know is by no means surprising. Even scientists, who were working on Germany's nuclear weapons research, were strictly forbidden even to utter the word 'atomic', outside the laboratories. Certainly the political leadership of the Third Reich, in their vociferous announcements of miracle weapons, were less reserved in that regard.

Heinkel 'Norway Bomber': the Mysterious Intercontinental Bomber

There may have been yet another German intercontinental bomber system, the existence of which is still being withheld. On 29 June 1945, the *Washington Post* printed a report from the AP news agency which has never subsequently been withdrawn.[55] The report stated that the German preparations, for bombing New York from Norway, had almost been completed by the end of the war. The statement originated from officers of the British Royal Air Force, i.e. the RAF, from the headquarters of XXI Army Corps on 28 June 1945. A 'huge airfield' near Oslo was to serve as the base for that attack. On the air base, according to a high-ranking British officer, the largest air force base that he had ever seen, the Allies found 40 giant bombers each with a range of 7,000 miles. Such aircraft were a new type of bomber that had been developed by Heinkel. According to AP, the Heinkel aircraft were dismantled by the Allies, for detailed evaluation. The report stated, that German ground crew had said that the aircraft were standing by for a mission to New York. A further statement asserted that special bombs, with a 'new kind of explosive power', were planned to be used on that mission.

Unfortunately, even now there has been neither a withdrawal of the AP reports, supplementary explanations, nor further reports, concerning the incident. Thus we do not know the details. There are also no German statements concerning the '40 giant bombers' near Oslo. The designation of the 'America Squadron' is not known, nor what aircraft type was to be used.

However, it is known that the Heinkel works were working on a rival design to the Ju 287. That aircraft, with the designation He 343, was a four-engined medium range bomber that only had a range of 1,620 kilometres. Thus it would have been completely unsuitable for a mission against America across the Atlantic. But it is striking too, that the history of the Heinkel He 343 has not been definitively clarified. At any rate, until now, it is still not known whether, or how many, aircraft of that type were produced, or even what happened to them.

Diplom-Ingenieur Siegfried Günther, the chief designer and director of the project office in the Heinkel aircraft works wrote a paper, on 1 October 1945, for the US Technical Service. He admitted that Heinkel engineers were busy on the design of four-engined long-range bombers right up to May 1945. The performance of the Heinkel long-range bomber projects would, he said, have been similar to that of the Horten and Junkers designs.[56] But the US report published no statement as to how far the work had progressed. It may be that the design and production of the 'Norway bomber' were deliberately hushed up. The planning, design, and preparation for action of 40 heavy jet bombers, however, suggests that a considerable number of designers, workers, ground staff and pilots were involved in the project. They may have been sworn to secrecy concerning all the details relating to the Norway bomber. Independently, on the Allied side, there must still be photographs and evaluation reports concerning those aircraft. One wonders where those documents may now be.

Another possibility is that the Heinkel 'Norway bombers' were in fact specially converted He 177s. Aircraft of that type, since the summer of 1944, had been parked in their hundreds on airfields in the north. The obvious thing to do would have been to convert some of them. It is quite possible that in the Washington Post report the figures relating to range, i.e. 'miles' in American, and 'kilometres' in German, were mixed up. Thus, if there was a mistake in translation from the statements of prisoners, the range of the Norway bomber was 7,000 kilometres. That happens to correspond exactly with the range of a He 177 with increased performance. (see corresponding chapter) But such an attack on America would have involved only 'one-way flights', with the aircraft afterwards ditching in the Atlantic. Plans for such kamikaze-type bomber flights to America, in He 177s, had already been contemplated in 1944. Because the chances of the crews being picked up by waiting U-boats were all too uncertain, the plans were personally turned down by Hitler. Under the pressure of what was happening in the war, the decision may later have been changed. The deployment of suicide pilots was rejected by Hitler. Nevertheless, in April 1945, they were regularly used on the Oder front.[57]

The next question is whether the 'Norway bombers' were aircraft belonging to the *Luftwaffe* or to the SS. In 1944 the SS had been pushing to have the production of He 177s, in the Junkers Oranienburg factory, placed under their control. Himmler's personnel may have appropriated some of the He 177s standing idle in the North. Perhaps there were connections to the He 177 conversions in Prague. (see this chapter) The argument that the He 177s in Norway were similar 'converted aircraft', thus has some weight.

A further possible explanation is that they were not 40 He 177s but He 177s of *Kampfgeschwader* 40. KG 40 retained its He 177s until the end of the war and was also stationed in Norway. Its long-distance bombers were specially fitted with HS 293 B missiles, which could be guided to their target by an interference-proof wire guidance system. The squadron was standing by for an annihilation attack on England. (For more details, see the following volume)[58] That may have been the real germ of truth in the story of the 'Norway bombers'. Perhaps KG 40 had to attack New York as an alternative.

The great airfield near Oslo, which in the spring of 1945 was to serve as the base for an attack on America, must also be investigated more closely. The same also applies to the largely unknown role that Norway was to play in the planned deployment of other *Vergeltungswaffen*. Until then, we must regard the reports concerning the 40 Heinkel 'Norway bombers' as unexplained. Perhaps those bombers were to be the weapons with which offensive intercontinental attacks were to be flown, in April 1945, against enemy capitals. That would serve to explain the fact that the existence of such aircraft continues to be hushed-up, because where there was no miracle weapon, of course there could not be any 40 aircraft to carry them.

3) Light Miracle Weapons' Carriers For Hitler's 'Five Minutes to Midnight' All-round Defence Plan

Suicide Junkers Ju 87: 'The Atomic Stuka'

Again and again in research, one comes across instances of overlap between the German nuclear weapons programme, and the so-called *Todesflieger*, i.e. SO-men, SO standing for *Selbstopfer*, i.e. suicide. Possibly such an incident occurred during the first days of May 1945, in Austria. At that time, 8 black-painted Junkers Ju 87 landed unexpectedly on a large field in Seitenstätten, in the forest area close to Loosdorf. But after they had landed the crews were to discover that there was no ground crew organisation, nor facilities for aircraft maintenance. In fact they had obviously been misdirected. Consequently, during the last few days of the war, they stayed in the village with the local population. They waited for orders that never came. While there they said that they had been ordered, after their landing, to pick up 'atomic bombs', in order to fly one more decisive attack with them. But it was to be a flight from which there would be no return, i.e. an SO mission. To which NSG unit the eight Ju 87s belonged, or what became of the pilots and the aircraft after the end of the war, is unknown. Perhaps it was all hearsay.

Little can be made of an apparently 'senseless' landing in some field, of an entire Ju 87 night bomber squadron, close to a small out of the way Austrian village. Naturally, in Allied documents that have been released, no confirmation of those events can be found. Possibly, however, the incident becomes clearer if one considers closely the place where the Stukas landed. The pilots of the 'atomic Stukas' said that they had been 'misdirected'.

Interestingly, looking at the map of Austria, there is another Loosdorf, close to which there is another Seitenstätten. Even more interesting, those places too can be linked with secret weapons. Close to the second Loosdorf was located the secret object 'Quarz', and the second Seitenstätten was less than 20 kilometres south-west of Amstetten. On the Amstetten railway station 30 lorry loads of 'explosives with exceptional explosive power' were waiting in vain to be picked up. (see later section 'Small Uranium Bombs')

Were the Ju 87s that landed in error in Seitenstätten, as had also happened previously with Bf 109s (see this chapter), to be fitted with the Amstetten 'bombs with exceptional explosive power'? However, the question is raised, in so far as the report is confirmed, as to why the Ju 87 squadron landed in the wrong place. In the chaos of the last days of the war, it may have been a case of simple confusion of place names. It may have been, once again, a case of sabotage. Whatever the case, a possible atomic night attack was prevented.

The night bomber groups were specialised units that flew attacks in darkness, or in twilight. Their targets had previously been precisely determined, and were at a relatively short distance from the front. The aircraft they flew, at the end of the war, were principally the Fw 190 and Ju 87. In those difficult flights the Ju 87, long since obsolete for daylight attacks, proved to be quite outstanding. On those missions the targets, which had been precisely determined, were marked with flares by other night bomber aircraft. Some of the attacks were guided by radar, i.e. the Egon procedure. So it is possible that some of the Seitenstätten Ju 87s were intended to be used on pathfinder duties, in the planned atomic night attack. Perhaps only a few aircraft from the squadron were actually to drop the bombs. Such an attack may have been previously practised elsewhere.

Unfortunately we have no information as to whether the eight Ju 87s had been converted for their planned special mission, nor whether they were normal production machines of the D-8 type. However, it is probable that the relevant documents and photographs could be found in some Allied archive.

Suicide Bf 109 with 'new types of explosives'

It is not known if tactical atomic bombs were to be used by suicide pilots. Under that scheme, the Messerschmitt Bf 109 single piston-engined fighter, in the spring of 1945, may have been intended to serve as a carrier for miracle weapons.

On 18 March 1945 the commander of a fighter squadron in the Munster area received orders to take over and unload three railway wagons. They had been sent to him, under seal, by the *Lufwaffenzeugamt.* The orders he received contained instructions and drawings detailing bomb suspension mechanisms. The installation material was to fit the Bf 109 aircraft, enabling them to carry and release a new kind of bomb. The commander was struck by the fact that it involved a bomb of the 250 kilogram class, but that the bolts which held the bomb away from

Messerschmitt Bf 109 K-4 (Works Number 330/75) of III/JG 51, taking off from the Junkerstroylhof airfield in April 1945. Under the fuselage it is carrying a completely unknown bomb. Is this perhaps the first photograph of Hitler's 'small uranium bombs'? (Photograph: Griel collection).

the aircraft fuselage were unusually long. The bombs, fixed in that way, would have a ground clearance of only 16 centimetres. Therefore the Bf 109, fitted with them, could only take off on smooth concrete runways.

Secret orders that followed a few days later, indicated that the plan involved deploying a new weapon which would have an overall destructive radius of 16 kilometres. At the same time it would mean that the aircraft was lost. Therefore, the orders stated, 'the mission was only to be flown by unmarried volunteers'. But when asked, all the flying personnel volunteered, including the married men.

Immediately after that, new orders, given by telephone, instructed the commander to direct two heavy tractors into Austria, via Linz, to Amstetten. There they would pick up bombs that were at the goods station. The orders also informed the commander that the new bombs would not be dropped in the usual manner. Instead, they were to fall to earth on parachutes, in order to give the aircrews the chance of getting away. It was planned that the bombs would be dropped from a height of 7,000 metres.

The officer in charge of the transport, a *Luftwaffe Hauptmann*, found at the Amstetten goods station thirty sealed lorries, marked with an inscription in white: 'Handle with care, new type of explosive'! Since then, an Austrian scientist, whose name is known to the author, has confirmed that the mysterious weapons at the station were really atomic bombs. He himself had inspected them there, together with Heinrich Himmler. Unfortunately, he does not specify a date on which that inspection took place.[59] The lorries were guarded by a unit of the *Waffen-SS* under the command of a *Hauptsturmführer* who refused to hand them over, citing the need for the authority of a Führer order. But the *Luftwaffe Hauptmann* had no written special orders with him, to authorise him to insist that the bombs were handed over, and the SS officer was taking no risks. Thus they all remained in Amstetten where the Americans found them. Having heard rumours of 'special' bombs, they had advanced with the greatest possible speed. The Americans arrived there only just before the Russians, because the Austrian specialist had told them about the bombs while in a prisoner of war camp.[60] How, and under what circumstances the eyewitness was taken prisoner, still remains unclear.

So what can be made of that report? In Münster-Hahndorf itself there were no fighter squadrons, but night-fighter units (1/NJG 1). It is true that in Münster there was a *Luftwaffe* testing station. But in the immediate vicinity there were units of JG 27, KG (J) 51, and JG 26. All three units were equipped with Messerschmitt Bf 109s and so are possible candidates. It is most probable that JG 27 was involved in the affair. Firstly, its units were concentrated around Münster. Secondly, its possibly converted aircraft were, as late as 15 April 1945, transferred to airfields around Prague. It was said that Me 262 units stationed there had specially requested that unit to protect its aircraft as they took off and landed.[61] In the Prague district, at the end of the war, there was concentrated an important part of the Third Reich's secret weapons development. The transfer of the squadron may have been ordered, so that they would be able to continue to fly missions from there with the new weapon. In the same area there were perhaps the similarly equipped Bf 109s of other units.[62]

Unfortunately, until now there are no other documents with precise details of the conversion of the nuclear SO-Bf 109s and the weapons they were to drop. But the fact that spacing bolts are mentioned suggests the use of an unmodified ETC 503 i.e. *Rüstsatz* 1. What the 250kg 'miracle weapon' looked like is unclear.

In view of the light weight of that bomb, the question must be asked whether, with the state of technology at the time, they could have been fully fledged atomic bombs, in the classical sense. It may be more likely that they were radiological bombs or other types of ordnance.

However, it must not be forgotten that within the Third Reich's arsenal there was a 'small A-weapon', with several hundred grams of atomic explosive charge. It was said to be already available, in small numbers. (see section 'Small Uranium Bombs') It too could have been considered for use on the Bf 109. Possibly there is even now initial photographic evidence. The photograph in question shows a Bf 109 K-4 of III/JG51 taking off from the Junkerstroylhof airfield in April 1945. Under the fuselage is suspended a previously unknown longish bomb of the 250 kilogram class. The nose of the bomb appears to be held in a kind of saddle that bears a striking resemblance to the American post-war T-28 weapons system. The T-28 saddle system was a special suspension system for transporting a tactical uranium bomb of the 'Hiroshima type'. The type of aircraft used was the single engined propeller driven Douglas AD-4B 'Skyraider'.[63]

Junkerstroylhof was in fact one of the most remarkable airfields of the *Luftwaffe*. It was located like a bridgehead in the Vistula estuary, i.e. in East Prussia. Open dykes protected it from attack on the landward side. The Germans continually reinforced that strongpoint, particularly from the middle of April 1945, with new supplies of personnel and material sent by air and by sea. They held it until the end of the war.

However, there may have been a special purpose for Junkerstroylhof. Until now it has been known only as a pure *Jägerplatz*, i.e. fighter airfield. As far as we know, the Bf 109s operating from there, were not 'misused' for bomber attacks. The photograph taken there, in April 1945, shows a Bf 109 K with a 'mysterious' bomb. It is known that Junkerstroylhof had close connections with the airfields on Garz, at Peenemünde, and at Bornholm. Both locations were also connected with the German atomic bomb programme.

It is therefore open to discussion whether or not the photograph was connected with test flights using atomic bomb casings. Trials were to examine to what extent it was possible to deploy the weapons from Junkerstroylhof. Perhaps that was to be the real purpose, although never carried out, of the 'bridgehead airfield' in the Vistula estuary. In that connection it is unclear if the Russians, after taking Peenemünde and Bornholm, found there the remains of such 'atomic' versions of the Bf 109 and if, eventually, they even found the weapons that were intended to be used against them.

Because of the use of the Messerschmitt Bf 109 G or K, the question is raised in that connection why, instead of the Messerschmitt, the Focke-Wulf Fw 190 A, F, or the new D versions were not used for such a decisive mission. The Fw 190 A or F, because of their greater loading capacity and, in conjunction with their rear-mounted engine, their lower vulnerability to fire, would have been more suitable than the Bf 109. One of the possible explanations is that the standard Bf 109 was still available in large numbers. That was a result of *Jägerstabprogramm* 226. It had achieved an enormous record in the production output of standard fighters, particularly in the autumn of 1944. In complete contrast to the new, rare aircraft types, the Bf 109s were standing around everywhere on the scattered airfields of the *Luftflotte Reich*, i.e. the Reich air fleet.

Apart from its ready availability, the Bf 109 had one great advantage over the Fw 190 A and F. At heights above 7,000m the performance of the latter versions rapidly declined. Above that level, with the exception of the few available Fw 190 A-9s, they were easy prey to enemy fighters. In view of the fact that for the intended special mission it was planned to drop the bomb from a height of 7,000m,[64] the choice of the Bf 109 as a carrier is easier to understand. In addition, the Messerschmitt aircraft that was planned from the outset to carry a bomb load of 500kg, was easily able to carry the 250kg bomb. It is also a fact that the Bf 109 type formed the backbone of the other German 'suicide' units in 1945.[65]

In March 1945 many piston-engined fighting units of the *Luftwaffe* were already being disbanded. That was a result of the dreadful casualties of the preceding months, of minimal fuel stocks, and the poor training of the young replacement pilots. Thus, from March 1945, the remaining piston engined units in the West mostly flew fighter-bomber missions only, against the advancing Allied ground forces. However, the Bf 109 was not considered by the pilots to be very suitable for such purposes, as is pointed out in other relevant sources.[66]

From a tactical point of view it is also unclear why the already-available specialised assault units, such as the night bomber groups, were not used for such an important mission. Some of the groups were already carrying out, with radar guidance, precise night attacks on important targets on the Allied front. They would have had greater experience for such a difficult mission than the fighter squadrons that from the outset were virtually untrained for such missions. But this is only one of the many curious aspects.

If the special weapons were really waiting on the Austrian railway station at Amstetten, near Steyr, they could only have been produced by the mysterious 'Quarz' works near Melk. The secret history of the location with the code name 'Quarz' has, hitherto, not yet been fully disclosed. But it shows many parallels with the Ohrdruf V-weapons factory.[67]

There is a somewhat adventurous ring to the story of the journey of the two tractor units from Münster. They travelled right across the Reich area, with its risk of air raids, to Amstetten. That would certainly have been a very large operation and it could not have been completed successfully in just one or two days. Also, in the conditions at the time, the journey could not have been undertaken without the highest authority, so that the story of the missing papers is not really convincing.

Perhaps it was the case that the SS wanted to keep the weapons under their own control, to use them in the future, or to use them as a 'dead pledge'. Thus, knowingly or unknowingly, they prevented the tactical use of atomic, or radiological, bombs on the Western Front, at the end of March 1945. It is not known if there was a 'Führer order'. Perhaps the weapons were not released because of an order from Führer headquarters. Perhaps there was sabotage by responsible but worried people at Fuhrer headquarters. Two tractor units could only have loaded up a small part of the load carried by the 30 lorries. That raises another question, as to which other *Luftwaffe* units were to be armed with such weapons? Evidently, however, none of that ever happened.

Finally, another possibility is that the new types of explosives from Amstetten were destined for other weapons systems, e.g. rockets, and were waiting there to be transported further.

The Mystery of the Me 262 V-555

The story of the Messerschmitt Me 262 A, is well known. It was the aircraft which, had it been used in time, could have reclaimed air superiority for Germany. Thus, considering the progressive nature of the design, it is no surprise that such an aircraft type could also be used for new types of bomb. The Messerschmitt Me 262 A-2a/U2, the 'fast bomber with Lotfe', was only developed in two prototypes. They bore the works numbers 110484 and 110555. It was no longer possible to put the version into mass production. The particular characteristic of the Me 262 was a wooden cabin in the nose of the plane. It accommodated an additional bomb targeter, who was to use the precise Lotfe 7H bomb-sight, to direct two 250 kilogram bombs on to the target. To carry its bomb load the aircraft was equipped with two ETC 504s.

The first prototype, with the white markings V-484,

flew as early as September 1944. On 7 January 1945, it was transferred to the Rechlin experimental station. But there all trace of it is lost. A second aircraft, with the white markings V-555, was completed in January 1945, and fitted with a modified Lotfe Cabin 2. The improved cabin, in addition to less drag, also provided less weight, in comparison with the cabin on the V-484. It was additionally fitted with two long exterior probes, one on each side. That aircraft was similarly transferred to the Rechlin experimental station and by the end of March had completed 22 test flights there.

Until now it was always unclear what function the antenna assemblies, alongside the bomb aimer's cockpit on the V-555, were meant to serve. They could have been a special range finder and altimeter used to detonate 250 kilogram antenna bombs, which were also tested in Rechlin. In action, the bombs would have been detonated by means of a signal from bomb aimers in the Lotfe cabin. At a precisely predetermined height over the target, in order to achieve the greatest possible dispersion of the payload, the signal would be given. It can be considered to be very probable that those antenna bombs were not to be filled with conventional explosive charges. (see relevant chapter)

On 30 March 1945, it was one of those weapons carriers, a Me 262 V-555, which was delivered to the Allies by a deserter. The aircraft landed at the Schröck airfield, near Marburg-Lahn. On landing, the undercarriage could not be lowered, so that the in the subsequent belly landing the jet engines of the aircraft were damaged. As far as is known, the Americans did not later fly the aircraft, although there are numerous photographs relating to its salvage.

The deserter's name was never made known. It may have been an Allied agent who was not sufficiently familiar with operating the aircraft. It may have been a German pilot who wanted to warn the Allies of the threatened development of the weapon. Perhaps premature use of the A-2a/U2 may have been prevented in that way. In this connection too, there are striking parallels with the timing of events in Ohrdruf. It is astonishing that one could say, 'once again', a Me 262 was lost without trace. Once again, no Allied evaluation reports relating to it were released. The ALSOS mission, acting according to instructions for German military nuclear research, shortly after the V-555 was delivered to the Allies in April 1945, was already searching throughout the Reich for evidence of antenna bombs.[68] Perhaps it was all coincidence.

Arado Ar 234

Although not as well known as the Me 262 jet fighter, the Arado Ar 234 *Blitz* was just as important for German war efforts. There was only a relatively short production run of fewer than 300 of these jet-powered two- or four-engined bombers and reconnaissance aircraft. However, the aircraft's progressive design and its outstanding flight characteristics made it an aircraft type which pilots liked to fly and which was respected by the enemy. The Ar 234 achieved great things as a single-seater jet bomber. But its greatest contribution, from the summer of 1944, was the fact that it was capable of flying over enemy territory higher and faster than all Allied fighters. In doing so it was able to take important photographs of every enemy movement. The only problem was that by then the German High Command knew all the important developments in enemy territory, including the exact co-ordinates of V-2 impacts. However, at that point in the war, they did not have the capability to be able to react to the knowledge.

An aircraft having such superior qualities as the Ar 234 might be considered to be one of the main candidates for dropping Germany's atomic bombs. Certainly, on that subject, there is much more data than for other aircraft types. The aircraft would have been capable of deploying special bombs up to the weight class of 1,500 kilograms. There are in existence striking sketch plans drawn on 16 December 1944, and 10 March 1945. On them the multiple-engined Ar 234 C is depicted with remarkable round, barrel-shaped 1,000 kilogram containers under the fuselage. Are they parachute-bombs, pictures of planned nuclear weapons, or simply conventional bombs?

The Arado Ar 234, together with the He 177, would have been one of the aircraft considered by Hermann Göring if he had wanted to direct atomic air raids on London in March, or April 1945. The Ar 234 was no stranger in the skies above England. From mid-1944, Arados of *Kommando Sperling*, and of the first flight *Aufklärungsgruppe* 123, flew reconnaissance missions over that country completely unscathed. At an operating ceiling of 10,000 metres, and a speed of 725 km/h, the British air defences could no longer keep up with them.

But there were also disadvantages that could have adversely affected the use of the Ar 234 as an atomic bomber. For one thing the Ar 234 Bs and Cs, which were available by the end of the war, only had a one-man crew. It is true that two-seater versions were being developed, but they were not yet available. In precision bombing raids from a great height, flying the aircraft and aiming the bombs often placed too great a demand on the pilot. That state of affairs would have had negative effects in an eventual atomic bomb attack. An additional factor was the range of the Ar 234. In the bomber version it was relatively short, particularly if the machine was flying with a heavy bomb load. Certainly there were attempts to improve its range by means of towing additional winged fuel tanks. But there was no longer time to bring those experiments to a conclusion.

A number of reconnaissance flights over Britain were

made in the last months of the war, from Stavanger, in Norway. However, at the end of the war when they occupied the air base there, the British troops found not only the Ar 234 reconnaissance versions but also bomber aircraft of the types Ar 234 B and Ar 234 C. On the Leck airfield, on the Danish border, there were also numerous Ar 234 bombers. With those, Britain could also have been reached without any problem.

Now there is the question as to whether the presence of the Ar 234 bombers, on Norwegian airfields, can be attributed to withdrawal movements within the framework of the threatening capitulation. Or had Hermann Göring, even then, given instructions to do something completely different with such aircraft?

4) Long-Range Escort Aircraft for Heavy Miracle Weapons' Carriers

Messerschmitt Me 329: Escort aircraft for V-bombers

By the end of 1944 a piston-engined long-range escort fighter for the *Luftwaffe* was under construction. The Messerschmitt Me 329 was one of the least-known *Luftwaffe* aircraft types. In the small amount of available literature concerning the aircraft, the Me 329 is mostly attributed to the team under the direction of Professor Dr Lippisch in Vienna. But it could have been a Messerschmitt development, under the direction of Dr Wurster, that incorporated the Lippisch design principles.

The Me 329 represented a special development which had no connection and was not in competition with the Dornier Do 335 project, underway at the same time. The Me 329 was a tailless aircraft with retractable tricycle undercarriage. Overall, the Me 329 looked like an enlarged version of the Me 163, having engine nacelles with pusher propellers set into the wings. The two-man crew of the Me 329 sat in a pressurised cabin, with a cockpit cover providing an all-round view. As armament, the pilot had four 20mm MG 151/20s in the nose, while the observer could use a remote-controlled 20mm MG 151/20 in the tail. By way of payload, in the bomb bay under the fuselage, either 1,000 kilogram bombs, or a corresponding fuel tank, would be carried. The aircraft had a wingspan of 17.5 metres, with a fuselage length of 7.72 metres and a height of 4.74 metres. Power was provided by two Daimler-Benz DB 603 engines, each with 1,900 hp thrust, to give the aircraft a maximum speed of 740 km/h, at a height of 6,000 metres.

After the end of the bomber programme, Hermann Göring himself gave orders for the urgent development of the Me 329 to create an escort fighter. But in that connection the question was evidently never asked as to what there was for this aircraft to escort. By that time almost all the heavy bombers of the *Luftwaffe* had already been mothballed or scrapped. Thus, from the perspective of the present day, Göring's orders could have only been related to one measure. With the Me 329 they would provide a superior long-range escort aircraft for the miracle weapons carrier aircraft that were being developed. The aircraft could have provided outstanding service as a fast fighter escort, a meteorological aircraft, a pathfinder and photo-reconnaissance plane.

That planned 'special purpose' may be the reason why the Messerschmitt Me 329, until now, has been given such scant attention in the specialist literature. Surely questions would have automatically been raised as to the purpose of such a development. Neither Professor Messerschmitt nor Professor Dr Lippisch let slip much in the post-war period, concerning the Me 329, although work was still continuing 1945. In actual fact, at the end of 1944, a flying model of the Me 329, without engines, was tested in Rechlin in flights under tow or gliding. But there was no time left for a construction project to develop the original design.[69] It was probably intended that a provisional replacement solution would be provided by the Ju 88 G-10, delivered to the *Luftwaffe* from March 1945.

Ju 88 G-10: the long-range escort aircraft

The Heinkel He 177 atomic bomber could have been used in two different ways. The first possibility would have been to use it as a long-range bomber against targets such as New York. As early as 1944, such missions would have

Junkers Ju 88 G-10 'escort aircraft' - where are the actual photographs of this aircraft type? (Author's model).

involved, as had indeed been planned in the case of the conventional He 177 A-7, kamikaze-type attacks. There was little chance of return for the crew, apart from the vague hope of being picked up by a German U-boat waiting along the coast. It is known that on 21 July 1944, Hitler specifically ruled out attacks of that kind.

Therefore there remains the possibility of a single night mission against such targets as, for example, London. The range of the aircraft would have been sufficient for this. But for such a mission to succeed it would have been necessary for support to be provided by so-called long-range escort aircraft. For that purpose meteorological aircraft, photo-reconnaissance, pathfinder and fighter-bomber escort aircraft were required that had a range corresponding to that of the Heinkel 177.

To examine the probability of such a planned mission, the available *Luftwaffe* aircraft stocks must be examined to see whether such aircraft were available. They would need to have shown the following characteristics:

- High performance, night flying capability and a long range. The same aircraft type would have to be suitable for all the uses specified.
- Only a short production run of the aircraft would be built.

Considering the war situation at the time, and the small number that were required, the long-range fighter aircraft project would not have involved any new development. However, the modification of an aircraft type already introduced into service would have been needed. On its own, that modification must represent to the contemporary observer, aware of the war situation at the time, a 'useless' waste of effort.

There is verifiable evidence that such an aircraft existed. It was a version of the Junkers Ju 88, the trusty workhorse of the German *Luftwaffe*. As the last variant of the long line of Ju 88 night-fighters, the Junkers Ju 88 G-10 was developed at the end of 1944. It was a modified Ju 88 G-6, the fuselage of which was extended from 14.35m to 17.88m. That enabled the aircraft, with a wingspan of 19.95m and a flight mass of 15 tonnes, to achieve a range of 4,680km, together with a speed of 585km/h, at a height of 6,000m. The G-10, designated as a long-range night fighter-bomber, was fitted with Jumo 213 A engines. The idea of increasing range by extending the fuselage had already been applied by Junkers, in 1942, when the Ju 88 H-1 and H-2 *Atlantikflugzeuge* were developed. But there seems to have been a remarkable degree of indecision, on the part of the German *Luftwaffe*, concerning the Ju 88 G-10.

The production of the aircraft began in 1944, with works number 460,000. However, the first prototype was only accepted in March 1945, by *Flugkapitän* Harder in Dessau. Only a short run of 10 to 20 aircraft was produced. One of them, works number 460060, was tested as a *Mistel*, only to be later re-converted, for reasons which remain unknown, into a long-range combat aircraft. Other G-10 aircraft were directly converted, in the Junkers works, into *Kampfmistel* and *Schulmistel*, i.e. *Mistel* 3 and *Mistel* 3A.[70]

It could thus be argued that the changing fate of the Ju 88 G-10 aircraft is connected with possible delays or problems with the conversion of the Heinkel He 177 V-38, and its sister aircraft. In any event, there is no other conceivable reason for instigating such a short production run of the very versatile Ju 88 G-10. The planned large-scale attack by *Misteln* against the Russian power stations, code named *Eisenhammer*, required no long-range night-fighters as it was to be carried out in daylight. But the G-10s were also not delivered to any known night-fighter unit. Thus they played no part in the defence of the Reich.

The expense then, seems to have been pointless. It may be a coincidence that the range of the G-10 matched fairly exactly that of the He 177. At the time they were in production, in March 1945, however, the *Luftwaffe* no longer had any 'normal' He 177 squadrons on active service.

At this point it goes without saying, that the published pictorial material is very scanty in this instance. That is the case of almost all, German, special weapons that can be connected with nuclear weapons planning. To date, the only known photograph, which shows a Junkers Ju 88 G-10, is a heavily retouched post-war photograph. Even so, it still only shows a *Schulmistel* variant of the type.

5) Special Developments: Special Misteln*, Large-scale Experimental Carriers and Atomic Propulsion for Aircaft*

Mistel 4 - *Misteln* as *Vergeltungswaffe*

The *Misteln* were already available bomber aircraft, i.e. Ju 88, He 177. They were converted into large bombs, on to which small controlling fighters were mounted. A single man could then attack, with a 3.8-tonne explosive warhead, targets within a radius of 1,500km. When it arrived at the target, the fighter would detach itself, while the unmanned explosive carrier underneath would smash into the target. Those astonishing weapons, improvised, it is true, but operationally practicable, brought into the realm of possibility German attacks on targets such as Leningrad, Gibraltar, Scapa Flow, and the Russian power stations. But, as the war proceeded, all the plans were shattered. It is true that during the Normandy invasion, at the battle for the Remagen bridge, and also in the final battle for the Oder crossings, hundreds of such dangerous *Mistel* composites were in action. But even they could not

Artist's impression of a Me 262/Me 262 *Mistel.*

bring about a change in fortune.[71] From July to August 1944, individual *Mistel* impacts were also recorded in Britain. However, it is unclear whether they were experimental *Vergeltung* attacks, or whether they simply involved *Mistel* aircraft that had gone off course during attacks against the Normandy fleet.[72]

The *Misteln* that were used were *Mistel* 1s, i.e. Ju 88 A4, with Fw 190 or Me 109, *Mistel* 2s, i.e. Ju 88 G1, with Fw 190, and *Mistel* 3s, i.e. Ju 88 G10, and H4 with Fw 190. Then, in November 1944, the *Mistel* 4 was proposed. The first design planned to use two Messerschmitt Me 262s as upper and lower components. The upper component was to be the Messerschmitt Me 262 A-2A/U2, with the so-called bombardier's cabin that was to hold a second crew member. The lower component was to consist of a Me 262 without the pilot's cockpit and undercarriage. It was converted into an explosive carrier, in the nose of which a remote-controlled warhead was installed. The bombardier of the guiding aircraft, by remote control, could direct the warhead by using a new type of televisual installation.

As a variant from the prototype of the Me 262 A-2A/U2, two Type MK 108 3-cm machine guns had been planned for the guiding aircraft. Thus, in possible dogfights, in addition to its superior speed, it would also be able to deploy reasonable firepower. The composite was able to take off with the aid of a five-wheeled take-off carriage, weighing 20 tonnes. It was given additional acceleration by four auxiliary rockets of the type HWK 109-501. For about 30 seconds the auxiliary rockets provided a forward thrust of 4,800kp. By such means the overall thrust of the composite on take-off, including that of the 4 Jumo 004-B engines from both aircraft, reached 8,400kp.

Three different versions of the explosive carrier were proposed, which were designated as models A, B and C. Version A was to have an armoured nose to the fuselage, with so-called liquid explosive, having a total explosive weight of 4,460kg. In Version B, the forward fuselage was to consist of a solid explosive, with similar materials in other parts of the fuselage, making a total explosive weight of 6,030kg. In Version C, it was planned to retain the forward fuselage of Version B, but to provide additional 'liquid explosive' in other parts of the fuselage, making a total explosive weight of 5.210kg.

The first composite had a total take-off weight of 16,000kg, the second 18,635kg, and the third 17,110kg. Two Me 262s were delivered, in December 1944, for conversion into *Misteln.* However, to date it is unknown whether those composites were ever flown before the end of the war.[73] What particularly distinguished the Me 262/Me 262 *Mistel,* as well as its pure jet engine that achieved such superior speed, was the planned use of so-called liquid explosives. That must have been the super-explosive 'Myrol', which even today is still shrouded in secrecy.

The explosive was developed by the Degussa Company in Frankfurt, after IG Farben had already done some preparatory work on it. It was a compound of nitric acid and methyl. It was said to be many times more effective than the German 'Hexogen', which itself represented a miracle substance, in the circumstances, at the time. According to British reports from German prisoners, IG Farben, in

Vienna, carried out an experiment in the open air to establish the power of the new liquid explosive. To do that the reports stated, a hole was bored in the middle of a cube of lead weighing 12 tons. Into the hole was placed a cubic centimetre of the new explosive. The hole was then filled with sand and sealed with molten lead. By means of that lead block test, prescribed by the Trauzl system,[74] the energy released, after the lead cube was shattered, would then be measured. But the lead block exploded while the experiment was in progress, killing some of the spectators.[75]

One does not need a great deal of imagination to envisage the explosive effect of the charges. They consisted of 4,400 to 5,210 kilograms of the substance, carried by the *Mistel* 4 versions A or C. Considerable expense was required for the industrial production of the 'Myrol' explosive. Although, in itself inexpensive, the system of production which had been planned, in the area of Silesia, had been repeatedly delayed. It is no surprise that further details concerning the location of the *Mistel* 4 Me 262 components, and the precise composition of the liquid explosive have not, to date, been made known. But a second aircraft composite was developed that went under the designation of *Mistel* 4.

In Nordhausen at Junkers, from the beginning of 1945, a composite was developed. It consisted of a normal Me 262 as the upper component, and a Ju 188 as the lower component. The Ju 188 was intended to carry additional jet engines under its wings.[76] Unfortunately, there is no information as to whether that composite was ever tested in flight, nor what subsequently became of it. A *Mistel* of that kind would have been suitable, without any problems, for the installation of a 4-tonne atomic bomb. By contrast to The *Misteln* 1, 2 and 3, because of their low speed before they jettisoned the lower component, were not used in daylight in the West. However, the Me 262/Ju 188 composite could have been used against targets, in Western Europe and Italy, with a greater prospect of success. It is known that in March 1945, officers of *Kampfgeschwader* 200, i.e. KG 200, went to Italy to make preparations for the *Mistel* 4 to be deployed there.[77]

The third *Mistel* 4 version, consisting of an Me 262/Ju 287 composite, was not developed. The design of the Ju 287 warhead shows that no normal hollow charge was intended to be used. (see section on Ju 287) In the absence of official documentation, indicating that the Germans intended to convert *Misteln* into atomic bombers, there was nevertheless a somewhat ominous British report.[78] It drew attention to the suitability of the *Mistel* for carrying the atomic bomb. Perhaps it was such fears which, on the night of 22 March 1945, led to a devastating RAF mass air-raid on the Junkers *Mistel* works in Nordhausen. That raid seriously disrupted further work on the *Mistel* projects.

Messerschmitt Me 323 *Gigant*: the experimental carrier

The Messerschmitt Me 323 *Gigant* was one of the largest piston-engined aircraft built at that time. It was developed from the Messerschmitt Me 321 heavy transport glider, and was powered by six Gnome-Rhone 14N engines, giving 1,140 PS. Although only a relatively small number of such ponderous giants were produced, there were a surprising number of special variants of the aircraft.

The most fascinating of all the many projects connected with those useful monsters, was a plan for them to transport an atomic bomb. It weighed 18 tonnes, other sources say 20 tonnes. It would be suspended under the starboard wing.[79] However, the weight of that experimental arrangement was so great, that a five-engined Heinkel He 111 Z tug was needed to assist the take-off. Unfortunately, to date, no more precise details are known concerning the conversions to the carrier aircraft involved in that giant bomb test.

Photographs from 1944 show a Me 323 with a Me 262 fuselage under its starboard wing for an experimental drop. They also show additional observation windows and a streamlined container, perhaps for cameras, under the starboard wing. The same aircraft, its markings and works number unknown, may also have been used for the later bomb drops.

In that experiment, carried out on a date in 1944 that still remains unknown, the huge experimental aircraft crashed, with the loss of the entire crew. The actual drop, and test of the bomb, before that is said to have been successful. (see section concerning the 20-tonne bomb. For the reasons for that crash, see section 'Giant Bombs'.) Apart from the specially modified Me 323 prototype, to date, no other conversions for carrying heavy bombs have come to light. There would have been no question of using the Me 323 in action, with such a huge bomb. Even in the experiment, the aircraft had already reached the very limits of its capability.

There is still no confirmation from other sources of the heavy bomb experiment, with Me 323s. The description of the incident, given by prisoners of war, naturally raises the question as to the general credibility of such prisoner of war reports. But experience within recent years has repeatedly shown how surprisingly accurate such reports can be.

There was also a plan that the Me 323 would carry V-2 batteries. It was intended to achieve rapid mobility of the *Vergeltungswaffen* batteries. It was calculated that to transport one V-2 battery, and its associated vehicles, an entire squadron of Messerschmitt 323s was necessary.[80] The idea from 1944 can be seen as a forerunner of present-day air transport of rockets. But, during the last phase of the war, it would have been impossible to carry out because of shortage of fuel, and Allied air superiority.

Night bomber Junkers Ju 290E: carrier for the giant bomb

The Junkers Ju 290 *Seeadler*, i.e. Sea Eagle, was a popular and reliable long-range marine reconnaissance aircraft. Nevertheless, essentially it was a converted transport, with all the disadvantages of that type of aircraft. The Junkers Ju 290 E was the planned final model in the Ju 290 series. It was a night bomber project based upon the Ju 290 C-1 series. The structure of its fuselage was radically modified to be able to carry a 20-tonne bomb load. That large bomb was to be carried in a huge wooden bomb bay. No other operational German aircraft was suitable to carry such a heavy bomb load. The aircraft's armament consisted of FDL 151V revolving gun-turrets, with four 20mm MG 151s in the nose and tail respectively. It had a hand-operated HDL revolving turret behind the crew cabin. It was planned to fit the aircraft with four Jumo 222 engines, each providing 2,500 pounds of thrust, but they were only ready for operational use in 1945. Until then, as a temporary solution, the 290 E was to be fitted with four BMW 801 TJ exhaust turbo-charger engines, each providing 2,000 pounds of thrust at take-off.

No data is available, relating to speed and performance for the E series. But the BMW 801 TJ was an extremely efficient turbo-charger engine, with full pressure at a ceiling of 11,000 metres. It was also used for the Junkers Ju 388 K and L high altitude aircraft, craft that even the fastest Allied planes could not intercept.

The Ju 290 E probably never got beyond the drawing board stage. In contrast to the Ju 290 C-1 and D series, however, there seems to have been a serious intention to develop the E series. How long work continued on the night bomber project, after the end of the bomber programme in the summer of 1944, cannot be estimated in the light of current knowledge. Even under the most favourable circumstances only individual prototypes could have been produced.

The planned purpose of the Ju 290 E was to deploy it as a high altitude night bomber that could drop a 20-tonne giant bomb. The planned operational range for the aircraft can only be surmised. Unfortunately there are no calculations available relating to the performance of the Ju 290 E. Therefore its chances of success cannot be estimated. But considering the large payload, at the most, what were planned could only have been medium-range operations. The proportions of the Ju 290 would, in 1945/46, have certainly made it essential for it to be painted in IG Farben's *Schornsteinfeger* radar-deflecting paint.

Nuclear Propulsion for Aircraft

From the end of May 1942, over the heads of Göring and Speer, a massive *Waffen-SS* research centre was built in Pilsen that worked in very close collaboration with the Skoda works in Prague. Under the special protection of Hitler and Himmler, that establishment, that today would be called the Third Reich's high-technology research centre, worked as a completely independent cover operation for the *Waffen-SS*. In the main its purpose was to develop 'second generation' secret weapons. The SS were also to press ahead, with all available means, in developing new jet propulsion technologies, laser and optical projects, and also nuclear propulsion technologies for aircraft and rockets.

The activities of those establishments, under the control of the so-called Kammler group, even today remain largely unknown. The relevant Allied archive materials have not been released. However, it is known that the work on the exploitation of nuclear energy, as a form of propulsion for rockets and aircraft, was already amazingly far advanced. It is possible that crucial work by the Kammler group, on the new nuclear propulsion systems, was also carried out in Melk, at Roggendorf.

In the mine tunnels, formerly used for secret weapons research, there is also a sort of engine test bed. What the test bed in the tunnel was for is not known exactly. It was certainly no coincidence that close to Melk, which would also have been connected with atomic bomb research and production, there was a large airfield. (see section on small uranium bombs) Even today, the place is known as a Messerschmitt establishment, even though Messerschmitt had nothing to do with the production of atomic bombs. But perhaps it relates to the Messerschmitt company's nuclear aircraft projects, on which work could have been carried out there.

According to Allied BIOS reports, there were plans to fit a version of the giant long-range bomber/carrier aircraft, the Messerschmitt P 1073 A with its 68m wingspan, with a nuclear reactor as a propulsion system. The P 1073 project came into being as early as 1940, as a design study for missions over the Atlantic and against the USA. It was to consist of the P 1073 long-range/carrier aircraft, with 3 onboard P 1073 B fighters. While the small P 1073 jet fighter is well documented, all further data, drawings etc. relating to the P 1073 A are still missing.

So what was the German nuclear propulsion system to look like? Most probably it was a nuclear version of the steam turbine engine for aircraft. The conventional version of this steam turbine engine was to provide 6,000 pounds of thrust and was commissioned, in August 1944, from Oser Maschinen GmbH. The plant consisted of four boilers of 0.9m × 1.22m and a main turbine of 0.62m × 1.83m, which drove two huge propellers. The conventional version was planned to run on fuel consisting of 65% triturated carbon, and 35% of crude oil. The Messerschmitt Me 264 V-1 was earmarked as the test aircraft for the new method of propulsion. However, before it could be used as a test aircraft for steam turbines it was destroyed in an air raid on 18 July 1944.[81] After the loss of the Me 264, a He 177 was enlisted as a test aircraft for the steam turbine engine. How far that plan then progressed is unknown.[82]

But further conjecture can follow the line that, as was later the intention for the American Convair X-6, it was planned to use jet engines driven by nuclear reactors. Possibly this is what is indicated by the sketch of a heavily-modified Me 264 with T-shaped tail, which under its wings shows four small Jumo 004 engines.[83] With the normal Jumo engines alone, that large aircraft would have been completely underpowered. For the standard Me 264, even earlier, significantly more powerful engine combinations were already planned, That forces the question of whether the advanced Me 264 version was not already to be fitted with nuclear-powered Jumo 004 engines. The aircraft would then have had sufficient power reserves, and unlimited range. Work may have been done on that project in Melk and Pilsen, but it is not known what became of it.

There are already clear indications that a nuclear-powered jet bomber was by then in existence. Otto Skorzeny, wrote in his book, *Meine Kommandounternehmen*, i.e. 'My Command Operations', Universitas, 1993, on page 117, that in April 1945 the designers of the Henschel O-122 bomber blew up the prototype. Its speed was 1,000km/h, and it had an operational radius of over 2,000km, and was fitted with a turboreactor. The British experts, he said, would have seized the wreckage and plans of the aircraft. They would have been more than amazed that such a German aircraft existed at all.

In fact it is known that the Henschel Company had a design under the designation HS P/122. That project, about which only little is known, even then, was a bomber design that was to be fitted with two normal turbojets. The aircraft had a tailless configuration with a short fuselage and with a normal tail fin. The cabin, constructed completely of glass, was to accommodate the two-man crew. In the low wing monoplane with swept-back wings, the two turbines were to be fitted in nacelles under the wing.

Those at least are the specifications for that aircraft type, found in Heinz J. Nowarra's standard work *Die deutsche Luftrüstung 1933-45*, Vol. 3, pages 37/39, Bernard & Graefe, 1987. It is not known if a connection exists between the Henschel O-122 and P/122. Possibly 'O-122' was a printing error in Skorzeny's book and in actual fact the designation was for the aircraft type '8-122'. With the number '8' before the type number that would then represent the usual designation for new aircraft development at the time Unfortunately, Skorzeny does not indicate where the British found the remains of the Henschel O-122. But the situation at the time suggests that it could only have been in northern Germany, Denmark, or the Norway area.

Independently it is known that, in the post-war period, German and Czech scientists who formerly worked in Pilsen, worked for the USA, on nuclear aircraft propulsion systems.[84]

In the 1950s, in the USA, an experimental reactor flew on board a converted Convair experimental aircraft. The subsequent projects, X-6 and WS-125 A, to create fully nuclear-powered experimental aircraft and weapons systems were, however, abandoned at the beginning of the 1960s. There was said to be 'no military need' for them.[85]

6) Further Types: Aircraft

Competitors of the Horten Ho XVIII

Arado Ar E 555

In the middle of December 1943 work began, in the Arado Company, in their Landeshut/Silesia works, on an all-wing project under the direction of Dr *Ingenieur* W. Laute. The project was then further developed, by *Diplom-Ingenieuren* Kosin and Lehmann, under the title 'Long-Range High-Speed All-Wing Aircraft'. Whilst at the beginning there was no direct connection between that project and the development of an intercontinental bomber, on 20 April 1944, a meeting chaired by *Diplom-Ingenieur* Scheibe and *Ingenieur* Haspe took place at the RLM with representatives of the Arado company. The requirements, for a jet bomber with the new Arado wing configuration, were confirmed. They had to create, from the Arado E 555 project series, a bomber that could carry a bomb load of 4 tonnes, over a distance of 5,000km, although other sources say 4,000km.[86] Over the Atlantic it was planned to refuel the Ar 555, with additional fuel from Focke-Wulf Fw 200 tankers.[87] It would be a dangerous operation, considering Allied air superiority.

The plan can serve as an indication that even at that time work was continuing on the 'America Jet Bomber Programme'. The Ar 555 was thus in direct competition with the piston-engined Ju 390 long-range bomber. Evidently they were beginning to understand at the RLM how vulnerable the heavy conventional giant aircraft were.

The Arado project can claim to be the first intercontinental jet bomber in the world. The number of designs within the E 555 project ran to 15. It included plans for strategic bombers, remote-controlled weapons carriers, and even heavy fighters. The most important was the Ar E 555-1 design, which also became well known through a 'Revell' 1:72 scale plastic model construction kit. It most closely matched the requirements of the later America Bomber programme. It would certainly, with appropriate further development, have been able to achieve the desired performance. The E 555-1 was powered by six BMW 003A engines. It was to be equipped with defensive armament, consisting of two Mk 103/30 cannon in the wings, a Mk 151/20 20mm twin-gun revolving turret behind the cockpit, and a further two Mk 151/20 20mm cannon in a remote-controlled tail turret.[88]

But the Arado Company did not know how to 'sell' their progressive designs effectively, to the relevant RLM departments. Instead they split up their efforts into a large number of variants of the E 555 project. So, on 28 December 1944, Arado were ordered to cease all work on the E 555 series. Only the designs from Junkers, Messerschmitt and Horten had been included on the final shortlist. The experience gained on the E 555 project was later put to use by Arado on the joint project EF 140.[89]

Blohm & Voss P.188.01-04

The P.188 bomber project was Blohm & Voss's contribution in the context of the America Project. The P.188 was to be of duraluminium construction and was particularly distinguishable by both positively and negatively swept wings. That meant the angle of attack could be altered. It had, too, an undercarriage in a tandem configuration beneath the fuselage. The fuselage consisted of three connected, but detachable, sections. There was a pressurised cabin for a two-man crew, a central section with bomb bay, fuel tank and undercarriage, and the stern section consisted of the tail assembly and brake.[90]

While the performance of the P.188.01 to P.188.03 versions was similar to that of the Ju 287, the P.188.04 would have been the actual design for an America bomber. It is true that the Blohm & Voss P.188 never had more than an outside chance. For that reason, work on it was probably not continued beyond the end of December 1944.

Junkers Ju 287 S

The Junkers Ju 287 S was Junkers' original contribution to Hermann Göring's America Bomber Programme of the autumn of 1944. It was a development of the Ju 287 model but was to be fitted with two Jumo 109/012 jet engines under each wing. According to other sources, however, power was to be provided by using four He S 011 engines.

It is true that the plans envisaged a slight reduction in speed as compared to the Ju 287, but a range of 8800km was to be achieved. The Ju 287 promised to be the aircraft that would involve the least development risk. That was because significant elements of the aircraft had already been tried and tested in the previous tests of the Ju 287 V-1. Out of all the projects, the Ju 287 S had the shortest range, with a maximum flight time of 5.7 hours, compared with 8.6 hours for the Horten Ho XVIII. Thus the aircraft had no chance of being awarded the contract.[91] For that reason, Junkers abandoned the development of the Ju 287 S, and turned to the further development of the normal Ju 287, and to the long-range bomber programmes EF132 and EF 140.

Messerschmitt P 1107

The Messerschmitt P 1107, with the Junkers Ju 287 S, was one of the projects in competition with the Horton Ho XVIII. It was included on the DVL shortlist for the creation of an America bomber. The P 1107 was a long-range bomber which, with a take-off weight of 29 tonnes, was planned to have a top speed of 1020 kilometres per hour. Its development was to make use of the experience gained with the Me 264 long-range bomber and the jet projects Me 262 HG I-IV. For the P 1107 project there were a large number of designs that significantly differed in wing and tail configurations and in the form of the nose cockpit. According to the promotional material, the aircraft was planned to have an overall range of up to 9600 kilometres. In its construction outline, Messerschmitt compared it with the previously mentioned Me 264 that had been built in 1942 for a similar task.

In the final evaluation on 26 January 1945, the DVL commission considered that the performance data provided by the Messerschmitt Company for their project were too optimistic. The company had not provided any evidence of their calculations. As a result, Messerschmitt further developed their design into the P 1108.

Messerschmitt P 1108

Included under the designation Messerschmitt P 1108 are further developments of the forerunner design P 1107, presented to the RLM between 1 January and 23 March 1945. Such developments represented a series of different designs, from delta-wing to fuselage aircraft that, in their aerodynamic configuration and design, were extremely advanced. The exciting history of the development of the P1107 and P1108, has been convincingly described by Dieter Herwig and Heinz Rode in their important work, *Geheimprojekte der Luftwaffe.* (Volume 2, Motorbuch Verlag, Stuttgart, 1998)

The construction outline of the P 1108 cites improved figures over the P 1107. When Hitler learned of that Messerschmitt proposal, he is said to have told Karl-Otto Saur, the representative, and later successor of Albert Speer, as Armaments Minister, to 'get the Messerschmitt P 1108 design into production'. Using this craft, Hitler wanted to be able to deliver retribution to the USA, for the destruction of German cities.

It is true that even the Messerschmitt P 1108 fell short of the merits of the Horten XVIII B. Therefore, on 23 March 1945, by order of the RLM, all work on the aircraft had to be stopped. Before that, the Messerschmitt engineers had had another try at meeting the specified requirements, with a flying-wing project, designated Messerschmitt P 1108/II.[92]

Junkers EF 132

The Junkers E F 132 long-range bomber was completely unknown for many years, although it represented one of the most advanced projects in German aircraft construction. With its newly developed wing configuration and with engines completely set into the wing roots it was, in the post-war period, the model for many Allied bomber designs. At the end of the war, the design of the E F 132 was already very far advanced. Even before May 1945 it had been possible to produce a 1:1 scale wooden mock-up in Dessau. After the end of the war, the Russian occupying forces ordered work on the EF 132 design to continue, first in Dessau and afterwards in Russia. Then, no doubt for political reasons, everything was stopped.

The aircraft was to have a wingspan of 32.40 metres and a fuselage length of 30.80 metres. The five-man crew was housed in a cabin constructed completely of glass. According to the plans, the armament consisted of two fixed 2cm cannon, and two FDL 151 twin-gun mountings. They could be lowered, and were to be fitted behind the cabin, and in front of the bomb bay. It was planned that the E F 132 would have a maximum service ceiling of 14,000 metres and a maximum range of 9,800 kilometres. The aircraft was powered by four Jumo 109/012 engines, each providing 2,500 kilograms of thrust. The EF 132 was also to carry the customary bomb load of 4,000 kilograms.

It is not clear what prompted the Junkers company to prepare such a design, as the E F 132 is never mentioned in connection with the America Programme. Certainly, in view of the war situation at the time, it would not have been possible to work on such a design without official support. It is thus possible that the E F 132 was an officially approved design in competition with the Horten XVIII B. That design would come into its own in the event that the revolutionary Horten design failed. However, that assumption still has to be confirmed by official documents.[93]

Junkers EF 140

The Junkers EF 140 was the so-called 'committee bomber'. It was planned to be jointly produced by Messerschmitt, Junkers, Arado and Horten in order to create a 'tailless America bomber'. To have the Ho XVIII A ready for active service, as quickly as possible, at the beginning of 1945 the RLM formed a committee. It consisted of Herrn Voigt of Messerschmitt, Zindel, Wocke and Hertel of Junkers, Kosin from Arado, and Reimar Horten from Horten. The industrial leadership was to take over control of the Junkers company. That explains why, for many years, in aviation books, the EF 140 was confused with the Ho XVIII B, and was said to be the same aircraft.

Unfortunately, it is not known how heavy the EF 140 was to be. The planned length was given as 19m and the wingspan as 42m. In the EF 140, a further development of the Ho XVIII A, a large tail fin was planned, in the forward part of which the crew would be housed. The maximum speed of 900 km/h was to be achieved with six Jumo 004, or BMW 003, turbojets that would be fitted under the wings in two nacelles. As defensive armament it was planned that the aircraft would be fitted with four remote-controlled Mk 108s.

Originally, it was planned to produce the EF 140 with great urgency in underground aircraft works in the Harz Mountains. But the Horten Brothers, by means of personal contact with *Reichsmarschall* Göring, were able to get the decision to produce the EF 140 overturned. Instead, work was to be expedited on the production of their own Horten Ho XVIII B. Work on the EF 140 was thus stopped, without having reached the design stage. The main argument against the EF 140 was that its range was inferior to that of the Horten XVIII B.[94]

Göring's Future Miracle Weapon Projects 1946

The Daimler-Benz 'Ultra High Speed Bomb Carrier'

The Daimler-Benz Project 03010256 was also drawn up as a project, in the autumn of 1944, by the technical director of Daimler-Benz AG, *Diplom-Ingenieur* Fritz Nallinger, together with his colleague, *Oberingenieur* Übelacker. Even today, the boldness of that project would be enough to fire the imagination of science fiction fans. But it was a serious design. It took account of the tactical realities of the time, and was an interesting variant on the theme of increasing range, and of transporting large bombs.

Synopsis of the Daimler-Benz/Focke-Wulf Weapons System 0301256:[95]

Project 'A': The weapons system consisted of a Heinkel He S 021 type carrier aircraft, with four turboprop engines, and a weight of 45,800kg, or six engines of the same type and a weight of 51,700kg. The wingspan was given as 54m.

Under that carrier aircraft would be suspended a two-engined bomber, with a V-shaped tail assembly, powered by two turbojets with 7,500 kg of thrust. The bomber's wingspan was 23.16m, and it weighed 71,800kg.

Project 'B': The same carrier aircraft, but it had a single-engined, twin-tailed bomber, powered by a Daimler-Benz turbojet, with 12,930 kp thrust. Weight 70,000kg.

Project 'C': An improved version of the carrier aircraft, powered by six Daimler-Benz DB 603s, each giving 1,900 PS. Four engines had puller propellers, two engines with pusher propellers.

Project 'D': A combination of 'B' and 'C'.

Project 'E': Comprised a universal carrier aircraft, as in Type 'C', underneath which were suspended 5 SO, i.e. suicide, manned flying bombs, each fitted with He S 011 turbine engine and ejector seat.

Project 'F': The existence of that project only became known many years after that of Projects 'A' to 'E'. It consisted of a carrier aircraft 'C', which was to carry underneath it 6 Type 'F' manned flying bombs. Each flying bomb would be powered by a BMW 018 turbine engine.

In the context of this book's concern with miracle weapons, Project 'E' is of no further interest.

Project 'C' was designed as a carrier aircraft, with a, so-called, ultra high-speed bomber between the legs of its undercarriage. That combination was intended to enable a 30-tonne bomb load to be transported over long distances. The ultra-high-speed bomber was to fly at a speed just bordering the speed of sound. That meant it would no longer be vulnerable to attack by enemy fighters.

In addition, it was intended that the ultra-high-speed bomber would provide good benefit, in relation to the cost of construction, i.e. in the relationship between its weight when empty, and its weight when loaded. Therefore, the payload of bombs had to be in a higher ratio to the cost of construction, than was usual in the construction of bombers at that time.

The attack aircraft itself had no offensive and defensive armament at all, but was to use its high speed as a defensive measure. The aircraft was designed with a very high control surface area loading of 500 kilograms per square metre. It was to transport a 30-tonne bomb load 1,000 kilometres into enemy territory, at a speed of some 1,000 kilometres per hour.

In order to achieve such a performance it was necessary to have recourse to additional auxiliary measures. That was because the undercarriage and the tyres of the ultra-high-speed bomb carrier would have had to be designed for a total payload of 70 tonnes. With those dimensions it would no longer be able to retract the undercarriage into the aircraft.

In addition, even if it had been possible to solve that problem, for the aircraft to take off would probably have required not only a concrete runway, but also a take-off carriage running on rails. As a result, the danger of failure at take-off, and the consequent destruction of the aircraft and its bomb load, would have been high. Also, as was correctly understood at the time, such arrangements for take-off would be very vulnerable to attack from the air. For that reason it was intended to construct the entire undercarriage of the jet bomber with dimensions which related only to the impact of landing, i.e. would only relate to the landing weight of the empty aircraft without fuel and bomb load. Correspondingly, the components were to be very light in relationship to the overall aircraft when it was loaded.

The aircraft was enabled to take off by means of a special carrier aircraft. It was designed as a huge mid-wing aircraft, powered by six Daimler-Benz D B 109 603 E or N piston engines providing 2,700 PS, or four Daimler-Benz propeller turbines of the type D B 109-021 each with shaft power of 6,800 PS. The three- to four-man crew of the carrier aircraft was to have a fully glazed pressurised cabin in the forward part of the cylindrical fuselage. The aircraft was carried on two long undercarriage nacelles, each of which housed three wheels in a tandem configuration. The ultra-high-speed bomber similarly possessed a fully glazed pressurised cabin in the nose of the fuselage, with a circular cross section. The wings and the tail assembly were swept-back, with the tail assembly being designed as a T-shaped tail without an actual vertical tail. The bomber was powered by a Daimler-Benz 109 016 jet engine with 12,000 kilograms thrust. The ultra-high-speed bomber, according to the plans as they developed, would be suspended on this underneath the carrier aircraft. The design, as against the piggy-back configurations already being used for other purposes, was proposed by the Daimler-Benz team, because such a scheme would enable the ultra-high-speed bomb carrier to be loaded from underneath, using normal bomb loading equipment.

For one carrier aircraft it was planned to use three ultra-high-speed bombers. It was hoped that it would be possible to get that combination into the air from normal grass airfields with a take off run of 500 metres at most. Almost every normal airfield would have been suitable. With the carrier aircraft it would have been possible to transport not only the ultra high-speed bomb carrier, but also a great many other special aircraft, weapons, or simple transport containers. Officially, in the Daimler-Benz design, i.e. drawing number 310256-05, a bomb load of 30 tonnes was proposed. It would consist of 30 SB 1,000 bombs, bundled together into five bombs, or 60 S C 500 bombs, bundled together into 10 bombs. Bundling the bombs in that way was a new technique and is described in a later section.

However, it is almost certain that the project was principally intended to carry the planned 30-tonne giant bomb. That mysterious special weapon is dealt with in a later section. Such a design would have been the only possibility of taking that weapon to the enemy, within a foreseeable period of time.

Although, understandably, those involved in developing the project did not go into greater detail in their design, concerning the 'super-weapon', nevertheless they incorporated within their project proposal an indication of its uses. They wrote, that 'with a single aircraft, it will be possible to carry out effective bombing of airfields, large railway installations, factories, ports, and gatherings of shipping'.[96]

It was planned that the composite would operate as follows. The carrier aircraft would take off with the ultra-high-speed bomb suspended beneath it. It would fly to the extreme limit of its range, and reach its maximum height. At this point the bomber would start its engines, and be jettisoned. Then the carrier aircraft would return to its base airfield, while the bomber with its unused fuel reserves flew on to its target. It was calculated that the high-speed bomber alone would penetrate 1,000 kilometres into enemy territory. Over time, many different versions of the Daimler Benz project were proposed for both component parts. One of the last proposals even planned to use the ultra-high-speed bomber as a long-range 'America bomber'.[97]

For that type of operation the bomber was constructed as an aircraft that was intended to be lost. To economise on weight, it only possessed minimal equipment and no undercarriage. After carrying out its long-range mission, the crew had to land the bomber, at a predetermined point on the enemy coast, where they would be picked up by a U-boat. A similarly risky use of U-boats, to pick up returning bomber crews, was discussed several times in 1944.

It was calculated that the overall composite on such a mission would have a flight distance of 17,000 kilometres, with the bomb load being 30,000 kilograms. There too, the concern was to find a way to be able to transport a 30-tonne giant bomb as far as the USA.

Nallinger's and Übelacker's design was then refined and completed in the Focke-Wulf design office which had been moved to Bad Eilsen. *Ingenieur* Nallinger, who was otherwise known for his cautious and reserved approach, on 15 January 1945, presented the project to those involved with it from the RLM and the aircraft industry. They met in the main committee *Flugzeugzellen.* It was suggested that an aircraft of that type could only be developed as a joint production of the entire German aviation industry. 'Certainly', Nallinger said, 'a decision would have to be taken immediately. In addition, all possible support for this development would have to be secured so that the development could be completed in the shortest possible time. The prospects which these projects will open up for the conduct of the war, are such that, in my opinion, this proposal should not be set aside, but must be tackled immediately'. As can easily be seen, there spoke an expert who knew exactly what decisive effect would result from such a proposed weapons system.

It is not known how far the project progressed. It is last mentioned, officially, in secret project documents of the Focke-Wulf company, dated 7 February 1945. But to turn the projects into reality would certainly have required a considerable length of time. Prophetically, Nallinger suggested that the greatest difficulties lay in the development of the jet engines. Those with a 13,000 kp take-off thrust would be required for the ultra-high-speed bomber. In a handwritten document, the designer even increased the planned performance to 15,000 kp. The engine would need to have ten times the take-off thrust of the most powerful engine being tested at that time. Difficulties, as can be imagined, were to be expected. There was also an alternative design of the bomber, with two BMW 018 air jet turbines, each providing 3,450 kp thrust. But they would not have given the aircraft the same level of performance.

Daimler-Benz Project 'F'

In the bewildering series of Daimler-Benz projects from 1944/45, Project 'F' occupied a special place. The existence of the project was only made known to the general public for the first time, in 1982, whereas the other Daimler-Benz projects had already been known of for decades.[98]

The 'F' Project was a so-called 'self-destruction aircraft', or rather a manned flying bomb. It was proposed that up to six of such aircraft, which bore a strong similarity to the Fi 103 flying bomb, could be carried underneath the project 'C' carrier aircraft. Compared with the Fi 103, Project 'F' was much larger, and had swept-back wings and pitch elevator. The pilot was to be accommodated at the stern, underneath the BMW 018 jet engine with its 3,400 kp thrust. The aircraft would have been able to carry an explosive charge of 3,000 kilograms, at a top speed of 1,230 kilometres per hour. It would fly faster than the speed of sound. The total weight for Project 'F' was given as 10.2 tonnes.

It is not clear what kind of attack method was to be used. Japanese-style suicide missions were still officially forbidden. In any event, the pilot would have had great difficulty in getting out of the aircraft in time, before the impact.

Two points connect the Daimler-Benz Project 'F' to miracle weapons. Firstly, the previously mentioned fact that Project 'F', in contrast to the other projects, was concealed from the public for so long, forced the suspicion that it had been deliberately removed from official documents published previously. Secondly, the other planned self-destruction aircraft, project 'E', was described from the outset in the most precise detail. Despite the fact that in the meantime other documents and drawings have been published, no official drawings and plans relating to Project 'F' have yet been published.

The solution to the mystery of that lengthy silence can only be in the other aspect of Project 'F', that is the 3-tonne explosive warhead. In contrast to project E, it was not a hollow charge warhead. The outlines given indicate that its composition was quite different. The first Russian nuclear missiles, in the post-war period, were designed for a 3-tonne explosive charge. The 'Redstone' nuclear missile, designed by Wernher von Braun for the Americans, was designed for a payload of similar weight. Knowing how the Allies tended to copy German designs, one is almost forced to conclude that the warhead in this instance must have been a planned nuclear weapon.

Göring's Ultra Long-range Bomber Project of Spring 1945

From the end of February 1945 there was another extreme bomber project which has not yet been fully explained up to the present. On 22 February 1945, at a meeting in Dessau at which the *Reichsmarschall* was present, tenders were invited for a bomber aircraft with a still greater range than that of the 'America bomber'. Unfortunately, the precise details of that tender invitation have not yet been found.

But it is known that it resulted in two aircraft projects. One of them was the Heinkel long-range bomber project, for a 60-tonne bomber. It was to transport a bomb load of 3 tonnes, and have a range of 28,000 kilometres. It was to be powered by four BMW 109-018 jet engines, each providing 3000 kp thrust, or by six Jumo 004 jet engines, each providing 1300 kp thrust. 3-tonne explosive warheads were also planned for the Daimler-Benz Project 'F', and also for post-war American and Russian nuclear missiles.

The Junkers company, under the direction of Professor Heinrich Hertel, in conjunction with the *Deutsche Forschungsanstalt für Segelflug* i.e. German Research Institute for Sailplane Flight, drafted the design for the other long-range bomber project, in which the two-part fuselage was part of the wing. With a wingspan of 51.30 metres and a bomb load of 8 tonnes, this bomber type was to reach a speed of 1030 kilometres per hour. The 90-tonne aircraft would have a range of 17,000 kilometres. With the end of the war it was not possible for those projects to be evaluated by the RLM. Even so, to turn them into reality could only have been achieved over a long period of time.

From the standpoint of the present day, it is not known what prompted Hermann Göring to invite such a tender. With an aircraft of that type, regular courier traffic to Japan would have presented no problems. Therefore, in March 1945 there must have been weapons that justified developments of the type, in the context of a situation where German air forces were entirely placed on the defensive.

Summary: The Miracle Weapons' Carriers of the Luftwaffe

In the summer of 1944 Adolf Hitler halted the *Luftwaffe's* conventional bomber programme and deliberately abandoned the idea of a 'strategic air force'. But during the course of the year a decisive change must have occurred. Once more, in the autumn of the same year, great efforts were suddenly being made to create long-range bombers.

However, in the meantime, the military situation had become far more disastrous. A change of policy was needed because the 'weapons which would decide the course of the war', were finally being completed. Means of transport for them was urgent, in fact more urgent than could have been envisaged. For that purpose, even small numbers of modern carrier aircraft would have been sufficient. But there were none.

The miracle weapons' carriers of the *Luftwaffe* can be divided into two different groups. One group involved modifications of existing conventional aircraft types, while the other represented aircraft with futuristic technology. It was a considerable fault on the part of the German armaments programme not to have completed the development of the Me 264 'America bomber'. It had already been flying since the end of 1942. From July 1944, when the aircraft was needed, there was only one prototype of the type, and it had not even been fully tested. From that group of conversions the Heinkel He 177 'nuclear bomber version' is the best known, having been mentioned in aviation reference works.

Until now, it has not been known why such a conversion was initially carried out. Besides, as far as is known, there was no German research going on to develop a German atomic bomb. In any event, in the Letov works in Prague, at the end of 1944 or the beginning of 1945, work was begun on the conversion of probably three Heinkel He 177 long-range bombers. At the end of the war, two of the aircraft were found by the Allies, incomplete and damaged. What became of the third machine, a similar conversion of which is indicated in photographs, until now is unknown. We also do not know whether the conversions on the He 177 were continued until the end of the war or whether they had already been stopped.

The atomic Heinkel He 177 would most probably have been deployed on individual missions against Allied capitals in Europe. Alternatively, a kamikaze-type one-way flight over the Atlantic to New York would also have been possible. The conventionally powered He 177, very fast for its day, could have made things very difficult for the Allied interceptor fighters. But despite all its modifications it could still have been at risk from the fast British DH 'Mosquito' night-fighter. A normal daylight raid in the West with that aircraft type would have been impossible because of Allied air superiority.

To be able to carry out a night attack with atomic bombs, the He 177 had to be accompanied by escort aircraft for pathfinder, meteorological, reconnaissance, and fighter escort duties. To achieve that, it seems that a short series of the tried, tested and efficient Ju 88 G6 night-fighter with extended fuselage was built. Because of its versatility, that aircraft type was suitable for all areas of operations. It could also be converted without great expense. In March 1945, the Ju 88 G10s of the *Luftwaffe* were at last available. But at the end of the war they had never been used for normal night-fighter or fighter-bomber operations. What became of them, and many other special aircraft, is still unknown.[99]

The Ju 390 V-2 was a hangover from a conventional 'America bomber' programme which had been begun as long ago as 1942. That programme ended prematurely, even within the context of the halt to bomber production, But in the summer of 1944, the second prototype, the Junkers 390 V-2, was completed. Because of its outstanding range parameters, it could have been used both for a transatlantic flight to attack New York, and also for courier flights to Germany's ally Japan. Where it finally landed is unclear, even today. The strong Japanese interest in the production of that aircraft, however, suggests that it is likely that it was transferred to Japan before the end of the war.

For a conventional long-range aircraft the Ju 390 had

excellent performance, and was heavily armed. But because of its relatively slow speed it would have been vulnerable to interception by enemy fighters.

Another example of conventional aircraft types, the Messerschmitt Bf 109, was intended to be used in the tactical deployment of miracle weapons. But the Bf 109 modification already showed the characteristics of an emergency solution. To judge by the reports, it was subjected to the confusion and chaos of the last weeks of the war. It was precisely the Bf 109 type that was chosen, and not the Focke-Wulf Fw 190 that was available in large numbers. The choice suggests that it was intended to approach, and the bombs to be dropped, from a great height. It also suggests a smaller weight for the tactical nuclear or radiological bombs. The available reports only speak of planned deployment on the Western Front. But it is completely conceivable, that within the context of Hitler's 'all-round defence', plans of this kind also existed for the Eastern and Southern fronts. It is said that it was planned to deploy the weapons systems in April 1945. However, supposedly, the plans were foiled by the resistance of SS guard units.

The weapons systems mentioned above used piston-engined aircraft. They had been developed technically at the same time as comparable Allied aircraft. However, in view of complete Allied air superiority, they could only be used under certain tactical conditions. Of course, things looked different in the case of the jet-powered miracle weapons' carriers. Even in the spring of 1945, they could have been deployed in daylight, in the West, with a great prospect of success. Despite the desperate fuel situation, which it is known did not even allow the already available jet fighters to be deployed, work was begun on two types of strategic bomber, by Horten and Junkers.

In the autumn of 1944, the Horten Ho XVIII was the winning aircraft of a programme commissioned for the creation of an intercontinental jet bomber. The aircraft was technically far in advance of its time. It found a worthy successor in the present day American B-2 Stealth bomber. On 1 April 1945, work was officially begun on the construction of that heavy intercontinental bomber, in an underground aircraft works near Kahla. It could be seen as an April Fool's joke if one was not aware of the background. Even today it is not yet clear how far advanced was the construction of that aircraft. In fact, it may be that work had already been going on, unofficially, in constructing the Horten. There can be no doubt that the aircraft was to be created exclusively for the purpose of carrying a nuclear or radiological bomb across the Atlantic to New York.

In addition to the Horten Ho XVIII programme, as late as March 1945, the Junkers company was commissioned by the RLM to produce their Ju 287 medium range jet bomber. However, it had already been announced in the summer of 1944 that the Ju 287 programme had been halted.

Considering the desperate military and industrial situation, those responsible could only have contemplated making individual aircraft. In a case like that, many raw materials and much industrial production capacity would have to be diverted from already heavily restricted emergency programmes for other weapons. There were prevailing, absolute priorities, given to defensive measures. So the diversions can only be explained, by the fact that the weapons that were deciding the course of the war were to be dropped, in favour of the two new types of bomber.

At the same time that work was resumed on constructing the Junkers Ju 287 aircraft, the programme of Heinkel He 177 aircraft conversions in Prague was halted. It would be interesting to know if that was because it had a better chance of a successful mission to drop an atomic bomb, than was to be expected from a fast jet aircraft. It would be supported by the fact that, according to verbal reports, the programme for conversion of the Heinkel He 177 V-38 was to be stopped, even before the end of the war. Because of the absence of official documents, however, that cannot be confirmed.

The heavy Junkers Ju 488, i.e. V-3, Junkers Ju 390, i.e. V-2, Horten Ho XVIII, and Junkers Ju 287 i.e. V-3, the miracle weapons' carriers, all have in common the fact that they were designed to carry a 4-tonne bomb load. Officially, there was no German 4-tonne bomb. That fact gives food for thought, if one considers the similar weight of the atomic bombs dropped by the Americans on Hiroshima and Nagasaki. One interior photograph of the bomb bay of the Heinkel He 177 V-38 was in fact published. Unfortunately, it does not allow any speculation concerning the planned size of the bomb load, nor what it would look like. The Heinkel He 177 V-38, like the aircraft types mentioned above, would also have been suitable to carry a 4-tonne bomb load.

The Messerschmitt Me 262 V-555 was the aircraft planned to carry antenna bombs. To what extent the Messerschmitt company planned further conversions of the same series, beyond the second prototype, is not known. The 250-kilogram antenna bombs, probably filled with radioactive substances, would have been used to irradiate an area occupied by the enemy. The mysterious Messerschmitt Me 262 prototype, of all aircraft, was handed over direct to the Allies in March 1945 from the secret *Luftwaffe* testing station at Rechlin. It may have been a coincidence.

There were other projects. There was the Ju 290 E project to drop a 20-tonne special bomb. Daimler-Benz had an ultra-long-range bomber project, to drop a 30-tonne special bomb. Daimler-Benz Project 'F' was to build a suicide aircraft with a 3-tonne special warhead. There were the designs for Hermann Göring's second intercontinental bomber project of February/March 1945. All were interesting, forward-looking projects, but they would have taken years to develop and produce.

It is not clear why the responsible Third Reich planners

wanted to tackle futuristic projects of that kind so late in the day, instead of concentrating all their efforts on the Horten Ho XVII and Junkers Ju 287 projects. It would seem that the fragmentation of developmental and production capacities, ran like a leitmotif through the entire Third Reich armaments programme, from 1939 to 1945.

In the case of the latter projects, it is interesting that from then on, a 3-tonne bomb load was specified. The 3-tonne charge happened to coincide exactly with the weight of the first American and Russian atomic warheads. In that instance, too, nothing was heard of plans for a German 3-tonne bomb.

B: Ordnance

1) Non-Conventional Luftwaffe *Special Armaments*

What were Hitler's airborne miracle weapons to look like? The results of research to date suggest that there was not something which was 'the' German atomic bomb, but a whole series of different nuclear and radiological weapons systems, from the small bomb to the 30-tonne monster. How far the various projects had progressed by the end of the war cannot yet be conclusively determined.

However, reports are piling up that indicate that the Americans, and no doubt the British too, had captured at least parts of those weapons in their advance, in April 1945. The Soviets can also have not gone away empty-handed. The only remarkable thing is the complete taboo surrounding the subject. Perhaps not everything was found at that time. That could be an important explanation for the stubborn culture of secrecy concerning the existence of Hitler's nuclear weapons.

Antenna Bombs

On 22 April 1945 Dr Edward O. Salant, on behalf of the American ALSOS Mission, issued an urgent memorandum to all American Air Intelligence Field Teams.[100] He appealed for a search to be made for German antenna bombs. At first the search was only for models of German *Luftwaffe* bombs with antennae on the tail. That was to involve bombs of the 150 kilogram and 50 kilogram classes. Probably, however, the writer wrote down the wrong figure with '150' kilograms, so that the correct figure was meant to be 250 kilograms. The agents were to inform the ALSOS mission of all the names of relevant researchers, factories or laboratories connected with the bombs, together with details of where they were located.

The antennae of the aluminium bombs were said to look like a motor car aerial, about 40 centimetres long and as thick as a finger, the thick end being screwed, as a base, into the tail of the bomb. The tail part of the bomb itself was said to be cylindrical, 22 centimetres wide, 40-70 centimetres long and probably fixed to the main body of the bomb with clamps. At the rear end of the main body of the bomb, it was said, was fixed a typical aluminium radio chassis. There, it was said, there was also a metal vacuum tube housing electrical parts, condensers, resistors, etc. In the search for the antenna bombs the teams were directed to Stade, Celle and Rechlin.

In a supplementary memorandum of 26 April 1945, the search parameters were extended to cover two other types of antenna bomb that had 25 centimetre long and 4-6 centimetre wide antennae on the nose of the bomb. The nose antenna, described in the hand-drawn sketch accompanying the memorandum, showed a spherical excrescence on the tip of the antenna and small holes covered with gauze.

It is not known whether the American secret service teams found any bombs matching that provisional description. It is very probable that the details of the bombs were compiled by the ALSOS Mission either on the basis of statements from prisoners of war, or perhaps after they had taken the cyclotron laboratory at Celle, on 17 April 1945. What is striking, at least from a present day point of view, is the fact that the secret memorandum of April 1945 was only recently released. But until today neither photographs nor drawings of such a weapon have been published. But it is striking that the German antenna bombs which the ALSOS Mission was seeking were also weapons connected with Hitler's nuclear programme.

For example, the fact that Celle is specified gives rise to mistrust. We know that the centrifuge workshop of Professor Harteck and Professor Groth was located in the Mitteldeutsche Spinnerei, in Celle. The aim of the two nuclear experts was to enrich natural uranium with isotope 235. From the beginning of 1945, the twin centrifuges, producing U 235 in Celle, were thought to be working round the clock.[101] It is not known how much fissile material could be produced by that process.

In the post-war years, at the beginning of the 1960s, Professor Groth caused rumours when he sent his closest colleague to Egypt to conclude contracts.[102] The Egyptian President Nasser for his part was believed to be looking for an explosive war-head that could be fitted to the missiles which he was said to be planning to direct against Israel. Professor Groth may have been involved in trying to sell a cyclotron to Cairo that would assist in the production of the necessary fissile material to build an atomic bomb.

In the summer of 1962 an Austrian scientist, Otto Frank Joklik, a former *Wehrmacht* officer, is said to have approached the Israelis. He said that he had just come from Cairo. It may be, that he believed that he had proof, that the German scientists in Egypt were producing 'an atomic bomb of the Little Boy type', by using nuclear waste. The radioactive materials, he said, if they were dispersed over Israeli territory, could possibly contaminate the ground and the atmosphere for months. It might be that Professor Groth wanted to revive a former second world war project, but not a war.

It is thus completely conceivable that the Celle antenna bombs were to be used as radiological weapons, and were to be filled with the radioactive isotope material that was enriched there. The purpose of the antenna would be to enable the precise detonation of an explosion, at a predetermined height, over a target. In that way it was expected to achieve the greatest possible dispersion of the radioactive substances.

A further indication for that is the existence of a 1949 photograph of the American experimental atomic bomb TX-8. The tail, strikingly, is fitted with the same kind of antennae as those shown in the ALSOS memoranda in 1945.[103] It is certainly no coincidence that the possible connection of the American TX-8 system with German developments was still under discussion.

In operational use, the antenna bombs would have been targeted by a special bomb aimer, and would be detonated by radio signal. To deliver them, in the circumstances of the aerial war in 1945, only a high-speed aircraft would have been suitable. There would also have been provided additional room for a separate bomb aimer. The single-seater Arado Ar 234 jet bomber was therefore disqualified. The only suitable carrier aircraft, in that instance, would have been the Messerschmitt Me 262 A-2/U2. The fast bomber version of the Me 262 had an additional bomb aimer in the nose of the fuselage. As further confirmation, there are photographs of the Me 262 V555 that show the final model of the type with two long antennae, like feelers, extending along the sides of the cockpit. The purpose of those remarkable antennae was, until now, still unclear in the relevant literature. However, it could have been indirectly connected with range finding, and detonation of antenna bombs.

It is known that the Me 262 V555 was at Rechlin. It was one of the other locations mentioned by ALSOS in relation to antenna bombs, where bombing trials were carried out. It may be a coincidence that it was precisely that aircraft that was handed over to the Allies on 30 April 1945. The reason why the Americans were trying to find antenna bombs in Stade is still unknown.

Radiological 1-tonne bomb: the V-weapon that Hitler turned down?

Germany's radiological bomb consisted of a container with radiating radioactive isotopes, in the middle of which a conventional explosive core was set as a detonator. The explosion of that core would disperse the radioactive material over a wide area. The consequences would have been death, radiation sickness, and genetic damage in the area in which the bomb had been dropped. The area would have been contaminated for a very long time, and would become totally uninhabitable.

The existence of the German radiological weapons programme was admitted by Professor Harteck and Dr Bothe in the post-war period.[104] The production of the radioactive waste products, necessary to produce those deadly weapons of mass destruction, was relatively cheap and comparatively easy. But it required chemical separation processes. The radioisotopes were to be generated by methane-dry ice reactors, cyclotrons, and other particle accelerators. The radioactive isotopes, such as caesium and strontium, which resulted from the process, would then be mixed with sand, silicon, and pulverised carbon.[105]

For storage, the dangerous substances had to be put into thick lead containers. All stages of production created enormous problems, in protecting the service personnel from the extremely strong radiation generated in the production process.[106]

As well as Harteck's group, there was also working on the isotope project the research institute of the *Deutsche Reichspost*, under von Ardenne and Houtermans. In addition to radiological bombs for aircraft, similar contents were being developed for the V-1, V-2, A-9/A-10 and the *Rheinbote*. (see following volume)

According to information provided by the British researcher Geoffrey Brooks,[107] a *Luftwaffe* bomb of about 1,000 kilograms was the real backbone of Hitler's radiological weapons system. It consisted of an 850-kilogram high-explosive, conventional warhead which was surrounded by 12 small bombs, about the size of a pumpkin, containing radioactive substances. The weapon was surrounded again by an additional radiation-proof shell. After it was dropped, it would descend by parachute, and was to explode in the air at a height of 30 metres above the target. In that way maximum contamination was to be achieved.

In dry weather, and under suitable atmospheric conditions, it was expected that all human life, within a radius of 2-3 kilometres round the impact point, would be annihilated. Persons who were within a 275-metre radius of the impact point of the radiological 1-tonne bomb, would be exposed to such a high dose of radiation that their death would have supervened within a period between nil and 10 days. Persons who were within a radius between 275 metres and one kilometre from the impact point would all die within a month.

It was calculated that dropping a single radiological

1-tonne bomb over a densely populated urban area such as, for example, Manhattan, would have claimed about 1 million victims and that afterwards the functioning of the infrastructure of the city of New York as a whole would be crippled in the most severe way for a long period. The only counter-measure would have been immediately to evacuate the affected area. Resettling in the area could only have been contemplated after the radiation levels had dropped.[108] The effects of an attack with radiological isotopes would, to be sure, rather resemble the results of the civilian reactor accident in Chernobyl, in 1986.

There are still no photographs or plans showing what the German radiological 1-tonne bomb would look like. Because Adolf Hitler had been aware, from August 1941, of the principle of developing radiological weapons,[109] progress by the end of the war must have been quite considerable. According to Brooks' information, the weapon was manufactured in an underground SS factory in the Harz district. Other likely places would have been Nordhausen, and also, because there is evidence of movements which would support this, S III, the Jonastal Troop Exercise Area, Ohrdruf.[110]

The radioactive life of the manufactured products was in some cases only days or weeks. In addition there was gamma radiation that could penetrate the thin walls of the bomb container.[111] Because of those disadvantages the bombs had, if at all possible, to be filled with the isotope material, near to where the aircraft were based. But in the case of rockets another solution became available. (see the following volume)

There was further information from the Director of the ALSOS Mission, S. Goudsmit. In evaluating the situation, he came across a report that described just such a weapon, left in an abandoned German nuclear research institute, following the capture of Strasbourg on 29 November 1944. The unnamed writer commented in his report, that a 'uranium machine' could be deployed as a huge dispersion bomb which, when it was dropped from an aircraft, could spray out deadly radiation. Goudsmit, completely unaware of the German radiological weapons project, considered it a crazy idea, to plan to drop an entire nuclear reactor over enemy cities, in the hope of creating a radioactive effect.[112] The original German report, describing a uranium machine as a bomb, is no longer to be found. There is only Goudsmit's uncertain, hand-written translation.

An American memorandum of 21 August 1943, expressed the expectation that Germany's radiological bombs would be ready between November 1943 and January 1944. It is not known why the radiological weapons were never used in action. However, Hitler probably equated radiological warfare with gas warfare. He turned down any first use of them, as long as there was no protection for his own civilian population against similar enemy retribution measures. In spite of great efforts, however, the German scientists did not succeed in finding appropriate counter-measures against the gamma radiation of the isotope weapons, which would have allowed Hitler to carry out a radiological V-attack.[113]

Probably the radiological weapons were among the four *Vergeltungswaffen* that Hitler mentioned to Marshal Antonescu on 5 August 1944. With regard to those weapons he stressed that, despite the fact that they were available, they could only be used when suitable protective measures were possible for the German people.

Nevertheless, radiological weapons might certainly have been dropped. Churchill was said to have threatened the use of poison gas and biological weapons against German cities, in retribution for the V-1 attacks on London. That intention was said to have been seriously considered, in the late summer of 1944. If it had been carried out, it could have resulted in the radiological contamination of the population of London and of other towns in the south of England.[114] The world appears to have had the great good fortune to escape a catastrophe of enormous dimensions.

The fact is that Germany's radiological bombs, despite being available, were never used. Perhaps the leadership of the Third Reich did have moral scruples. However, where those weapons were, at the end of the war, is still unknown.

The isotope weapon was not restricted to Germany. In 1968, the People's Republic of China was said to have recently incorporated the former German concept into their weapons planning. The information was given to China through a spy of Chinese origin, by the name of Dr Tsien. As a US Army colonel he had evaluated the German procedure for America's Manhattan project.[115]

Although the existence of such weapons was never admitted, there are indications that the USA also had radiological weapons at its disposal in the Korean War. Thus, on 11 February 1951, General MacArthur proposed to cut off North Korea from its supply areas in Chinese Manchuria, by means of a radiological 'circle of contamination'.[116]

Small Uranium Bombs

The 'official' opinion is, that it is a matter of certain knowledge that the stage that had been reached in nuclear technology, in the mid-1940s, only allowed large, heavy nuclear bombs. However, that may not be true, considering the absence of any evidence. As incredible as it may at first sound, another form of German miracle weapons were small bombs, about the size of a pumpkin.

The existence of those weapons was revealed by Henry Picker, in his book, *Hitler's Table Talk*. As a historian, who was also an eyewitness, Henry Picker is one of the few reliable sources for events in Adolf Hitler's immediate circle. The authenticity of his statements and writings was confirmed by many members of the Führer Headquarters, and also by Adolf Hitler's *Wehrmacht* adjutant. If the former *Bundespräsident*, Professor Dr Theodor Heuss, had not enabled the publication of that collection of documents in 1951, the facts would never have become known. But since Dr Henry Picker's work[117] is a source beyond any doubt, the following account is now given here.

Hitler's last visit to the front was on 11 March 1945, to the central section of the Oder front, and to the 9th Army in Schloss Freienwalde. Hitler implored the commander, General Theodor Busse, and his officers, to hold up the Russian assault on Berlin, at least until his 'new' weapons were ready to be used in action. He pointed to the example of *Generalfeldmarschall* Ferdinand Schörner, who with his *Heeresgruppe* Mitte was defending Silesia and the Bohemian area with undiminished ferocity. Hitler declared as he left: 'Every day and every hour is precious in allowing us to produce the terrible weapons that will turn the course of the war.'

According to Julius Schaub, who was Adolf Hitler's personal adjutant, the 'terrible' weapons Hitler meant were principally the 'uranium bomb'. It was about the size of a small pumpkin, the design of which had reached the stage where a prototype could be built.

According to further information from Picker, the design for a prototype of the German 'uranium bomb' was, in actual fact, fully developed by a team from the *Reichspost* research institute in Berlin-Lichterfelde and Klein-Machnow. The development had been carried out in parallel with work by a team under the direction of Professor Heisenberg. Unfortunately his group was unsuccessful.

When he was in Berlin, Hitler often visited the *Reichspost* Research Institute run by the Minister, Dr Ohnesorge. However, on those visits *Militäradjutant* Engel, who escorted Hitler, was not allowed to see the documents relating to the research. Among Ohnesorge's colleagues in the *Reichspost* Research Institute, were such luminaries as the nuclear physicist, Baron Manfred von Ardenne. After the end of the war, Baron von Ardenne continued to work on nuclear projects for the Russians, and was later awarded the Stalin Prize, Second Class, for his work.

Of course in the case of the small uranium bombs it would be vain to search for official plans and drawings. But there are a few indications of what this weapon looked like. The weight of the complete 'small uranium bomb' could not have exceeded 250 kilograms. The actual pumpkin, with its 100-gram nuclear explosive charge, like a tennis ball, was located in the narrow oblong body of the bomb. The length of the bomb must have been necessary, to accommodate the detonator.

An accompanying document to Führer Order 219, from the period October 1944, describes the small nuclear weapon, as one of two types of uranium bomb. It gives precise detail, right down to details of the outer shell and detonator mechanism. If the information from Professor Rose is to be believed, in his *Heisenberg and the Nazi Atomic Bomb Project* (University of California Press, 1998) a copy of the order, demanding the immediate production of the nuclear weapon, is still in the Wiesenthal archives in Jerusalem.

It is not known where the small uranium bombs were produced. There are two likely places. According to Picker, the production was to take place in an underground SS works, in the southern Harz mountains. It had a production capacity of 30,000 workers. After Germany's unconditional surrender, the works were transferred by the Red Army to the USSR.

But it is also possible that the secret factory, 'Quarz' near Melk (Roggendorf) had significant involvement in production. The importance of Melk, as a location for the production of secret weapons, was discovered by the Austrian researcher, Schmitzberger.[118] The underground tunnels there are up to 7 kilometres long, and could provide accommodation for 10,000 workers. According to the official line, Melk was only supposed to have been an outstation of Steyr. But there is evidence for incredibly high levels of water and electricity consumption that do not match that of a normal factory. To provide energy, even in the middle of the war, a new dam was purpose-built on the Danube. Also, the great Markersdorf airfield lay close to Melk. It appears that Melk was mainly responsible for the production of relatively small nuclear charges that were to serve to fill 250-kilogram bombs. They could also be used as bundled explosive warheads for rockets, or as propulsion for the planned uranium engine.

Some of the completed or almost completed uranium bombs were stored in secure places in the Alps, e.g. in the Salzkammergut, in the first instance in mine tunnels. Later, some were also deposited temporarily near Henndorf.

Thus, as early as 1944 small atomic bombs were being developed, whereas today the basic assumption is still being made that World War II technology only ran to producing the very heavy bombs of the 4- to 5-tonne class as A-weapons.

The small uranium bombs could have been envisaged as the backbone of Hitler's planned 'all-round defence'. It was planned to deploy them on the Western Front, as soon as the front lines could be stabilised, and there were sufficient numbers of the bombs.

The mass production of the weapon, that could kill every living thing within a radius of several hundred metres of the impact point, was supposed to run from mid-October 1944. The details were discussed at a secret conference of officers, in Stockerau, at the beginning of October 1944. It was the conference concerning which a secret American report had already been drafted by 7 November 1944.[119] The extent of treachery was simply unimaginable.

Sources among which there is a consensus,[120] speak of 'at least' one atomic test that was said to be linked to that weapon. Thus, for instance, the eyewitness, Frau Cläre

Werner, states what she observed during the 1940s. From Wachsenburg, close to the Ohrdruf troop exercise area, where she lived as a custodian, she saw striking flashes of light over the exercise area. The flashes of light were huge, and lit up the sky from horizon to horizon, so that 'you could have comfortably read a newspaper, at night, for minutes on end'. Moreover, the eyewitnesses to those incidents, Frau Werner and two other persons, felt completely shattered for three whole days. Such a state very probably had something to do with what they had observed. Scientists explain the feeling of being shattered as being due to a shock, caused by waves of gravitational field energy that result from a nuclear explosion. Cläre Werner's report also matches information, from a reliable source, that reports a small atomic test of that kind took place on the troop exercise area.

Frau Werner's statements have also been reported several times in the regional Thuringian press. On the other hand, experts maintain that Frau Werner, had such an explosion actually taken place, would have been irradiated. That line of argument, however, would only apply to the use of a bomb of the Hiroshima type, but not for small tactical atomic bombs that, as has been described, were indeed available.

The weapon being tested in that instance may well have been the same weapon that was also mentioned at the officers' conference in Stockerau. The fact that details of the deadly, effective radius of the small uranium bombs were already given at the conference in 1944, leads to the conclusion that tests of this kind had also taken place. Supporting evidence for such a test is also given by reports [121] that, in 1944, a test explosion had been carried out in the North Sea in the presence of selected observers. The explosion had caused a small island to completely vanish into thin air. Ostensibly, a small atomic bomb was used in this instance. Unfortunately, to date there is no further information concerning the location and precise date of the incident. Nevertheless, we can be relatively certain that the development and production of such bombs had gone far beyond the mere prototype stage.

But then, apparently, deployment of the small uranium bombs was delayed. Probably, it was necessary first to build, and test, a secure mechanism for suspending and releasing the bombs. At that stage too the Type AS 12/44 parachute solution was probably being developed. But also, independently, 'suicide' pilots were found who, according to statements by Himmler, were prepared to drop the atomic bombs without a parachute. (see section concerning *Selbstopfer* Bf 109) [122]

According to Picker's account, Hitler also wanted to deploy the weapons in another way. He wanted to use several of the 'dangerous pumpkins' as the explosive warhead, for the A-9/A-10 America rocket.[123]

It is more than probable that there were similar plans for installing the charges in the A-4, A-4B, Fi 103 and 'T' flying bombs. How far those developments had proceeded will be the subject, among other things, of the following volume.

Whether the atomic bombs that were supposed to be deployed in the winter of 1944/45 in the Ardennes offensive [124] were also small uranium bombs is not certain, but probable. According to various sources of information, six or twelve 'atomic bombs' were supposed to bring about the decisive breakthrough in the last great German offensive effort. Why they were not used, it is true, still remains unclear. Unfavourable westerly winds, with the resultant threat of nuclear fall-out for the German-occupied area, could have been one of the conceivable possible reasons. But perhaps once again the sabotage factor was at work. When the atomic bombs came to be needed for use, they could not be found anywhere near the airfields from which the attack was to be launched.

'Operation *Bodenplatte*' was the last desperate, large-scale attack by all the German fighter aircraft still available in the West. It began on 1 January 1945. That attack, in which large numbers of Allied aircraft were destroyed on their airfields, was principally intended to hit enemy fighter airfields, ground organisation, and radar control stations. The consequence of *Bodenplatte* was that the Allied fighters were temporarily crippled for about a week. Certainly, the price that had to be paid for that attack was terrible. 300 German aircraft were lost.[125]

Perhaps the attack was also intended to prepare the way for the planned deployment of German atomic bombs. But the temporary interruption of the enemy fighter defences could have opened wide the doors for the German atomic bombers to attack, if they could have been deployed. We do not know, unfortunately, which aircraft it was planned should be used in the Ardennes, for A-attacks.

Far more is known about later plans for deploying the small uranium bombs. But there again the weapons were not deployed, although at the end of March 1945, the German *Luftwaffe* had dropped leaflets over the planned target areas. The leaflets told the civilian population to evacuate the areas in question by the 1 April 1945. They were dropped over the Westerwald and Siegerland and requested the evacuation of a zone extending 50 kilometres up from the Rhine. They said that, on 1 April, new weapons would be used that would decide the course of the war, and bring German victory. (see also section on the Bf 109)

The American General Groves, who was responsible for the Allied nuclear weapons programme, also expected German atomic bombs to be used from 1 April 1945.[126]

The 'defensive' form of deployment, however, would have meant that the nuclear weapons would have been dropped over German territory. That would have inevitably led to Germany's civilian population also being hit by the effects of the bombs. In the chaotic circumstances that already prevailed at the end of March 1945, evacuation of the target area, in time, despite the leaflets, would have been out of the question. There are indications that Speer and certain SS circles, possibly for that reason, may have prevented that kind of 'five minutes to midnight' deployment of the weapons.[127]

It is not known what became of the weapons at the end of the war. In their 'coincidental' lightning advance into Austrian Amstetten, in May 1945, the Americans, in a race against the Russians, probably captured most of the bomb material that was loaded on lorries and railway wagons.[128] Incidentally, the Americans had been informed, by an Austrian source, of the Amstetten 'treasures'. According to the source, they had been shown to him by Himmler. The 'source' may have been acting on behalf of Himmler, or other SS circles, when he gave away the location of the weapons.

Amstetten was taken by the Americans on 8 May 1945. The SS, with no attempt whatever at defence, were waiting in the marketplace for the Americans. When the Americans marched into Amstetten at midday, they met the SS there, completely peacefully, not a shot being fired. When a Russian air-raid 'happened' to hit that meeting, Americans and SS together, ran into the air-raid shelter. Some of the Americans later withdrew with the SS, no doubt taking 30 lorry loads back across the Enns, while others drove on towards Melk.[129]

Like Ohrdruf in Thuringia, Melk was fanatically defended by the SS for a long time. The same troops, who could not hold Vienna and the *Ostwall*, dug themselves in there and defended a firm front until 8 May 1945. In Thuringia it was the 6th SS *Gebirgdivision* that put up dogged resistance to the Americans. Fighting in Melk was the 6th SS *Panzerarmee*, comprising the remnants of 8 Panzer divisions including units of the *Leibstandarte Adolf Hitler*, *Das Reich*, and *Hohenstaufen*, and also parts of the SS Division *Hitlerjugend*. In addition, there also 'happened' to be at least 15 *Jagdtiger* tanks between Ybbs and Steyr. They were the most powerful tanks in the world at that time, and no enemy tank could withstand their 12.8cm cannon at 4,000m range.

The Russians had already taken St. Pölten in the middle of April 1945. Then, surprisingly, three kilometres before they reached the Markersdorf airfield, i.e. 10 kilometres from Melk, they shifted over to the defensive, and reinforced their positions with deep trenches. Their loudspeakers announced, in German, that the 'greatest betrayal in the history of the world' was about to take place, and asked the Germans to desert to them.

What were the Russians afraid of? Perhaps there were secret negotiations between the Western Allies and the Third Reich, about which, to date, we still know nothing. Perhaps the Russians feared that agreement between them appeared to be within reach.

The two attempts at negotiation, by Hermann Göring and Heinrich Himmler, are well known. Both were predestined to fail. Both, independently of each other, were trying to negotiate a separate peace on the Western Front. Nothing came of either.

Perhaps, in April 1945, there were other negotiations between the 'official' Third Reich and the Western Allies. One clue to this could be that on 12 April 1945 *Grossadmiral* Dönitz, later to be Hitler's official successor, was in Bern for 24 hours. Later, the same evening, he met Hitler in Berlin.[130] With what mission had Hitler sent him to Bern? All kinds of speculation are possible. There may have been connections between those puzzling events and the behaviour of the Russians near the secret factory in Melk.

After the 'betrayal' they had feared evidently did not happen, the Russians, on the morning of 8 May, began a gigantic heavy artillery barrage. Following this, they broke through the German front at Merkersdorf. They captured Melk, and shortly afterwards met US tanks on the outskirts. The Americans had taken Linz at the beginning of May and were likewise moving up at top speed towards Melk. In the 'published' history, however, it says that the US Army only got as far as Enns.

But then the inconceivable happened. There was a fierce firefight between the tanks of the two sides. The Russians, after having just come 'second' to the Americans in Amstetten, evidently did not want to have the prize snatched from under their noses, this time in Melk. According to the available information, the Red Army held the field in the battle and, after clearing up this 'misunderstanding', the Americans withdrew again.

It is not known what the Russians found in Melk. However, after the Russians had taken the town, 10,000 people who were formerly employed there, also went missing from Melk. There are, clearly, parallels with what happened in Ohrdruf/Crawinkel. However, after the war, the Russians spent two years 'scrapping' the complex in Melk.[131]

In that way the Austrian atomic booty was divided between the Americans and the Russians. The Americans had Innsbruck and Amstetten, and thus no doubt most of the completed weapons. Meanwhile, with Melk the Russians captured a significant, main bomb production site. The only unanswered question is whether, as was the case in Ohrdruf, there had previously been extensive destruction, or sealing up of tunnels, by the Germans. Was everything handed over to the Allies at the time, or is there somewhere, in a secret hideaway in the Alps, a 'poisonous atomic pumpkin' still slumbering in its hiding-place?

1-tonne Uranium Container: the 'Swabian' atomic bombs

It is not known if there were also uranium weapons in the southern part of the Reich. According to an account by the American author, and former secret serviceman, Dr David Myhra,[132] even in 1945 German physicists produced, as an emergency solution, two containers, each weighing 1,000kg, filled with alternating layers of uranium and paraffin. Those scientists, whose names are not known, evidently believed that by dropping that device from an aircraft, they could set off a nuclear explosion of enormous power.

As they marched in, French Army soldiers found the two containers sunk in a huge water tank, in a nuclear research laboratory that was housed in a former textile factory. The factory is said to have been in Haigerloch, but probably there is some, perhaps deliberate, confusion in the report concerning the location.

Before the American ALSOS Mission could reach the French troops in this 'location south of Stuttgart', the French blew up the entire plant. This destroyed all the installations including the containers filled with uranium.

According to the same account, the Horten Ho XVIII, if it had been ready at the beginning of 1945, was to have dropped another of the containers on American targets, either on New York or Washington. Dr Myhra, however, is of the opinion that the bomb would have failed. Dropping the containers from a height of some 11 kilometres or less, he maintains, would just have made a 'nice round hole' in a building or a street, before the containers came to rest deep in the ground, without exploding. What can be made of all this?

According to the English author and nuclear specialist, Philip Henshall,[133] a processed uranium bomb of the kind mentioned in Myhra's account would have been quite conceivable as a weapon. However, its detonation would not have caused a proper nuclear explosion, but only expelled the contents of the container. Nevertheless, because of the radioactive contamination that would result, it could have caused serious consequences in the target area.

Unfortunately, there is no further information concerning the appearance of that improvised weapon at the end of the war. In the form described in the account, the 1-tonne uranium containers would certainly not have been capable of causing an explosion. On the other hand, the entire district would have been affected when the French went about destroying the textile factory. If it is possible to discover the exact location of the atomic bomb factory, then work must also begin immediately on researching any cases of radiation sickness that may have appeared after the war.

Haigerloch was clearly not the location of the nuclear factory that needs to be found. Certainly, the place was known, because it was the location of Professor Heisenberg's heavy water pile. However, the ALSOS mission had captured, and dismantled, the atomic research installation located there, before the French arrived. The French Army, as it marched in later, then found only minimal traces of the German nuclear plant.

The description in the above mentioned account is more likely to fit the nearby small town of Hechingen. The Americans and French were involved in fighting and occupying that town from two directions. There was a great deal of fighting, perhaps because of the important known nuclear research laboratories. One of the laboratories was housed in the Grotz textile factory and was known to contain the prototypes of Dr Bagge's isotope sluice. Therefore the French and the Americans would have had equal opportunities to gain access. The literature published to date, however, only mentions that, in the case of the Grotz textile factory, the Americans retained the upper hand over the French and were then able to dismantle everything undisturbed. Nothing is mentioned of the water tanks and bomb containers that were located there, nor that the factory was destroyed.[134]

However, the containers being searched for could have been at another location in the district. It is known that there were nuclear research laboratories in Tailfingen, in Bissingen and possibly in another place south of Stuttgart. That area remains to this day a centre for Swabian textile manufacture, so that at the time there would have been a great number of textile factories and spinning sheds that could have been considered as locations for such a nuclear laboratory. In Tailfingen, Professor Hahn's nuclear laboratory was housed in the Roller textile factory. But again, nothing is known about that factory being destroyed at the end of the war.

But there are a few more important clues that support the accuracy of Myhra's account. In March 1945, Professor Gerlach acted for the Reich Research Council and was responsible for nuclear research. In addition to travelling to Stadtilm, he undertook a tour to Haigerloch and Hechingen. Gerlach asked the astounded Professor Wirtz whether the 'uranium machine' that was located there could not soon be dropped on an enemy city. Professor Wirtz connected the question with the Haigerloch uranium pile. It was definitely not suitable for use as a nuclear weapon.[135]

However, American authors, on whose translations we have mostly to rely nowadays, have had difficulties in establishing the precise meaning of the word *Uranmaschine*. That is because the word means far more than the usual mechanical concept suggested in English. In a more recent edition of the Duden dictionary, there are 50 different meanings of the German word *Maschine*, filling almost a page. Thus the word *Uranmaschine*, which is used again and again by the German scientists, could not only relate to mechanical uranium machines, in the sense of nuclear reactors, but could equally well have referred to an atomic bomb, i.e. *Atomhöllenmaschine.*

Consequently, it is not the case that Professor Gerlach wanted to drop entire atomic reactors on cities, but that in speaking of this he was referring to a 'proper' uranium, i.e. atomic bomb. The false assumption, that the German scientists had so little idea of how an atomic bomb functioned, that they wanted to drop the entire reactor, is something that even today haunts the specialist literature.

The additional question is raised, as to whether Professor Wirtz was informed at all about the activities of the other researchers in the vicinity, or if he knew about the purpose of their laboratories, or if in fact he was deliberately hushing something up. Remarkably, attempts in the USA to gain access to the interrogation records of Professor Gerlach, by appealing to the Freedom of Information Act, were completely unsuccessful. Obviously those documents are still being kept under lock and key.

On the basis of the current status of research, we may be sure that the group around Professor Heisenberg, which mainly worked in Haigerloch, had not by the end of the war worked on the development of a German atomic bomb. However, that is not the case for the other researchers. Some of them had their nuclear laboratories in the area, but even today their names are not known.

The ALSOS Mission pressed by time, and in competition with the French, had concentrated on the principal group around Professor Heisenberg. It is perfectly conceivable that, in doing so, they either overlooked other researchers in the area, or only discovered their importance after the French units had already got to them.

That applies, for example, to the Swiss physicist Dr Walter Daellenbach who was working for the German Reich. According to American information, the scientists Werner Heisenberg and Max von Laue met with Daellenbach every Wednesday in Bissingen. They discussed with him the construction of his 'super cyclotron'.

The significance of that machine is the subject of conflicting opinions in specialist circles. Colonel Boris Pash from ALSOS, found it 'not particularly interesting', but French physicists under the direction of Colonel Frederic Joliot seized the machine in Bissingen, and designated Daellenbach's work as having 'great importance for the war'. If Daellenbach's accelerator made any contribution to the construction of Germany's atomic bombs, it was because it made it possible to produce sufficient plutonium.[136]

It is therefore entirely possible that work was also going on, in the south of Germany, on atom bomb projects. The uranium bomb containers that were destroyed could have been atomic weapons that had not yet been completed, or at least atomic weapons without detonators. There the operational principles are not yet clear.

2) Special Bombs of the 4 to 5 tonne Class

Bundle Bombs

Among the weapons developments of 1944/45 that have been, perhaps deliberately, disregarded to date in the specialist literature, are the so-called bundle bombs.

Two combinations of that weapon were known. One of them involved coupling together 10 bombs of the type SC 500. The other involved connecting together five bombs of the type SB 1,000. The available documentation does not precisely indicate how the bombs were to be connected, but it must have been by some kind of clamp. To stabilise the bombs when they were dropped, it was planned to use a parachute arrangement.

A bundle weapons system of that kind could essentially have offered two advantages. Firstly, previous tests had indicated that the destructive effect of a 5-tonne bomb was less than that of five individual 1-tonne bombs. Secondly, bundling the bombs together made it possible to subject a single target area to the effects of the contents of different bombs. That would have allowed, for example, explosive, splinter, gas and radiological charges to be combined. It is known that isotope charges require normal explosive components to disperse them over the target. Thus, by combining radiological and explosive bombs, a many times greater dispersion effect could have been achieved with simultaneous destructive effect.

Unfortunately, however, there are no written documents relating to those weapons. The only project in which it is known that plans existed for bundle bombs to be used, is the Daimler-Benz ultra-high speed bomber project of February 1945.[137] Incidentally, today the Americans possess so-called cluster bombs that were used in the Gulf War with devastating effect. Such weapons could perhaps represent a further development of the earlier German design.

SA 4,000

The heavy aerial mine, also designated as ML (Mine, Luft) or Ml 4000, was developed by the Rheinmetall-Borsig Company. It was composed of 5 nipolite cylinders, each with a diameter of 1m, and had an overall length of 4m. To stabilise it, and to reduce its rate of fall after it was dropped, a parachute developed by the FGZ (Ferdinand Graf Zeppelin) research establishment, with an opening diameter of 1.6m was to be used.[138] On the flattened forward end of the bomb were 4 delayed-action detonators. Shaped like hollow rods, they were connected to the core of the bomb that was then filled with the detonator explosive.

The bomb had a relatively thin casing, and was stabilised by numerous screw rods on the block construction system. The shell of the bomb was made of nipolite. This was a solid detonator explosive based on di-ethylene glycol di-nitrate (DEGND). The solid mass of the explosive was relatively inert. It therefore possessed considerable mechanical strength, so that it could be used instead of metal, as an outer shell for the bombs.[139] Strangely, it was never said which material was intended to be used to fill the interior of the nipolite cylinder.

By the end of the war a whole series of bombers was designed to carry a 4-tonne bomb offensive payload. It has been presumed that the SA 4,000 never reached the stage of experimental prototypes being built. However, that seems barely credible, because in American bomb-disposal documents of the post-war period, precise reference is made to that quite recognisable weapon. There must have been reasons. If one considers the published design drawings of the SA 4,000, one is struck immediately by the circular filler openings in the nipolite cylinders. Their design suggests that it is unlikely that they would be used within a conventional atomic bomb.

But it was very likely that the bomb could be filled with radiologically active substances. They included for example, silicon, carbon or cork fillings mixed with radioactive strontium or cobalt isotopes. Because the bomb was divided into individual cylinders it would have been possible to fill it with various substances, in a co-ordinated scheme. The design of the SA 4,000 would have seen to it that the substances were dispersed to the greatest possible extent. Perhaps this could be the 'silicon bomb' of the Ho XVIII.

4-tonne Stratosphere Bomb

A special type of 4-tonne bomb was planned for the Sänger Antipodes bomber.[140] The craft would circle the earth on an undulating trajectory, at a speed of 26,000 kilometres per hour. After about 19,200 kilometres in orbit it would release a 4-tonne bomb from a height of 40 kilometres. Because of the 'dropping' conditions prevailing in the stratosphere, special adjustments had to be made to the weapon.

Concerning the appearance and configuration of the bomb there is only little information. According to that, the bomb was to have a length of 6.10 metres and a diameter of about 1 metre. Its appearance matched the ballistic requirements for a drop from a great height. Its form rather resembled a smaller V-2 without tail fins. The same principle was used, as with the SB 30,000 bomb. An FGZ parachute, fitted in the tail of the bomb, had to serve to slow the rate of descent.

It is almost certain that the 4-tonne bomb of the Sänger project involved a nuclear weapon. In August 1944, Dr Sänger put forward his proposal, with design documents and hypothetical bombing charts, to the German leadership and the prominent scientists of the time. The proposal was known as the affair of the famous secret command, 'No. 4268/L XXX 5'. The synopses were allowed to be delivered by courier only, and had to be passed from hand to hand. The target plan of New York, which among other things was contained in those papers, and which was published by the US Air Force in the post-war period, could have been the bombing plan that had been worked out for the 4-tonne stratosphere bomb. The circular radii of destruction, shown in this plan, corresponded fairly exactly to those of the later Hiroshima bomb of August 1945. In the radius of destruction they resemble very closely the secret weapon described by Hitler. It too was to have a radius of destruction of 4.5 kilometres. In considering that design we must ask how the writer could know so much, as early as August 1944, concerning the expected effects. A conclusive explanation would be that the originators of the bombing plan, in summer 1944, must have already had experience of previous nuclear test explosions.

Judging by its size and design, the warhead must have resembled the Stadtilm uranium bombs of the 'Hiroshima' type. (see relevant section) We also know that the ballistics expert, Dr Stuhlinger, one of the leading colleagues of Wernher von Braun, worked for several months in Stadtilm, in the spring of 1945. Perhaps the striking resemblance of the bomb casing of the stratosphere bomb, to the form of the V-2, was a result of his collaboration.

For the stratosphere bomber there was also the design for a 1-tonne stratosphere bomb, which in appearance resembled a smaller version of the 4-tonne bomb. The planned contents of that bomb could have been either radiological isotopes, or the 'TX-8' Type 850kg nuclear warhead which was also being developed for the A-4 and A-9/A-10. (see following volume)

Both the 4-tonne and the 1-tonne bombs could have been dropped from other aircraft types such as, for example, the He 177, Ho XVIII, Ju 287 and Ju 390. Nothing is definitely known concerning the stage which development of the bombs had reached by the end of the war.

Large Uranium Bomb: the mystery of the Stadtilm 'container'

What type of large bomb was to be transported by aircraft such as the Ho XVIII or the EF 132? In addition to the SA 4,000 and the stratosphere bomb, also possible is another weapon, the 'heavy uranium bomb' from Thuringia. The development of that miracle weapon was already at a very advanced stage.

There is evidence that the principle of the uranium bomb was known to German scientists. On the same lines as in an artillery shell, enriched uranium is caused to explode by a beryllium detonator. That evidence was provided in post-war statements by Professor Heisenberg, during his captivity in the prisoner-of-war camp at Farm Hall, England. There is also the statement of the Hamburg chemist, Dr Edse, who was an important member of the team around Professor Diebner.[141] Both statements were made before details of the Hiroshima bomb had been officially publicised. Thus the two official groups most closely connected with Germany's nuclear research, i.e. Heisenberg and Diebner, knew very well how such a bomb functioned. The evidence is in the published history.

But there was at least one more research team, under SS control. The importance of the SS nuclear researchers connected with that team, who to all intents and purposes remain unknown even today, cannot be overestimated. Certainly, at the moment, only a small amount of information can be suggested in that connection.

The information available indicates that the German 'Manhattan Project', which was to lead to the creation of a uranium bomb, was carried out underground, in the so-called *Objekt Burg* in the Ohrdruf/Crawinkel area.[142] It appears that the uranium bombs were the result of a programme of collaboration between the SS group, and the group around Professor Diebner. Competition for 'research victory' among the teams, however, hindered the operation. The decisive breakthrough was achieved in July 1944. But afterwards, for reasons that are not quite clear, there appears to have been a delay. That had a significant influence on the production of atomic bombs to be ready for deployment.

The causes of the delay could have been friction, power struggles, or even deliberate sabotage. Perhaps there was even a connection with the failed assassination attempt on Adolf Hitler, on 20 July 1944. In the event of a successful *coup d'état*, perhaps the conspirators wanted to use the nuclear weapon to force a peace deal with the Allies. In any event, there are indications that close connections existed between the Stadtilm researchers and the '20 July officers' circles'.[143]

The work, in *Objekt Burg*, must then have been continued in dreadful conditions for the prisoners who worked there. In addition to German researchers, Japanese scientists were also involved from time to time in the research.[144] There is confirmation for the presence of Japanese in the nuclear weapons project. After the

Zinsser's He 111: Tail view of one of the specially-converted He 111s with tail-mounted antennae to monitor rockets (Source: Peenemünde B1359/44; photograph: Deutsches Museum, Munich).

Some of the measuring instruments installed in the Peenemünde He 111s (instrument assembly with oscilloscope, type unclear, 1944) (Source: Peenemünde B1533/44; photograph: Deutsches Museum, Munich).

View of the cabin of the He 111 (Source: Peenemünde B1535/44; photograph: Deutsches Museum, Munich).

occupation of Japan, the Americans found documentary evidence that, during the war, there was a regular exchange of nuclear scientists between Japan and Germany.[145]

Strikingly, the facts were not mentioned in any written American account. Many decades later, they were given by Robert Nininger to the American author Robert Wilcox, who had written a book about Japanese nuclear research. Nininger must have known precisely what was going on. Besides Major R. Furman, Nininger was the second section leader of the American 'Group Three'. The group was the Asiatic counterpart of the American ALSOS Mission in Germany. Unfortunately, to date we know nothing of the names of the German and Japanese scientists involved in those exchanges, or what became of them at the end of the war.

Calibration of a time-lapse camera in a He 111 observation aircraft for photographing rocket take-offs. Were nuclear tests also observed by these specialist aircraft in October 1944? (Source: Peenemünde B1537/44; photograph: Deutsches Museum, Munich).

The way in which 'second class' nuclear experts were dealt with at the end of the war, however, gives us reason to fear the worst. Thus, when the Americans marched into Stadtilm, three Siemens engineers were found in the nuclear laboratory. It is believed that they were immediately executed.[146]

Kapitän Falcke, too, vanished without trace while in US captivity. The naval officer, who knew the secret purpose for which uranium had been loaded on to U-boat U 234 to be sent to Japan, was never seen again. After the surrender of the U-boat on 19 May 1945 we may assume that he too met a violent death.[147] U-boat U 234 was surrendered on 19 May 1945. Incidentally, the history of U-boat U-234 is so complex that it would require a separate book.

But even the people who worked on the construction of Hitler's uranium bombs during the war, in Germany, paid a terrible price in blood. One immediately thinks of Professor Dopel's prophetic words from 1942. He principally refers to the people who were working in *Objekt Burg*, on making the bomb a reality. To a certain extent he is supported by the fact that, shortly before Ohrdruf was captured by the Americans, the Germans dealt ruthlessly with many of the people working there.

Rumours, which have been circulating for years, suggest that some 12,000 people vanished without trace.[148] They were not only prisoners, but also scientists, and elements of the SS guard personnel. Also included were miners working in that area towards the end of the war. There was talk of 3,000 men who had to be of 'pure Aryan stock'. It is not known what happened to them.

The Miracle Weapons of the *Luftwaffe*:

Winged miracle weapons climbing away. The Dornier P.247/6 and Lippisch Me 329 escort fighters are peeling away over the French coast from the aircraft they have been escorting, a Horten Ho XVIII A (reconnaissance bomber), which must continue on its mission alone. The American artist Richard L. Mendes set the time of this imaginary 'New York City Nuclear Mission' as 19.23 GMT on 13th February 1947.

Looking ahead to volume 3 of *Hitler's Miracle Weapons:* circular aircraft of the type BMW Flügelrad V.2, on its first flight in October 1944 from the Munich airfield (Neubiberg) (Richard L. Mendes).

'The Third Reich strikes back': Horten Ho XVIII A and B with escort protection over the French coast, 13 February 1947, 4.15pm, the 'New York City Nuclear Mission'. Two Horten Ho XVIII aircraft will escort the actual nuclear bomber across the Atlantic, while the protective escort must turn back (Richard L. Mendes)

'The Eagle's Last Attack': 4 April 1945, Lower Rhine region. Messerschmitt Bf 109 K-2 (SO[suicide]) aircraft, adapted in Münster to carry small uranium bombs, carry out a dawn suicide attack on enemy river crossings (Richard L. Mendes).

Heinkel He 177 A-7 high-altitude bomber for the planned SO (suicide) attack on America; Germany: Autumn 1944. Paint scheme: Upper surfaces: RLM 70-71; undersides RLM 76; fuselage RLM 02 over RLM 76 (commissioned work, Igor Shestakov)

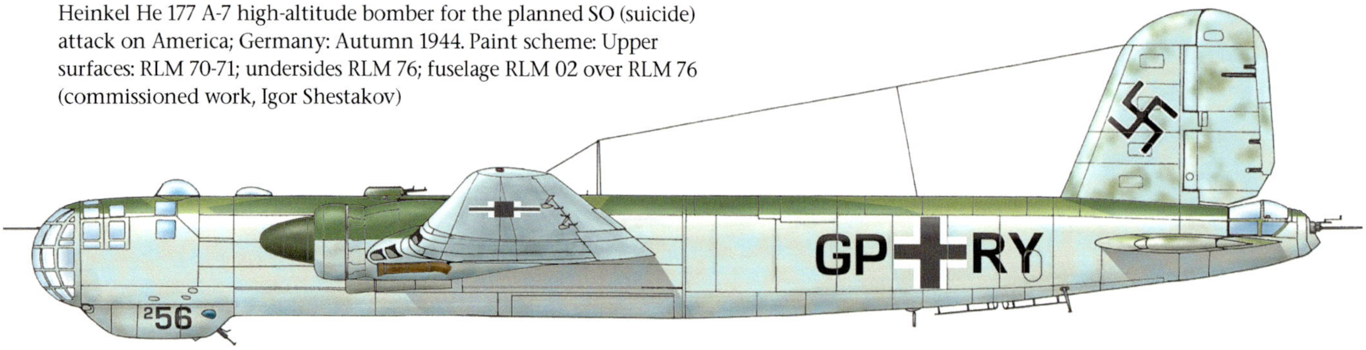

He 177 A-5 *Amerikabomber* with radiological SA 4000 bomb and Blohm & Voss aircraft suspended beneath as a flying fuel tank; Project 1944. Paint scheme for He 177: Fuselage and undersides RLM 76 + RLM 70; paint scheme for BV 40: underside RLM 65, remainder RLM 70 (Igor Shestakov)

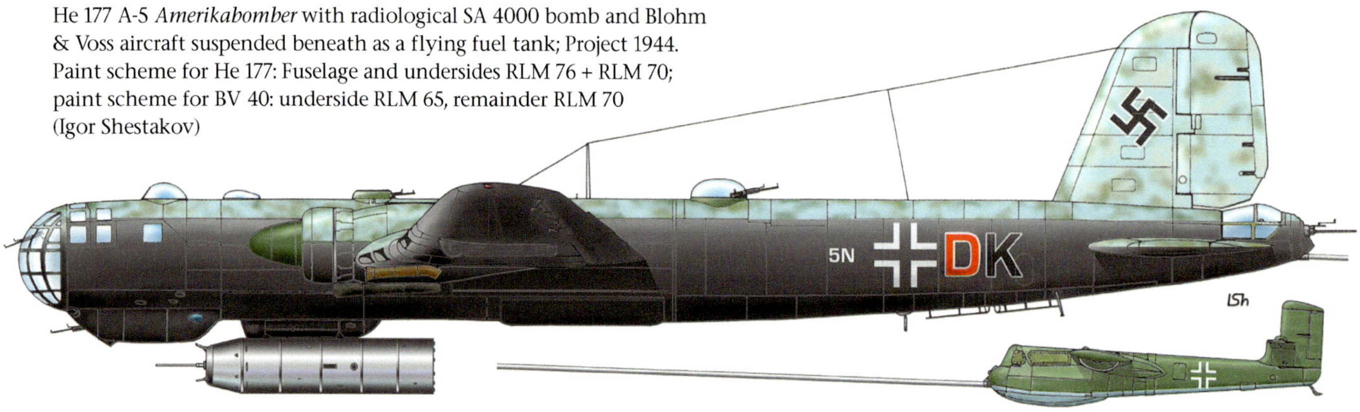

Heinkel He 177 A5 mother aircraft for Me 323 onboard bomber with small uranium bomb; Project 1944. Colour scheme He 177: RLM 02 overall, upper surfaces camouflage marking with RLM 70; colour scheme for Me 328: underside RLM 65, upper surfaces RLM 70 (Igor Shestakov)

Heinkel He 177 A5 transatlantic aircraft with reduced armament and additional fuel tanks; suspended beneath: Messerschmitt Me 410 B (SO) with radiological 2-tonne bomb; Project 1944. Colour scheme for He 177: Upper surfaces RLM 80/82, underside RLM 76; colour scheme for Me 410: undersides RLM 76, fuselage and upper surfaces RLM 80/82 over RLM 76 (Igor Shestakov)

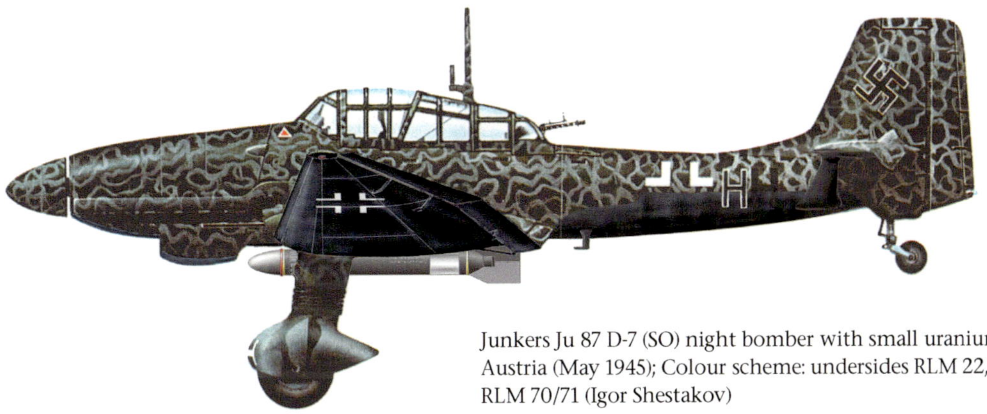

Junkers Ju 87 D-7 (SO) night bomber with small uranium bomb, Seitenstätten, Austria (May 1945); Colour scheme: undersides RLM 22, upper surfaces RLM 76 over RLM 70/71 (Igor Shestakov)

Blohm & Voss destroyer project with small uranium bomb (Igor Shestakov)

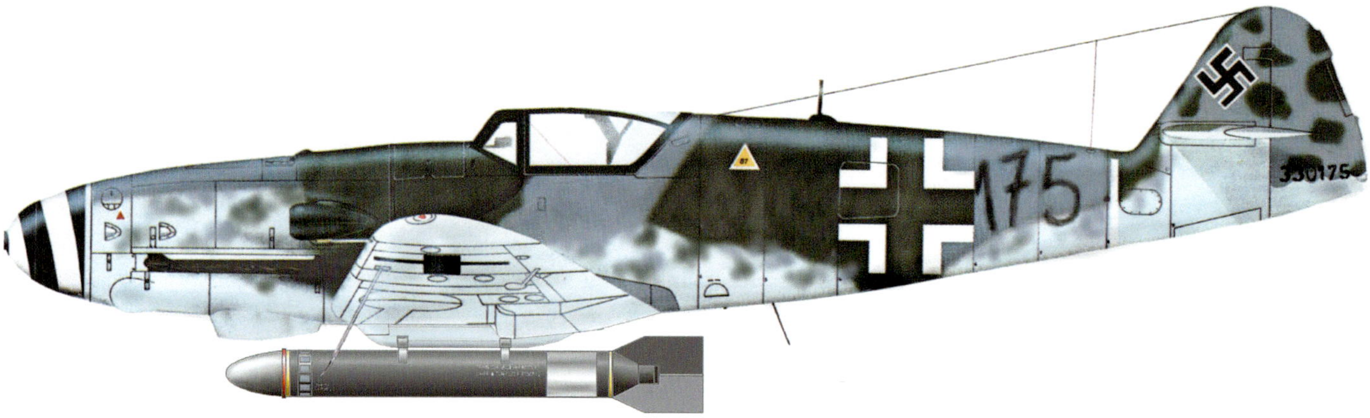

Messerschmitt Bf 109 K-4 (SO) with small uranium bomb: fixed bomb mounting, Eastern Front, Junkerstroylhof, East Prussia (April 1945). Colour scheme: undersides RLM 76, upper surfaces RLM 75/82 (Igor Shestakov)

Meserschmitt Bf 109 K-4 (SO) with small uranium bomb: detachable bomb mounting, Western Front, Münster (April 1945). Colour scheme: undersides RLM 76, fuselage and underside RLM 84, remainder RLM 80/81 (Igor Shestakov)

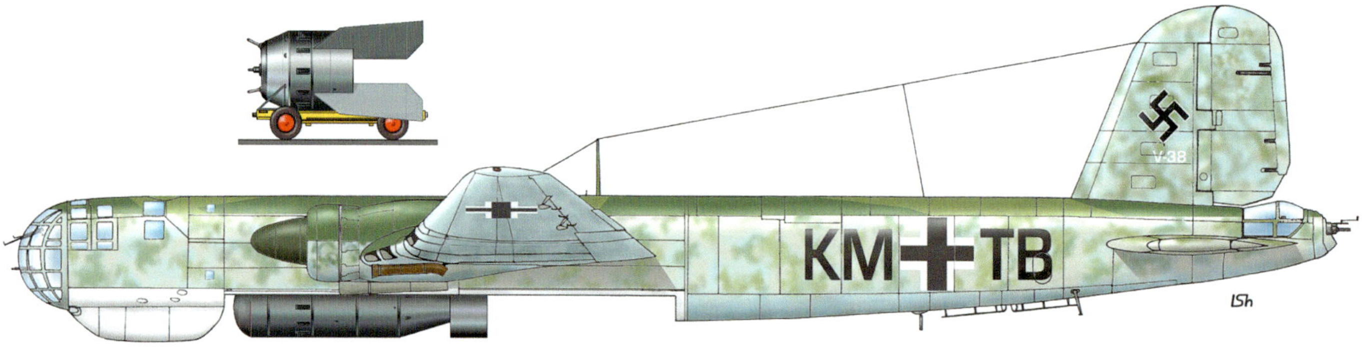

Heinkel He 177 A-5 (V.38) nuclear bomber with 4.5-tonne uranium bomb of the 'Hiroshima' type (Stadtilm/Ohrdruf?); alternative payload: 4.5-tonne plutonium bomb on transport vehicle (Innsbruck, May 1945), KdE Prague (1945). Colour scheme: undersides RLM 76, upper surfaces RLM 70/71, sides RLM 65 and 70 over RLM 02 (Igor Shestakov)

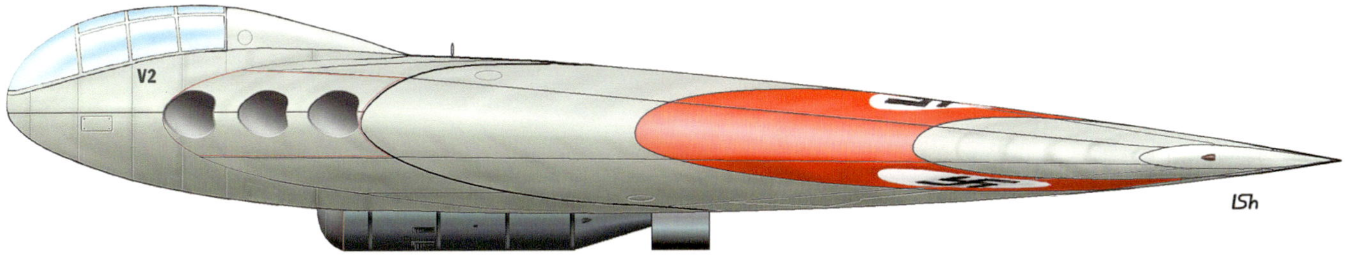

Horten Ho XVIII A (V.2) prototype with 4-tonne uranium bomb of the Hiroshima type, Thuringia (1945). Colour scheme: RLM 22 overall (Igor Shestakov)

Horten Ho XVIII IB with 4.5-tonne uranium bomb of the 'Innsbruck' type, Kahla 1945. Colour scheme: RLM 22 overall, upper surfaces with RLM 81 and RLM 82, sides with RLM 22 and RLM 82 (Igor Shestakov)

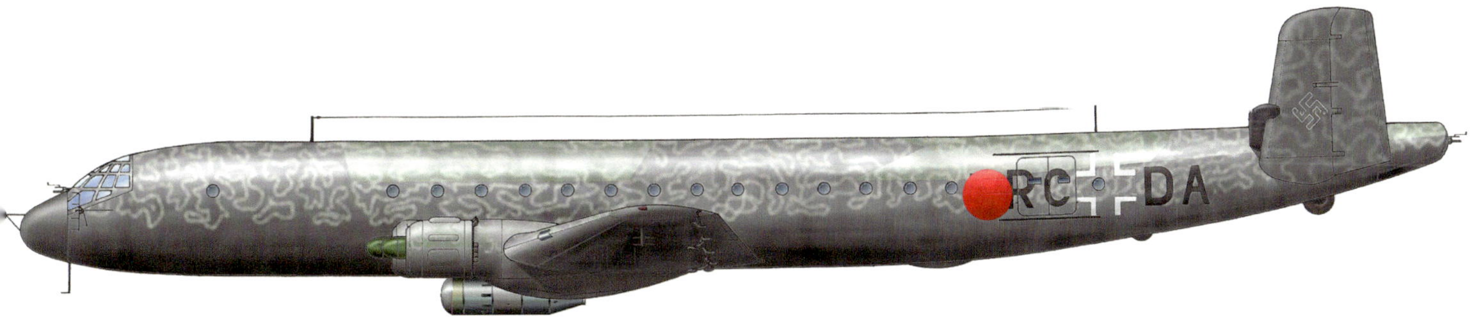

Ju 390 V.2, intercontinental bomber/transporter with 4.5-tonne uranium bomb of the Ohrdruf type. Defensive armament 2 x 3cm Mk 108 keyhole gun mountings in the nose cabin and tail with German/Japanese markings (March 1945). Colour scheme: undersides and fuselage sides RLM 22, upper surfaces and upper half of fuselage RLM 76 over RLM 75/76 (Igor Shestakov)

Ju 287 medium-range bomber, intended to carry nuclear weapons, flying low over the North Sea (Richard L. Mendes)

Messerschmitt Me 264 V.3 America bomber with small uranium bombs, S. Kdo Nebel, Augsburg 1944. Paint scheme: RLM 72/73, undersides RLM 22 (Igor Shestakov)

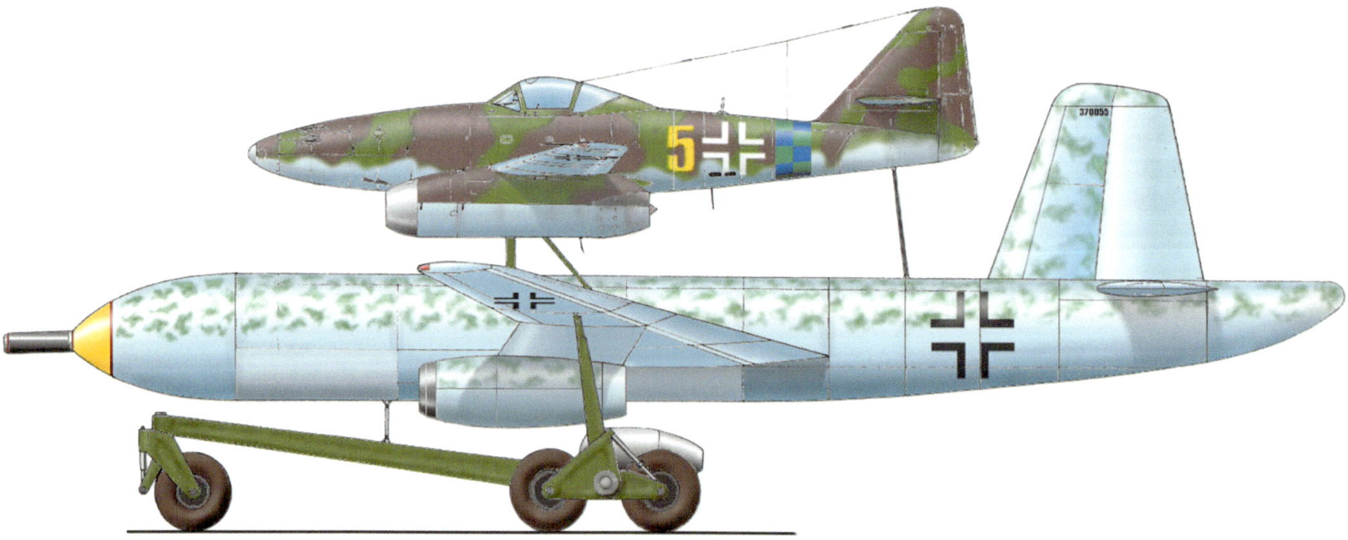

Junkers Ju 287 B *Atommistel* with Me 262 A-2 aircraft on Rheinmetall/Borsig take-off vehicle. Payload: one nuclear weapon of the 'Ohrdruf' type or one plutonium bomb of the 'Innsbruck' type. Paint scheme: Undersides of both aircraft RLM 76 and RLM 24, upper surfaces of Ju 287 RLM 76 and RLM 24, upper surfaces RLM 76 with RLM 81 camouflage markings. Me 262: undersides RLM 76, upper surfaces RLM 80/82. Take-off vehicle: olive green (Igor Shestakov)

Messerchmitt Me 329 escort aircraft - flying mock-up model, Rechlin 1944 (Author's model, base model by Frank-Modellbau)

Mistal-4 variant comprising Me 262 and Ju 188 with additional BMW 003 engines under the wing roots (Author's model)

Grossmistel comprising He 177 and Fw 190. This composite could have carried (almost) any bomb load. Although some of these Grossmisteln were produced, here too there are, to date, no available photographs and plans... (Author's model)

Junkers Ju 88 G-10 escort aircraft (1945) (Author's model)

Arado Ar 234 C-3 jet bomber with a 'barrel bomb' (Author's model)

Proposed design for Junkers intercontinental bomber project with Me 262 onboard fighter (similar to EF 132) (Author's model)

LTV-N-2 'Loon', US Army version in Fort Bliss, Texas. The flying bomb is based on the technology of the German V-1 (Author's collection)

Fieseler Fi 103 with auxiliary rocket for take-off, remote control antennae and RLM 72/65 paint scheme on a transport vehicle (Author's model)

20-tonne bomb in experimental paint scheme on a Büssing transporter. The first post-war hydrogen bomb, MK 17, was originally to weigh 21 tonnes (Author's model)

Above: Kaelble heavy load tractor Z 6 G 3 R A with 30-tonne bomb on 'Gotha' trailer (Author's model)

Experimental reconstruction of the 'small uranium bomb' (Author's model)

Experimental reconstruction of a 250kg antenna bomb (Author's model)

German 'Castor transporter' 1945? This is what the reported movements of nuclear material from Ohrdruf could have looked like! Fully-wheeled Kaelble Z 6 R 3 A heavy load tractor with nuclear container on a special vehicle and Kaelble Z G 4 pushing tug vehicle (Author's model)

SB 30000 on 'Gotha' heavy load trailer (Georg model).

Comparative sizes: 30-tonne bomb (Sänger), SA 4000 'Ohrdruf bomb' (Author's model)

Comparative sizes: SA 4000 and German 'Hiroshima' bomb (Author's model)

Comparison of Sänger 4-tonne bomb, SA 4000 'Little Boy' and bundle bombs (Author's model)

Sänger 4-tonne bomb and German Hiroshima bomb of the 'Ohrdruf' type (Author's model)

Kaelble heavy load transporter type with SA 4000 and German Hiroshima bomb of the 'Ohrdruf' type (Author's model)

The Miracle Weapons of the *Kriegsmarine*:

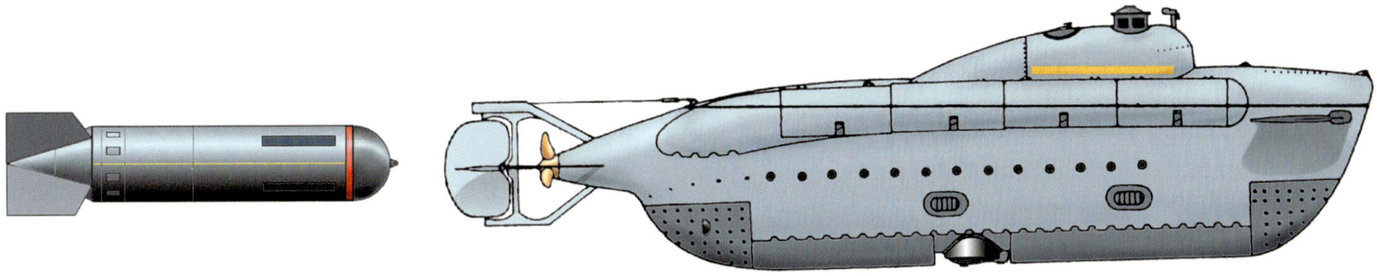

Caproni CA 3 midget submarine for carrying frogmen (Ex R.S.I., Ex *Regia Marina*) shown with a nuclear underwater tow mine; Germany (1944/45); colour scheme: 23b, 58, aircraft recognition marking 63 (Igor Shestakov)

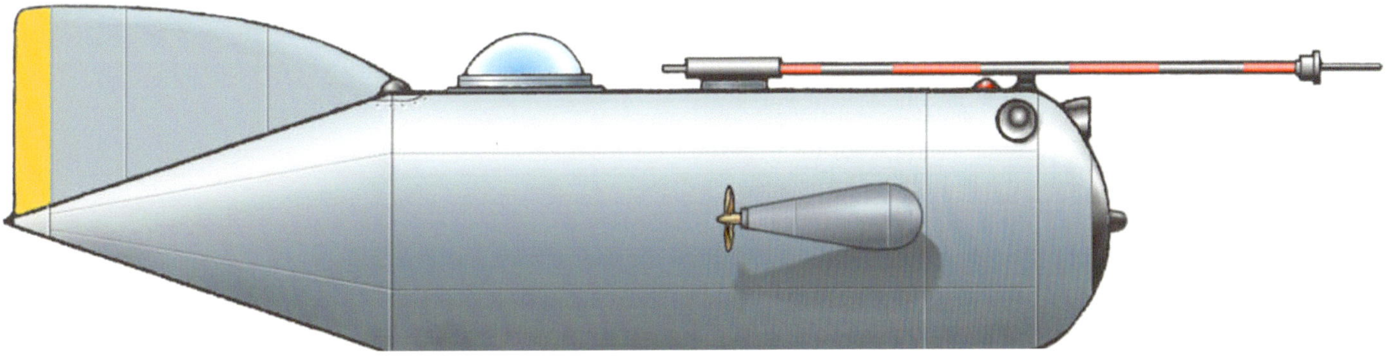

Grundhai midget submarine project (1945). Typical colour scheme for North Sea training. (Igor Shestakov)

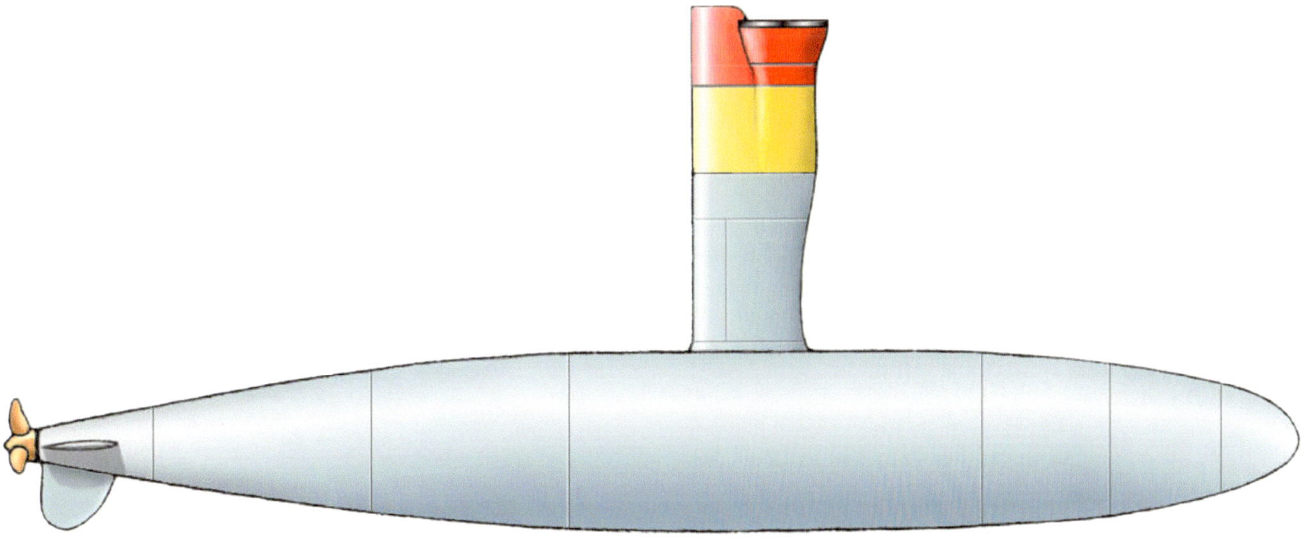

Tropfenform (drop-shaped) research U-boat. German Reichspost Research Establishment project (1944). Training paint scheme for experimental vessel (Igor Shestakov)

U-boat Type XXI 'Kangaroo' with CA 3 midget submarine for mission against America, Germany (1944/45); paint scheme of both boats 23, 58; aircraft recognition markings yellow 63 (Igor Shestakov)

U-boat Type XXI with V-1, project (1944/45). Paint scheme 23a, 58; camouflage pattern 32, yellow aircraft recognition marking 63; V-1: RLM 73, 65 (Igor Shestakov)

U-boat Type XXI with rocket launcher for *Vergeltungswaffe* 'Ursel' underwater missiles, Kiel (1945), colour scheme 23b, 58 (Igor Shestakov)

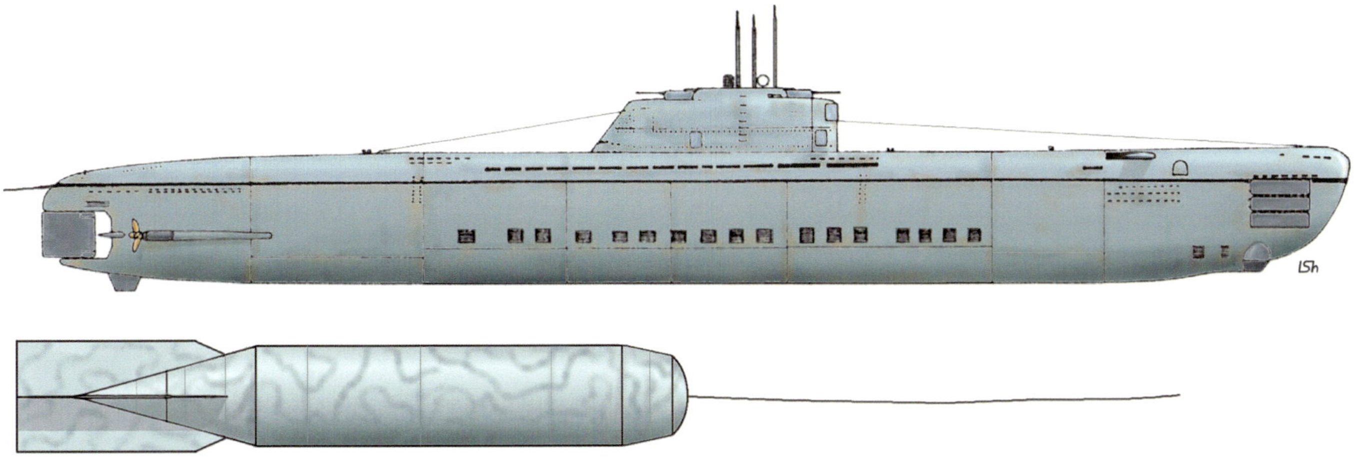

U-boat Type XXI with 'Laffarenz' underwater tow container for V-2 rocket, Gotenhafen (1945). Colour scheme XXI: 23, 58; Lafferenz container 32 (3), 32 (1) (Igor Shestakov)

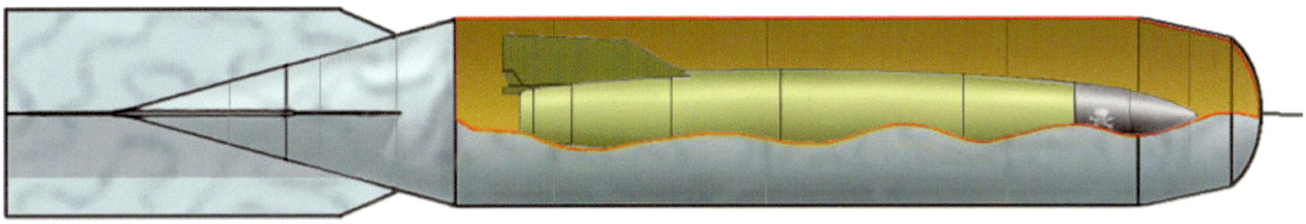

Cross-section of a V-2 launch container with a nuclear V-2 (Igor Shestakov)

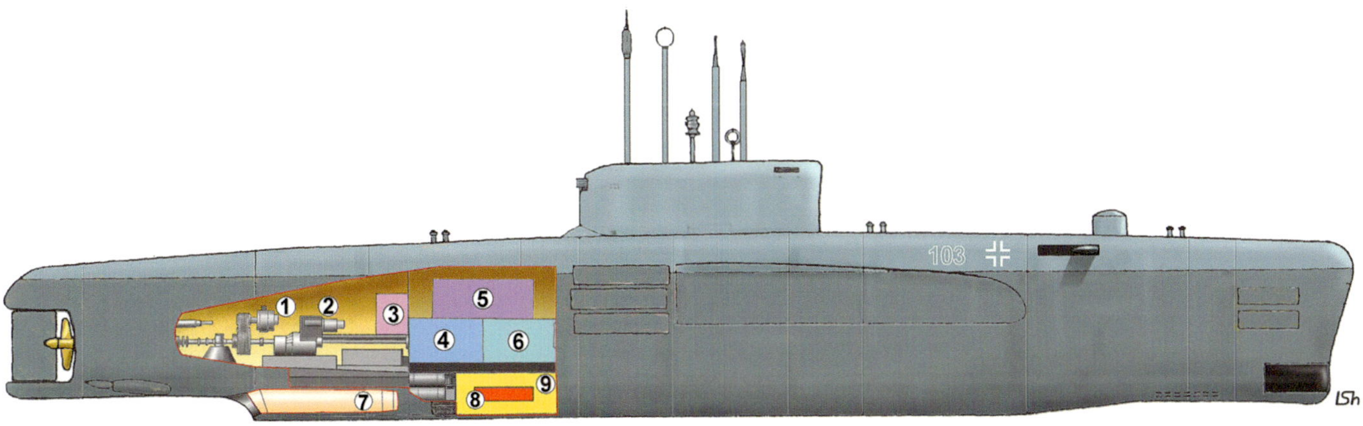

Type XXVI nuclear U-boat project (1945); colour scheme 23, 58 (Igor Shestakov)

DKM 44 28cm light cannon for nuclear ammunition on Panther chassis, Rheinmetall/Skoda/Hanomag, prototype (1945). Colour scheme: red, brown, dark yellow over olive green overall base colour (Igor Shestakov)

Said to be an original American development: US T-131 nuclear cannon (Author's Model)

In *Objekt Burg*, by the end of the war, a number of small and large uranium bombs, called 'containers', are supposed to have been produced. It is only with great difficulty that any information can be obtained concerning the number of bombs, and the production stage they had reached.

In the meantime, there have been indications that numerous tests of uranium bombs were carried out in the Third Reich. The macabre fact is that those experiments also took place on troop exercise areas that were close to populated districts. In 1944, the area ruled by Hitler had already grown very small.

Particularly notable among the various reports is the test of October 1944. The description of that test, by the anti-aircraft missile expert Zinsser,[149] contains the most precise descriptions of the side-effects of a nuclear explosion. In reading the report we should recall that, on the 19 August 1945, i.e. when the Zinsser report was written, no details whatever were yet publicly accessible concerning such 'secondary' effects. Thus, at the time he wrote his report, Zinsser could not possibly have had recourse to such knowledge.

The entire sequence of the explosion was described by Zinsser in meticulous detail. There was the flash of light lasting two seconds after the detonation. There then followed the pressure wave, the formation of the mushroom cloud with rings, the changing colour of the explosion cloud, the atmospheric and electrical disturbances. He continued right up to the details of height. Nothing was omitted.

The real problem with the Zinsser report is in determining what location he is describing. Where did this test take place? In the published version, Zinsser gives the location of the 'Atomic Bomb Test Station' as being 10-12 kilometres away from the Ludwigslust airfield. In a later observation he added that the place in question was 'further east' from there.

At this point, it needs to be taken into account that the Zinsser report is only available as an Allied abstract, in English translation. The original statements, of the putative prisoner-of-war Zinsser, can thus not be directly compared, to see whether they agree. The details of the location, in the available version, may have been concealed for reasons of security. Subsequently, it may have made it more difficult for the test area to be found.

As likely locations, researchers who have worked on the Zinsser report, suggest the troop exercise areas at Lübtheen, Garz, i.e. Peenemünde, and an exercise area near the island of Rügen.[150] Others are of the opinion that the suggested direction 'east' has been deliberately confused with 'west', so that perhaps the troop exercise area at Kummersdorf is a likely location. Near to that exercise area was the Gottow nuclear laboratory of Dr Diebner. American aerial photographs, taken in 1945, also show in Kummersdorf a large unusual-looking round explosion area.[151] That may have been the test site.

To date, there has been no conclusive success in establishing the definitive location of the October 1944 atomic test. If that test involved an atomic explosion set off at great height, it would be futile to look for a crater or

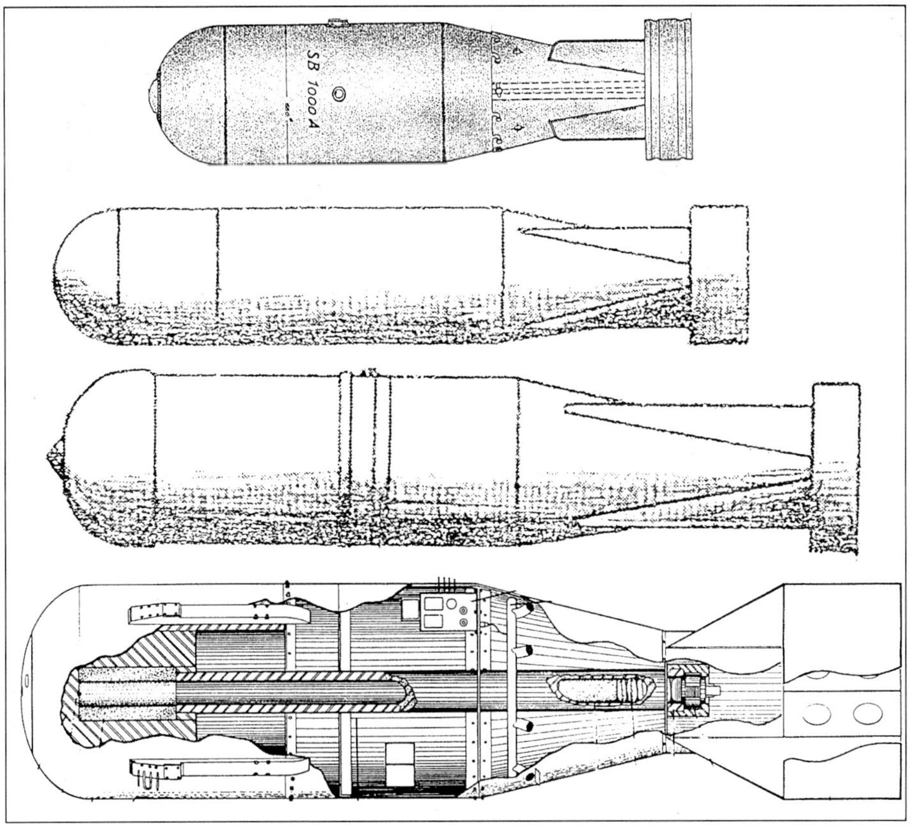

German special bombs: above, the SB 1000 A; below, the SC 2000 and the SC 2500. The diagram at the bottom is a cross-section of the – allegedly American – 'Hiroshima' bomb. Remarkably, it has a typically German appearance, if one compares it to the above bomb types...

anything like one. In any case, it would certainly have to be possible, even today, to establish by ground tests, that a nuclear explosion took place there in 1944. Further research is needed.

If the further statements in Zinsser's reports are to be believed, then there also must have been American eyewitnesses of the nuclear explosion. Zinsser's He 111 would have had to avoid American P 38 fighters that were operating in the area. Such a fantastic sight as a nuclear explosion could scarcely have escaped the crews of those P 38s. Therefore their observations should be able to be found in American operational reports.

Certainly Zinsser's report, in the form in which it has reached us from the Allies, contains an important key that could indicate the actual location of the nuclear test. The key concerns Zinsser's actual activity, and his aircraft. Zinsser maintains in the report that he had happened to pass the area because he had to make a courier flight. It is believed that he went up again, a second time, a little later. Most importantly, it is not known who could have given him permission. Therefore the question is what did an anti-aircraft missile expert want with a He 111 at a nuclear test?

Many converted Heinkel He 111s were used by the Karlshagen test centre near Peenemünde for testing new types of rocket. At Karlshagen, as at Peenemünde, the aircraft were a fixed element of the complement and were used by both test centres, until they were evacuated in

The two American atomic bombs which fell on Japan. In the pictures: the 'Little Boy' bomb dropped on Hiroshima, with a slim design shape, was a uranium bomb, while the somewhat more voluminous bomb, suitably called 'Fat Man', was a plutonium bomb which destroyed Nagasaki.

the spring of 1945. The reliable Heinkel aircraft were used there as launch, survey or photographic aircraft. Every individual rocket flight had to be documented to the last detail.[152] That suggests the conclusion that the anti-aircraft missile expert Zinsser had actually taken off in his special He 111 from Peenemünde, and not from Ludwigslust. There is thus added weight to statements that place the nuclear test in the Peenemünde area.[153]

The question as to whether Zinsser 'happened' to come across the test area at the time must, on closer examination, be discounted. In actual fact, he had probably been given the task of documenting the individual stages of the nuclear test, from a special Heinkel He 111 that was otherwise used for anti-aircraft missile tests. In a test as secret as a nuclear explosion, he could perhaps have 'happened' to fly close to the test area, but he could never have made a second flight within an hour. He must then have been given the task of continuing his test observations by a second flight.

Of course, the information given in the Zinsser report is not yet final proof. Interestingly, in addition to Zinsser's report there also exists a statement from an Italian officer, who attended the same test as an observer for Mussolini. That officer states precisely that the nuclear test was carried out on 11 October 1944 in the area of the island of Rügen, i.e. close to Peenemünde.[154]

Particularly notorious is a test in which there could have possibly been many victims. Concerning that nuclear explosion, near to Auschwitz, not a great deal of information has subsequently come to light. However, it was actually used at the Nuremberg Trials, as an argument, by the prosecution. The test, at which IG Farben also collaborated, is said to have been carried out, in order to test the destructive effect of a nuclear bomb. To do that, a temporary town had been built which was populated by 20,000 Jews. If the reports are to be believed, that test ended with the annihilation of practically all the test persons.[155] However, the truth of the matter is not confirmed.

Post-war reports dated 1958, from former prisoners-of-war in France, also tell of a test explosion, probably also nuclear, that was caused by the impact of a manned rocket shell. In that test a town, which had been temporarily built, was completely destroyed. But that report contains nothing concerning 'victims'. (for details see the following volume)

It is not known if those reports refer to the same test as was carried out near Auschwitz, or if there were several 'target cities' of that kind. In a last experiment in March 1945, at the Neuruppin/Glewe troop exercise area, a uranium bomb is said to have been dropped 'on a parachute'. Apparently, that test went off to the complete satisfaction of the research teams from the *Wehrmacht* and the SS who were involved in it.

Perhaps the tests which were carried out before the end of the war already led to the 'large containers' being ready

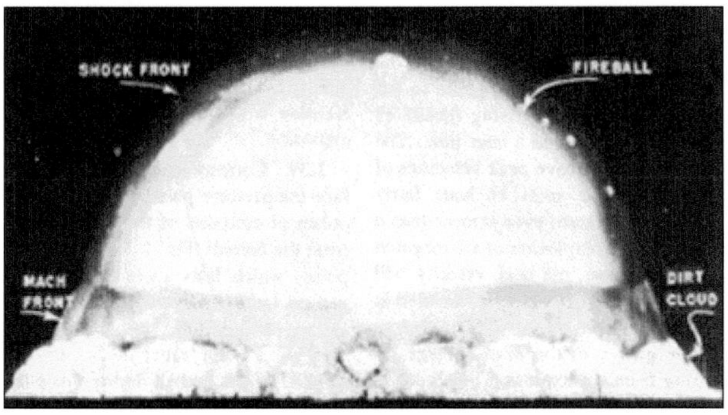

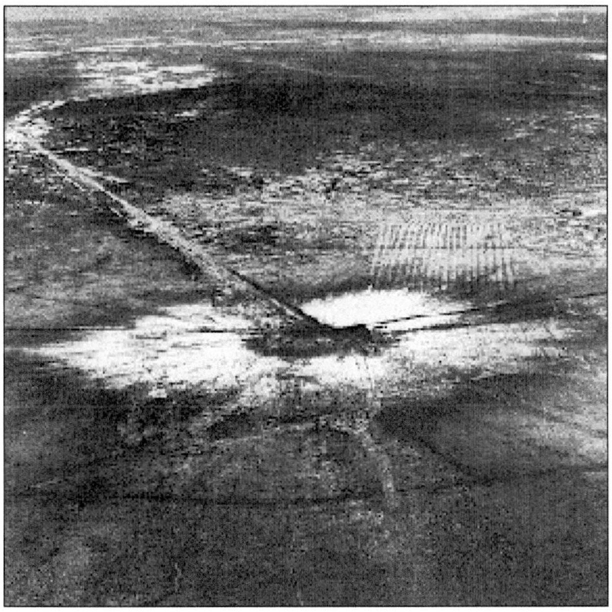

The American plutonium bomb 'Trinity' was tested in every detail before being used. For the detonation on 14 July 1945, it was mounted on a 40-metre-high steel tower in the unpopulated Alamagordo Desert. There are detailed test results, including film footage and photographs and also eyewitness accounts, relating to this test. If such an expensive test was carried out for the plutonium bomb, the mechanism of which functions differently to the uranium bomb, why was it not done for the predecessor of 'Little Boy'? Was it that this type of bomb did not need to be tested because German scientists had already tested it? Did the American military know, on the basis of German experience already available, that the uranium bomb would succeed in any event?

for use in action. It goes without saying that such a new type of weapon as the atomic bomb involved breaking new scientific ground. To solve the many problems that arose, particularly under the conditions of 1944/45, was an almost superhuman task. In particular, it is not known if the problem of delayed action detonation had been solved completely. Certainly, there were investigations of barometric detonators and radio-operated detonators. Particularly suitable for such purposes was the Schnabel apparatus.[156] It was a variation of the FuG 101 altimeter. At the time that was the best altimeter in the world.

Unfortunately, to date, there are no plans or photographs showing what the large Stadtilm bombs looked like. According to eyewitnesses, the amount of atomic charge in the 'large containers' was 8,000 grams. In the 'small containers' (see section concerning small uranium bombs) it was a few hundred grams. For dropping the bomb from a great height it was planned to use a 'braking' parachute.[157]

From the area close to Professor Diebner's Stadtilm test laboratory there are eyewitness accounts, given on oath. They say that the German nuclear weapons could actually be seen there. One eyewitness spoke of 'small scale models in an armour-plated cupboard'. The other witness reports that she had even seen 'the actual warheads'. The eyewitnesses agreed that what they had seen there resembled at least one of the atomic bombs dropped on Japan.[158] Could that, possibly, be true?

If one considers the 'Little Boy' bomb dropped by the Americans on Hiroshima, one is immediately struck by its appearance, which is untypical of American bombs used in World War II. In the 'published' history this is explained away by saying that, because of the improvised design of the 'Little Boy' bomb, a '*howitzer* barrel' had to be used as the bomb casing.[159]

If one considers the published pattern of the 'Little Boy' bomb, and compares it with designs of well-known German bomb types of World War II, one can see great external similarity. It is almost as if a line of descent can be established from the German SB 1,000, through the SC 2,500, directly to the 4.5-tonne 'Little Boy' bomb. It may simply have been coincidence, once again. Only the typically American angular stabilisation fins, on the tail, suggest US production. German bombs almost all had cylindrical ends.

However, apart from the post-war mock-ups of the 'Little Boy' bomb, there are still no published photographs of the actual pattern of the 'Little Boy' bomb that was used in action. The actual appearance of the weapon may even now be kept secret. With a cylindrical end to the bomb, the Teutonic origin of the design would have been all too obvious. Technically, however, it would have been no problem to exchange a cylindrical end for an angular end. Another possibility is that the Americans still had to complete development of the 'braking' parachute system, and therefore added an 'original American' end to the bombs.

In his books, the author Harald Fäth[160] describes the remarkable events that occurred when the Americans occupied Stadtilm and Crawinkel. It may be considered to be beyond doubt that something happened there which remains mysterious even today.

What was the captured material on the American convoy that transported away German containers marked with the Death's Head? Why did the population have to black out their houses while the convoy drove through? Also, the fact that behind the convoy an American jeep with a loudspeaker drove through Stadtilm and announced that because of what had been found there, Germany's war guilt was redeemed, shows that they must have found something quite extraordinary. What were they so thankful to the Germans for? It would be interesting to find out who was responsible on the American side for authorising the use of those words over the loudspeaker. However, the 'redemption of war guilt' did not last very long.

One might conjecture that they were the same Stadtilm 'containers' to which the contested and much discussed statement of a leading American nuclear researcher refers. It was said that 'the atomic bombs dropped on Japan came from German arsenals'.

Apart from the Teutonic appearance of the later uranium 'Little Boy' Hiroshima bomb, there are a whole series of curious things which point in that direction. The first version of an American uranium bomb is said to have been so big that it could not even fit into the bomb bay of the B 29 carrier aircraft. But then, after a long period of research, the size of the bomb was reduced so that it could fit. Comparing the sizes of the 'Little Boy' with the bomb bay of the B 29, however, shows that the bomb dropped on Japan was small enough for several 'Little Boys' to have easily been accommodated there.

The casing of the 'Little Boy' bomb, according to official historians, had been ready since July 1944. Why then did the Americans only fly test missions with the so-called 'pumpkin' bomb casings of the later plutonium bomb? Does this curious fact not indicate that until April 1945 there were in reality no uranium bombs in the form of the 'Little Boy' bomb in the American arsenal? Was it therefore only possible to practice with 'pumpkins'?

According to another American reference work, it was only on 23 July 1945 that the first empty 'Little Boy' casing was assembled on the island of Tinian and a successful test drop completed.[161] Where did the bomb parts come from?

Another question is also of great importance. Why was the uranium bomb dropped by the USA on Japan, before the plutonium bomb, without any previous test? Seen from a military point of view, it would be extremely dangerous to use a completely untested weapon, for the first time, in a mission which might decide the course of the war, if instead there was another weapon available which had already been tested. Had the Americans simply forgotten to carry out a test, or had somebody else done it before them?

The Pacific island of Tinian served as the base for the American nuclear bombers against Japan and thus was subject to the strictest security. According to official information, the command structure on the island was divided between the three military commanders, General T F Farrell, Admiral Purnell and the expert, Captain Parsons.[162] But it is practically never mentioned that the actual field command was exercised on the island by Major R.R. Furman. Why is his name not even mentioned, even today, in reference works relating to Tinian? Probably this can be attributed to the fact that, during the war in Europe, Furman was one of the leading people of the ALSOS espionage mission. Major R.R. Furman was the personal adjutant of nuclear General Groves, and accompanied the ALSOS mission as his representative. He had plenipotentiary powers to deal directly with the highest ranking officials in Europe, including Churchill.[163]

Major Furman was demonstrably the direct connection between the ALSOS nuclear espionage mission and the American nuclear bomb project. In fact it was

Major Furman himself who brought the functioning warhead of 'Little Boy' by air to Tinian.

It is worthy of note that at the end of his command of the mission to drop the nuclear bomb, Furman was once again head of an investigating mission. His task then involved the Japanese atomic bomb programme.[164] It is true that on this mission he was not able to bring out so much material to the USA, as perhaps had been hoped at a higher level. The main complex of the Japanese uranium bomb programme was in the northern part of Korea, which was already occupied by the Russians. American nuclear spies were not exactly welcome guests there.

What conclusions can we draw from all those remarkable circumstances surrounding the Hiroshima bomb? All the notable events immediately make sense if, in reality, the Tinian Hiroshima bomb was a weapon that had already been tested, perhaps even a number of times. It may have been captured in Germany by ALSOS. In that case, therefore, the mysterious role of Major Furman on Tinian would become understandable.

Supporting that would also be the fact that the actual radius of effect of the later Hiroshima bomb exactly matched the radius marked on captured German target impact plans for a planned attack on New York.[165]

Of course, such arguments are not direct proof that 'Little Boy' was a captured bomb. But the many indications that this might be the case should give even the most stubborn doubters cause for thought.

There were extraordinary American uranium bomb plans. Although the uranium bomb was used before the plutonium bomb, the impression arises that in American eyes a bomb like that remained a 'white elephant', in other words, surplus to requirements.

When in 1945 planning of the invasion of Japan was under way, Groves and Oppenheimer only wanted to use plutonium bombs of the 'Nagasaki' type.[166] Why no uranium bombs? The unthinkable answer that immediately presents itself is that perhaps, with the exception of 'Little Boy', there were no other uranium bombs in the American arsenal.

According to available sources, in the post-war period the Americans never followed up in any consistent way the concept of the artillery shell-type uranium bomb.[167] Most of what has become known about American uranium bomb plans, from 1945, seems to relate quite strikingly to former German weapons systems.

There are nuclear versions of the V-1, V-2 and the 28-centimetre nuclear cannon. Either one must believe in three further coincidences or one comes to the conclusion that they were actually the result of plans to develop and produce captured German projects.

Germany's Plutonium Implosion Bomb

Hitler's 'birthday present', or the Third Reich's last trump card? Did Germany also win the race to produce the first plutonium bomb? The uranium bombs of the 'Hiroshima' type, which worked on the artillery shell principle, in present-day specialist literature look primitive in comparison with the uranium-saving plutonium bombs.[168]

The first known test of such a weapon took place on 14 July 1945 in the Jornada-el-Muerto Desert near Alamogordo in New Mexico. In that explosion, 14 pounds of plutonium and 5,000 pounds of explosive were caused to implode. The bomb was placed high up on an aluminium tower, surrounded by thick armour plating for reasons of safety. It was necessary to be able to retrieve the valuable material in the event that the test failed. But that safety measure proved to be completely superfluous, because the explosion of 'Trinity' had a strength of 15,000 to 20,000 tons of TNT and could be seen from 200 miles away.

The origins of 'Trinity' are not known. It appears that the principle of the implosion plutonium bomb had been discovered before World War II by the Viennese Professor, *Physicist-Ingenieur* Friedrich Lachner. He had outlined it in a lecture to the Vienna Technical University (TU) to German and foreign physicists.

At the time it was assumed that, once so-called 'critical mass' was exceeded, the radioactive chain-reaction process would happen very quickly. Professor Lachner heard of this in a Vienna University lecture given by Professor Adolf Smekal. As a result, Lachner gave thought to industrially safe design possibilities, that could be implemented in spite of the uncertainty concerning the level of 'critical mass'.

That 'Lachner atomic bomb design' was planned to use casings in the form of concentric cylinders. The explosive, i.e. hollow charge, on the outside, detonated uniformly, and was to hurl the masses of uranium inwards towards the centre. In doing so, they had first to penetrate a protective skin of neutron-absorbent material, e.g. graphite or cadmium, then draw closer and closer together, so that before they combined the effect of a 'critical mass' should be achieved.

Thus, Lachner's invention of an atomic bomb was published before World War II. But apart from simple demonstration models it was not built at that time. A few years ago, the date is not known, a picture of a functioning pre-war model of that kind was shown in the Vienna weekly newspaper *Wochenausgabe*.

During the war Professor Lachner could have been a member of the group of the Vienna professor, Dr Stetter, which operated an atomic bomb research laboratory close to Innsbruck, perhaps at Schwaz. As well as the attempts to produce large and small uranium bombs, the German plutonium bomb project was the other, large, German atomic bomb project.

A method of producing plutonium itself had been

confirmed. As early as 1940, Professor von Weiszäcker had informed the HVA (*Heereswaffenamt*) that in an *Uranbrenner*, the early German name for a nuclear reactor, apart from the products of uranium fission, the isotope U 239 could be produced. Later it was called plutonium. This could, he said, be used as a nuclear explosive. Similar conclusions were also reached by Professor Houtermans at the RPF (*Reichspostforschungsanstalt*). As early as 1941 he had recognised the method of plutonium production later used in the USA. In contrast to what we are told today, Germany's ten-year competitive edge was not thrown away, but consistently exploited to the full.

One gets the impression that the plutonium bomb project, in contrast to the construction of the uranium bombs, had a more 'official' character, and a longer period of preparation. By contrast, the uranium bomb project gives more the impression of an improvised project born of necessity.

In contrast to the joint production of uranium bombs with the Diebner group (HWA), in the experimental factory 'Burg' in Ohrdruf, the plutonium bombs were constructed by the research establishment belonging to the SS. Work on their development is said to have been carried out in several different places, such as Hirschberg, Bad Sachsa and in the Technical Office of the SS itself. The actual production of the bombs then took place in underground secret factories near Innsbruck, perhaps at Schwaz. In Schwaz the population told convincingly of a secret factory that was still thought to be underground.[169]

The establishments there, and in the uranium preparation plant in Treibach, may possibly have been connected with the production establishments of the Stetter group. Whether the complex in Melk is connected with the plutonium project, in addition to its other tasks, is unclear.

The plutonium programme gives the impression of being a very decentralised operation. It seems that some of the Vienna specialists were evacuated to Kärnten in the spring of 1944 by the Technical General Staff of the SS, and continued their researches there.[170] To date, little is known about those activities. According to Lachner, many experts were involved in this plutonium project, but if they are still alive today, they have never dared to admit it. Many prominent names, Lachner says, even Nobel Prize winners, were thought to be among them.

Professor Heisenberg had informed the *Heereswaffenamt* (HWA), who were in competition with the SS, that atomic warheads could be produced using plutonium. However it was the research group around Professor Stetter, in Innsbruck, who succeeded in producing the first plutonium bombs on 20 April 1945. They described it as 'damned hard graft'.[171]

But the detonator cartridges, which consisted of a new kind of isolator material, were the real bottleneck until well into April.[172] Moreover, they were produced in another area and had first to be brought to the Tyrol. But, in spite of all the problems, the bomb designers had been able to keep their word concerning the completion date. *Gauleiter* Eigruber from the Upper Danube had, shortly before, sent a telegram to Adolf Hitler which read: '*Mein Führer*, the six detonators will be ready for your birthday'.[173]

FIG. 23. SELECTED BOMB MODELS used in the subsonic ballistic tunnels of the Luftfahrtforschungs-Anstalt Graf Zeppelin (FGZ).

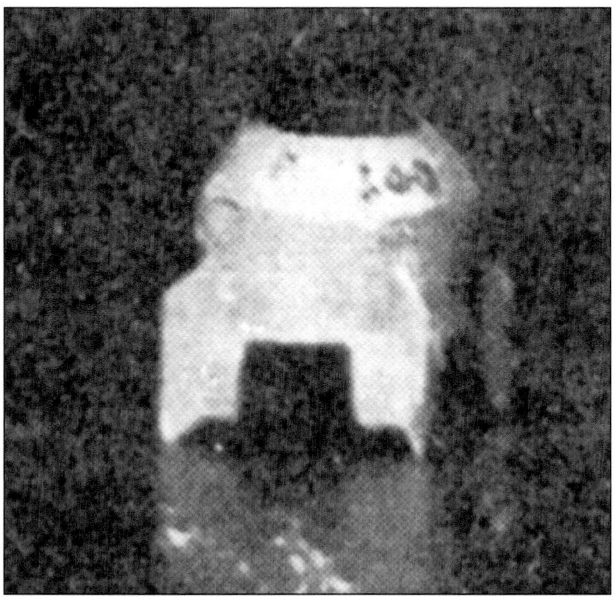

Various bomb models which were tested in the wind tunnel of the Ferdinand Graf Zeppelin (FGZ) aviation research establishment. Among them is a bomb which could be the German plutonium bomb (enlargement right).

Then a dramatic situation arose for the German leadership. After the Nordhausen and Ohrdruf secret factories had fallen into the hands of the advancing Americans on 12 April 1945, they had once again been handed another weapon to play as a trump card. Actually, it happened too late to be of very much use, because on 20 April 1945 the remaining area of the Third Reich had already been split into a northern and a southern part. On the same day, the Soviets also succeeded in decisively breaking through the Eastern Front at Cottbus, which led to the collapse of the defensive front and to the encirclement of Berlin. Hitler had therefore already decided to move the Führer headquarters, the OKW and the Army General Staff and the *Luftwaffe*, with the exception of small, staff, working groups, into the so-called *Alpenfestung*. The withdrawal of the staffs from Berlin was already well under way.[174]

All those events made it extremely difficult for Hitler to use the nuclear weapons. He ordered the transfer of the bombs into the northern area of the Reich. In addition to operational airfields, the destinations of the transports were the North Sea ports. That was with a view to planned transport by U-boat to Japan.

At the same time, contrary to his original announced intentions, Hitler decided not to flee to Berchtesgaden, the area of the planned alpine fortress, but to remain in Berlin. The reasons for that change of mind remain a puzzle even today. Perhaps knowledge of the new plutonium bombs had something to do with it.

It is unknown whether the bombs were to be transported by land or by air. It seems that an attempt was actually made to move them, but had to be called off because of sabotage of the detonators when they were being transported.[175] Another version suggests that the detonators were not sabotaged when it was attempted to move the bombs, but had already 'quite suddenly' disappeared when they were being brought up to Innsbruck.

To replace the detonators required another six weeks' production, time that the Third Reich no longer had. All this was reminiscent of similar incidents which arose in connection with the plans to use the uranium bombs. The plutonium bombs were therefore taken back into storage in one of the grottoes near Innsbruck. After some to-ing and fro-ing, they served as a 'dead' pledge in the negotiations for surrender in May 1945. After they had served that purpose, the Innsbruck bombs were handed over to the Americans as agreed, and the Americans, only 48 hours later, sent them to Genoa. An armada of ships and air transports took everything from Genoa to the USA (see section 'Why were they never used'?).[176]

Possibly the Americans went on to complete the production work on the bombs captured at Innsbruck by fitting them with a more resilient casing of greater diameter and with a parachute. No certain figures can be estimated concerning the precise number of the atomic bombs of all types, including uranium and plutonium bombs, which were almost completed or semi-finished. Rumour has it that the Americans captured at least three of them. One of them was tested at Alamogordo, before the two other bombs were used against Japan. In addition there were two accidents with bombs. The Russians also captured a German bomb, so that at least six were captured.

There is no confirmation of what was really exploded on 14 July, by the USA in Alamogordo. During the course of World War II the Americans exploded another two plutonium bombs. One of them was the 'Trinity' test bomb at Alamogordo, the other the 'Fat Man' bomb dropped on Nagasaki. The dumpy looking 'Trinity' bomb was photographed before it was detonated. Was 'Trinity' really of genuine American origin?

A photograph of captured German bomb models that were tested in the subsonic ballistic tunnels of the Aviation Research Institute of Ferdinand Graf Zeppelin (FGZ) shows something quite striking. In addition to other normal bombs there can be seen a picture of a model bomb which looks like the small-scale model of the 'Trinity' bomb. On the nose of the bomb can even be clearly seen the round nose cap which was typical of later US plutonium bombs. But in contrast to 'Trinity', on the box-like end of the bomb fuselage four tail stabilisation fins were fitted of the kind used on a V-2.

This wind-tunnel model resembles no other German bomb and forces the reflection as to whether these photographs represent a planned German plutonium bomb of the Trinity type. The resemblance between the FGZ wind-tunnel model and the later Alamogordo bomb is so striking that the question can be asked as to whether at least part of the 'Trinity' bomb came from Hitler's arsenal.

3) Special Case: the 3-tonne bomb

There are indications that finally, in 1945, in addition to the 4-tonne bombs, another light 3-tonne nuclear bomb was planned. To date, such a weight class is not shown in any list of German bombs. There must have been some designs for such a weapon, since the last intercontinental bomber projects of March 1945 were designed to carry just such a load.[177] The flying bomb Project 'F', of the Daimler Benz Company, also planned to use a three-ton warhead. It too could be connected with the above mentioned designs.[178] But plans or photographs of wind tunnel models of the German 3-tonne bomb have never been published. This is all the more remarkable because, at the end of the 1940s, the Russians mounted similar 3-tonne warheads on their first nuclear missiles. On the other side of the Atlantic, at about the same time, the first operational US nuclear missile of the 'Redstone' type, designed by Wernher von Braun, was similarly fitted with a 3-tonne nuclear warhead. These parallels between the early American and Russian missile developments can hardly be attributed to coincidence.

It may be the case that here is an instance of both great powers having recourse to captured German plans. The use of the former German 3-tonne bomb project, by the victorious powers in the post-war period, could also explain why further information has not been available to date.

4) Giant Bombs

From 1943, in the final phase of the Third Reich, there were verifiable plans for bombs of truly gigantic proportions. 20- or 30-tonne bombs, made anything seem possible. But why did the Germans want to create such extreme bomb loads for which suitable carrier aircraft still had to be constructed? Certainly conventional explosives seem to make no sense in that connection. Was it necessary to create such gigantic atomic bombs? In actual fact, however, such heavy weights were not necessary for 'normal' nuclear weapons.

Even at the beginning of the 21st century, the transport of such large payloads would be no simple task for present-day military aircraft. But perhaps the giant bombs were necessary to provide casings for bomb charges that would carry our normal ideas off into the realm of fantasy. One has only to think here of the oxygen bomb or the cold bomb. (see following volume) The precise 'purpose' of those very heavy weights is unclear even today. Whether it was simply a question of technical gigantism is doubtful.

20-tonne Bomb

The 20-tonne bomb represents a similar project to the SA 4000. Its origin can be traced back to an investigation ordered by *Generalfeldmarschall* Milch, in August 1943, into the feasibility of a 20-tonne bomb load.[179] It is striking how often one comes across the year 1943 in connection with the beginning of such projects.

The planned Ju 290 E, high-altitude night bomber could have been intended to be used as the carrier aircraft. The large Me P 1085 aircraft that was originally planned for that purpose had long since been discontinued.

Nothing has to date been published concerning the name of this bomb and what it looked like. However, a captured photograph from the FGZ wind tunnel, shows an extended bomb with circular tail, which resembles in appearance an extended version of the 'Little Boy' Hiroshima A-bomb.[180]

All those bomb projects are said to have been axed, with the end of the bomber programme, in summer 1944. In spite of that, there are indications of the production of an experimental prototype, and of a test drop of the prototype in 1944.[181]

At that time, there was not a bomber that would have been suitable to carry such a heavy bomb load. For that reason, it was thought it would be possible to adapt the six-engined, Messerschmitt Me 323, large transport as a test aircraft. There was already some experience in dropping heavy loads with that aircraft. Thus, from the spring of 1944, two experiments are known in which artificially weighted Messerschmitt Me 262 fuselages were dropped into the Ammersee and Lake Constance by the Me 323.[182]

The Me 262 hulls were dropped in order to achieve a maximum rate of fall. However, in both instances they were destroyed because a rescue system failed. In each instance the Me 263 carrier aircraft remained undamaged. It is striking that nowhere is there documentation relating to those tests, although they are substantiated by photographs and eyewitness accounts.

But things were very different in the test drop of the 'giant' bomb, whose weight was said to be 18 tonnes,[183] and carried out by the same aircraft type. Both in the case of the Me 262 fuselages and the 'giant' bombs, take-off could not be achieved without the help of an additional five-engined Heinkel He 111 Z, tug aircraft. The difficulties with such take-offs can be easily imagined.

In all three instances the teams of the Me 323 and He 111 Z succeeded in taking off. But then there was a disaster with the 'giant' bomb. After taking off, with the bomb suspended under its right wing,[184] the Me 323 did slowly gain height. Shortly before it reached the planned dropping height the *Gigant's* fuselage fractured. The aircraft plunged to earth, but the crew managed to release the bomb in time. It fell and functioned as planned. But the entire Me 323 crew lost their lives.

A commission is said to have established that a spar supporting the fuselage had been snapped in an American air raid on the airfield a few hours previously. That damaged supporting spar was then, according to the commission, the cause of the accident.

Confirmation that the incident occurred was passed to the author by British sources. However, to date, no confirmation has yet been found in German documents. This means that this particular bomb drop is confused with similar drops of Me 262 fuselages. But the weight details alone show that the bomb could not have been a Me 262 fuselage. A complete Me 262 of fuselage, wings, undercarriage, etc. weighed only 4,420kg. Even if the fuselage had been filled with sand, it would certainly not have reached the weight of 18-20 tonnes.

It seems that every reference to these events in 1944 has been removed from the available documents. It is therefore not known from which airfield that bomb experiment took off, nor who carried it out. The British account could therefore come from captured documents, or from the statements of prisoners of war.

The question is now raised as to whether that was the only test drop of such a large bomb. There are no known results. It is not known if the drop was connected in some way with the large explosion on an atomic testing ground. Dated October 1944, this is mentioned in the so-called 'Zinsser report'. (see section 'Uranium bombs')

Was the true cause of the accident really structural damage? Perhaps the large, slow, clumsy, transport-plane was in fact caught in the gigantic explosion of the experimental bomb and therefore it crashed. The Me 323, even with a normal pay load, did not reach any great height. If then the test drop of the bomb were carried out from no great height, without a parachute, the carrier aircraft would have had only a slim chance of getting out of the way in time. In any event, after that incident there appears to have been no other test drop involving a Me 323 carrying the same weapon.

Supplement: According to new information, the test of the 'giant' bomb took place in the second half of July 1944. The information states that the place where the test and development of the bomb took place was the *Luftwaffe* research establishment at Karlshagen, near Peenemünde. There, tests of other new types of bomb such as the Fritz-X and the Hs 293, etc, also took place.

As a large carrier aircraft for such bombs, a special Messerschmitt Me 323 Z is said to have been built. This design involved two Me 323 *Gigants* being linked together, along the lines of the Heinkel He 111 Z, by a common central wing. The *Doppelgigant* thus produced, with its nine BMW 801 engines each providing 1750 PS, was certainly the largest aircraft in World War II. Its appearance must have been mind-blowing. However, there are no known plans or photographs. Shortly before the planned first test drop of the large bomb, however, the *Doppelgigant* is said to have been structurally damaged in an Allied air raid on Peenemünde, possibly on 18 July 1944. Failure to carry out repairs was then the cause of the aircraft crashing in the subsequent test. There are no reports of other aircraft of the Me 323 Z type.

This heavy transporter would also have been suitable to carry other bomb loads, such as the 30-tonne bombs from the Sänger project, and test versions of the A-9/A-10 air-launched flying bombs. (Source: Gary Hyland, Anton Gill, *Last Talons of the Eagle - Secret Nazi Technology which could have changed the course of World War II*, Headline, 1998, p.89).

SB 30000 30-tonne Bomb from Space

In August 1944, Dr Sänger and Dr Bredt planned a bomb weighing 4 tonnes for their rocket-powered stratosphere bomber. It was to be dropped from a height of 40 kilometres above the target. (see section on the Stratosphere Bomb)[185] In addition, to attack the largest individual targets, a bomb weighing 30 tonnes was designed. It could penetrate 110 metres of earth or 10 metres of reinforced concrete. This giant was 11.2 metres long, 1.4 metres wide, and in size and appearance was something like a V-2 rocket. No stabilisation fins or control surfaces were attached to the tail of the bomb, because all surviving parts would have been melted away in the hypersonic re-entry into the atmosphere and the resultant temperatures. It was also possible to attach a parachute arrangement, designed by the FGZ research establishment, in order to slow the speed of the bomb in the lower levels of the atmosphere.

To carry out the planned tests, an expedition had already been planned to go from Norway to Greenland. However, it was not possible to produce a prototype of such a bomb before the end of the war.

For the 30-tonne bomb, and for the 4- and 1-tonne bombs that were also planned for the same bomber, there were hypothetical targets. The plans had been developed for the area of Manhattan, New York, in the USA. They formed part of a secret synopsis, 60 copies of which were prepared and handed to *Reichsmarschall* Hermann Göring, *General* Milch and to specialists such as Wernher von Braun and Professor Heisenberg. One of the target plans contained in that synopsis was published several times in the post-war period. It was attributed to a great many different projects, such as A-9/A-10 attacks on New York, or planned conventional raids by America bombers in 1942/43. Only recently has there been convincing evidence that the target plans related to a nuclear attack.[186] Unfortunately, to date, only the target plan for smaller bombs has been published, while the target plan relating to the 30-tonne bomb still awaits publication.

It also became known, from American post-war reports,[187] that craters caused by nuclear explosions could have an extremely important effect as weapons in themselves. There are certain targets both on the surface and underground that need a contact impact, i.e. the formation of a crater, to cause significant damage. Massive concrete fortifications, underground structures, heavy industrial machine plants, aircraft runways, tunnels and dams are good examples of such a target. For tactical reasons the effect of large craters was increased by radioactive contamination. The radioactive radiation that the crater emitted could prevent repair work from being carried out for a long time. If a crater were to be used as an impediment, its effectiveness depended upon the relationship between the radius and the depth of the crater. All this may be one explanation why the hypothetical target plans for the 30-tonne bomb have not been published to date. The other reason lies probably in the nature of the weapon itself.

There is added significance, if one considers the fact that this 'monster' could not be tested in areas created for the purpose on German territory, but had to be tested on the almost deserted island of Greenland. It raises the question as to what devastating effect was expected by the Germans, from such a weapon, if such a remote test site was needed. Moreover the test site could only be reached with great difficulty. The use of a conventional explosive would certainly not have justified such expenditure. It has also never become known whether this Greenland expedition was only used to observe the test drop of the 30-tonne bomb, or whether it was planned to take the bomb along with the expedition and to explode it in a suitable area. The latter becomes less likely if one considers the almost complete lack, at that time, of any suitable air transport to carry such a heavy payload. The Daimler-Benz 'C' ultra-high-speed bomber project, which had been designed for the same 30-tonne payload was, at that time too, only at the planning stage. It would have taken some years to be fully developed.

It is also extremely questionable whether there would have been any point in having a bomb of that kind filled

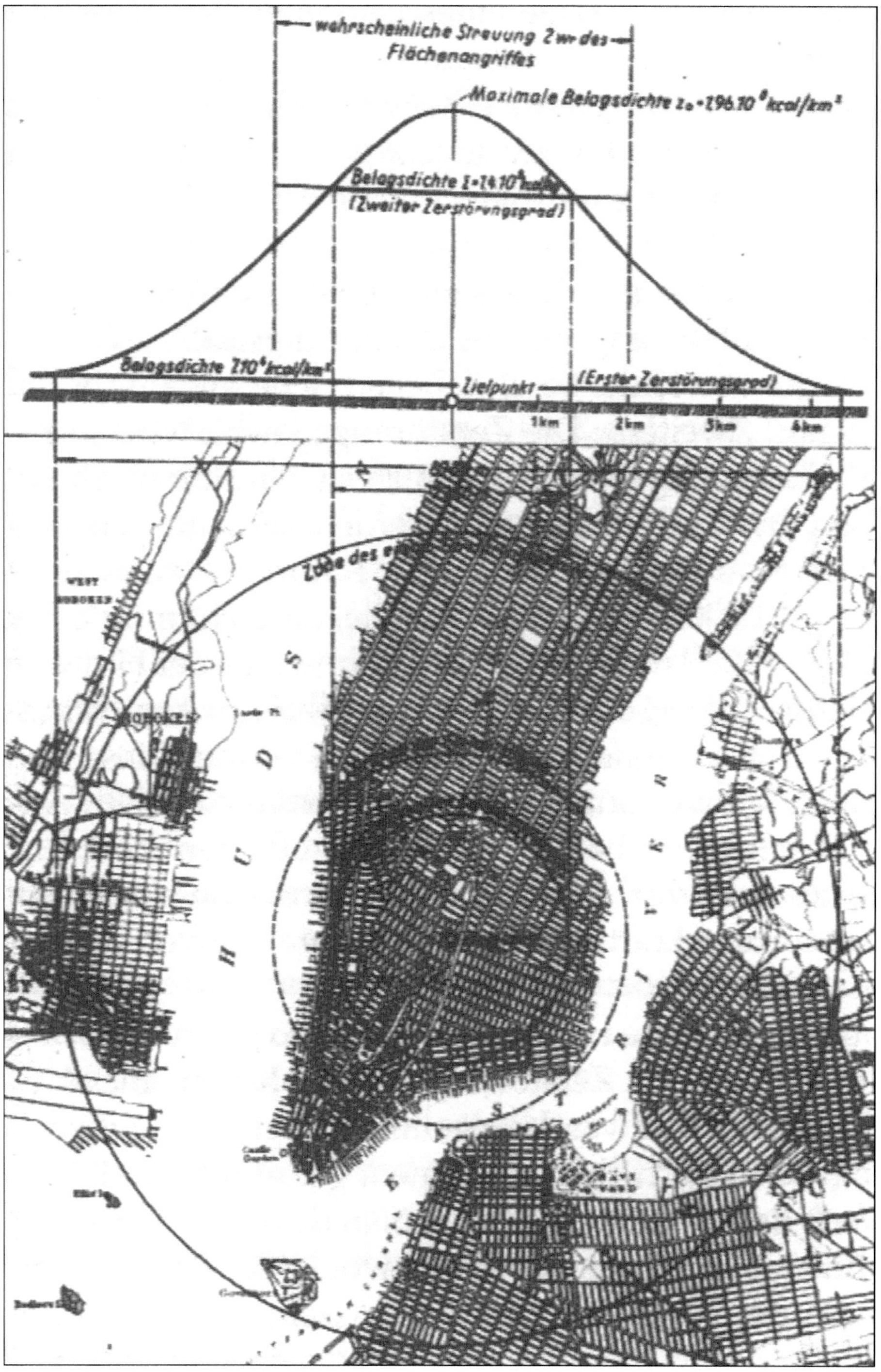

German *Luftwaffe* target plan for an attack on the Manhattan area of New York. Note the circles which have been inserted showing the zones of destruction. Such an effect is impossible to achieve with saturation bombing by many bombers - the plan shows the use of a single weapon, an atomic bomb!

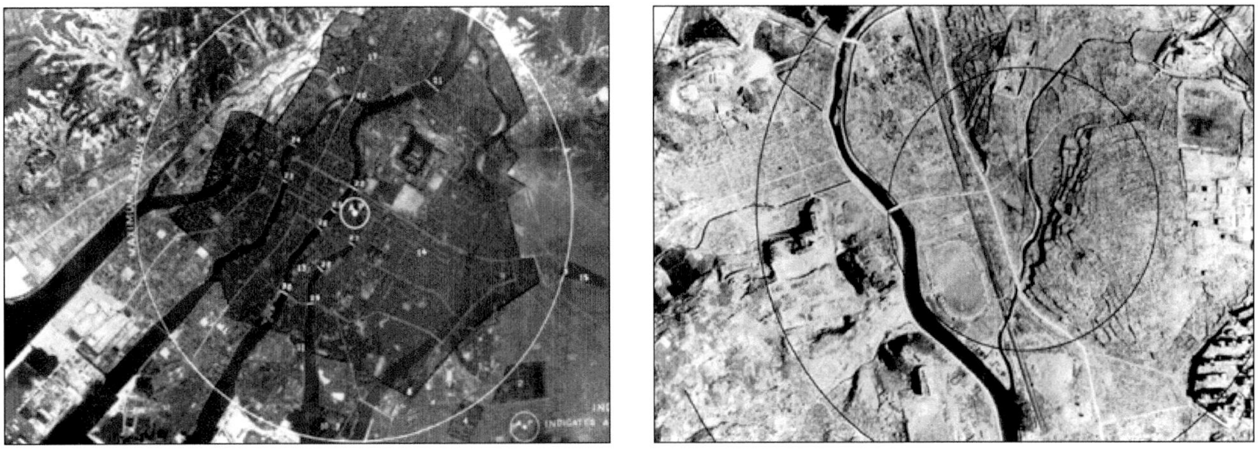

US Air Force aerial photographs taken after the use of the atomic bombs on Hiroshima (above) and Nagasaki (below). The circles mark the zones of varying destructive power. Is there a connection to the radii which are shown on the German target plan for an attack on New York?

with conventional explosive. With the resources available at the time, it was not possible, using an unguided bomb, to hit a precise target accurately, from a height of 40 kilometres. It must therefore be assumed that the giant bomb was to be filled with special material, the precise composition of which is not known even today.

One could speculate about the use of nuclear materials in that instance, but equally one could start from the premise of other ambitious miracle weapons. There are some projects about which even today only fragments of very disjointed information are available. For example, endothermic weapons, the proper functioning of which possibly required a large but stable casing.

5) Nuclear Weapons - Special Developments

The Thorium Atomic Bomb: Bomb or Toothpaste?

At the end of the war there were huge quantities of thorium metal in Germany. To date, no one has suggested a practical explanation as to why this metal was so carefully hoarded, nor what purpose it was supposed to serve.

At the beginning of 1944 Dr Nikolaus Kriehl, the leading chemist of the *Auer Gesellschaft*, had bought up for his company all the supplies of thorium in occupied Europe. After the war, the explanation for this urge to hoard thorium in large quantities was simply in order to gain a monopoly in the production of a radioactive toothpaste called *Doramat.* It was believed to be seen as a logical explanation because, before the war, the *Auer Gesellschaft* had produced such a toothpaste.

However, purchases of that kind by civilians were out of the question at the end of the 'total war'. To try to buy metals in that way for civilian purposes could have cost the instigators their lives. Even if the project had succeeded, the *Auer Gesellschaft* would afterwards have had to supply every citizen in the world with their toothpaste, for decades, in order to use up the reserves of metal that had been purchased. So, something was out of the ordinary.

The real reason for storing reserves of thorium could have been that it was the intention to use thorium as the fuel for a reactor or a nuclear weapon. Nuclear scientists such as Heisenberg or Harteck never mentioned that they had been involved with thorium. However, there is a telegram from the ALSOS Mission, dated 3 September 1945,[188] in which the nuclear scientist Professor Houtermans describes, in precise detail, how thorium can be used to create the fissile element U 233, in a nuclear reactor, or in a nuclear bomb.

Professor Houtermans, as one of the leading nuclear scientists in the Third Reich, worked with Professor Manfred von Ardenne in the Lichterfelde laboratory of the *Reichspost* Research Institute. (RPF)

That ALSOS report is the first evidence that a German physicist, from the period of the Third Reich, mentioned that they were certainly aware of the suitability of thorium as a reactor element or as a nuclear weapon. It could well have been the real reason for building up German thorium reserves in 1944.

The fissile element U 233 is produced from thorium in a similar manner to that which produces fissile plutonium 239 from uranium. But in the production of U 233 some waste products are released which have a very strong level of gamma radiation. That material could have been used as an additional radiological charge in A-weapons. However, at the same time, the waste products would have made it very difficult to prepare the thorium. Extreme care, and remote-controlled methods, would have been necessary in production as a result of the radiation.

The fusion process of U 233 is similar to that of plutonium. It would have to be detonated, like the plutonium bomb, by means of the implosion method. Otherwise it would have been caused to prematurely blast out its contents without exploding.[189] It is known that German scientists were thoroughly familiar with the implosion principle. (see section 'Plutonium Bomb')

An atomic bomb, based on thorium, would also have been a practical solution for producing a German nuclear weapon in World War II. The various references to a bomb the size of a pineapple, or a pumpkin, could also relate to the core of such a thorium bomb, without protective casing and detonator assembly.

Therefore, with regard to the reserves of thorium which were accumulated, it is certainly open to discussion as to whether thorium experiments of that kind were also undertaken in *Objekt Burg* or in Stadtilm. Apparently coincidentally, there was a branch office of the *Auer Gesellschaft* quite close to Stadtilm.

Incidentally, in the same ALSOS report, Professor Houtermans predicted that the Russians would no doubt also produce their first atomic bomb by means of the thorium method. We know today that this prediction was wrong. But what was interesting were the reasons on which Houtermans based his prediction. For instance, in Berlin the Russians captured the complete nuclear laboratory of the RPF. Could it mean that in the place where Houtermans was working they had been engaged in detailed work on the thorium bomb, and that the Russians then had possession of those documents?

It is thus completely probable that, in the Third Reich, work was continuing on the thorium bomb, as well as on the uranium and plutonium bombs. How far this work had progressed is still unknown. The implications of such a thorium spectre only lead to total disbelief when one regards the persistence with which the story of the radioactive toothpaste is still in circulation today.

The German Hydrogen Bomb

In 'published' opinion, it is contested that from June 1942 there was no German atomic bomb programme at all. Remarkably, however, it is admitted that German researchers were already working on thermonuclear fusion. That was nothing other than a hydrogen bomb.

In 1944, at the Kummersdorf firing range, the research area for the Army Weapons Office for Explosives, a remarkable series of nuclear experiments began. A nuclear and chain reaction was introduced by the explosion of explosives. These nuclear experiments, concerning which precise details have never been published, were under the energetic direction of Dr Diebner.[190] At the end of May 1944 Professor Gerlach mentioned that 'the question of obtaining nuclear energy by different means than the uranium decay method has been tackled comprehensively'. The nuclear processes that resulted were to have increased the effect of explosive materials. In those experiments, small cylindrical or spherical bodies of TNT explosive of various diameters were used. Into the centre were inserted either heavy paraffin or heavy water as deuterium carriers. In the explosion, almost all the energy that was contained in the large quantity of conventional explosives was to be focused on the tiny mass of heavy water or paraffin at the centre and lead to a chain or nuclear reaction.

Similar experiments were undertaken in the chemical-physical experimental establishment of the *Kriegsmarine*'s Explosives Research Establishment in Dänisch-Nienhof, near Kiel. That was done with the collaboration of Herr Professor Otto Haxel. He is also said to have worked on another larger uranium project. Unfortunately, very little has become known concerning such nuclear research experiments carried out by the *Kriegsmarine*.

Several German thermo-fusion experiments were undertaken, but no radioactivity is said to have resulted. That supposed failure is, however, only based on two publications of documents by the ALSOS Mission. The data suggests that they were indeed going in the right direction, but that the experiments had been carried out on much too small a scale.

But on the basis of material that has recently come to light, it appears that on the German side this problem had been fully recognised. It was therefore planned to use small uranium bombs as detonators for the hydrogen bombs. (see section 'Small Uranium Bombs')[191]

Afterwards, all was again silence on the subject of the German hydrogen bomb. But this does not exclude the possibility that in the future surprising results will come into the public arena concerning that weapon. Perhaps it may reveal that the accepted wisdom of scientific history is wrong.

There is already one indication that points in that direction. As early as the end of the 1930s, the Vienna physicist, Karl Nowak, is said to have possessed a system, ready to be implemented, for the development of a hydrogen bomb. That system, it is said, was sabotaged by the German nuclear physicist Otto Hahn.[192]

The Neutron Bomb

Was work also being done in the Third Reich on the neutron bomb? There are indications that in addition to radiological and atomic bombs it was also planned to use the revolutionary neutron bomb as a miracle weapon.[193]

While, to date, it is unknown in which location, and by which scientists, the work was carried out, American information suggests that a research unit of Rommel's Afrika Korps had carried out the neutron bomb tests in the Libyan desert.

Dave Dunn, the commandant of a prisoner of war camp in Roswell in America, reports that among the inmates of his camp were German soldiers from the Afrika Korps. They possessed remarkable postcards produced by their original unit showing the destruction of New York by an atomic mushroom. Questioning of the prisoners indicated that the explosion shown on the postcard was of the test carried out in the desert by their unit, on to which the skyline of New York had been superimposed by trick photography. Today Dave Dunn still has one of those postcards in his possession. In any event the test must have taken place before the surrender of *Heeresgruppe Afrika* in May 1943.

How did work continue on the supposed German neutron bomb in the next two years of the war? If that weapon was ready for testing in 1942 or 1943, there was enough time for its further development and production. However, there is no accessible information about this. The same report[194] says that it was planned to mount neutron warheads on special U-boat V-2 rockets.

But given the assumption that the Germans did have some kind of neutron weapons technology, it appears that the Allies were not able to find or evaluate it at the end the war. Otherwise there would surely not have been an interval of 30 years until the neutron bomb was introduced into the American and Russian arsenals

A simpler explanation would perhaps be that in the report there is some confusion between the neutron bomb and the German radiological isotope bomb. Could it be a fact that a radiological bomb was detonated in the Libyan Desert? Will this question ever be clarified?

Heavy Water Bombs

At the end of the war there was much talk that the Germans were planning to deploy 'heavy water' as a weapon. Thus, in February 1945, local defence committee member *Ingenieur* Marsch gave a report to the Wetzlau *Kreisleiter,* Haus and his area economic adviser Dr Hensoldt. It concerned new weapons and the 'heavy water' which were soon to be used and which would decide the course of the war.[195]

In actual fact,[196] before the end of the war, a quantity of heavy water, i.e. deuterium, which still remained, was poured into the empty casings of conventional bombs.[197] According to Professor Lachner, it was his idea, since deuterium would be safest there from thieves and spies, and because no one would risk touching a bomb.

So, there were indeed German heavy water bombs, even if they were really more a sort of safe keeping measure, born of necessity, than a weapon which it was planned to use in combat.

After the end of the war, the Allies found these heavy water bombs when they occupied the area. It seems they did not properly investigate their contents, because the heavy water was thought by the soldiers to be ordinary water and was simply poured away![198]

SECTION 2
Miracle Weapons of the *Kriegsmarine*

Until well on into the war the *Kriegsmarine* was the poor relation among the German armed forces. At the end of 1942 Hitler called the German navy a 'wretched copy' of the British Navy and contemptuously called the ships that were stationed in Norway 'dead iron'.

Very soon afterwards, in 1943, all construction of large capital ships was halted. The traditionalist, *Grossadmiral* Raeder, was replaced by the dynamic *Grossadmiral* Dönitz, who was a decided advocate of the U-boat. But 'Fleet Construction Programme 43', which Dönitz initiated together with Armaments Minister Speer in June 1943, came a year too late. Based on U-boats and light naval vessels, that programme, the largest in the history of the German navy, was doomed to failure from the beginning. There was a shortage of men, material and above all, time. But, in spite of all that, a great number of conventional U-boats, of the tried and tested Types VII and IX, was achieved. However, from the spring of 1943, after the German naval code was cracked, they were too slow to be able to escape the Allied defence systems that were growing ever stronger.

As a response, *Grossadmiral* Dönitz tried to replace the old U-boat types, whose technology was still based on First World War designs, with superior new electronic and Walther U-boats. It cannot be disputed that if the new types of U-boat had been deployed in time, the war at sea could have turned in Germany's favour. However, as in the case of the jet fighters, the chances were thrown away because it was all 'too little, too late'. Apart from the construction of a superior revolutionary U-boat weapon, and because of the constant withdrawal of the fighting fronts, the *Kriegsmarine*, which was already far too small, had to take on an increasing number of other tasks. It had to transport refugees from the threatened areas in the East. Their tasks also concerned the defence of the Reich.

Despite such depressing developments, at the end of the war the *Kriegsmarine* was preparing offensive plans that could have turned the course of the war. Even today they provoke astonishment.

1) Long-Range Guns for Atomic Artillery Shells: America's Atomic Cannon and its German Predecessor, the DKM 44

In the early 1950s the US Army succeeded in bringing into service the 28-centimetre T-131 atomic cannon. At the time, a long-range cannon of that sort was more accurate and less susceptible to the effects of weather than airborne atomic bombs. In addition, such nuclear artillery was to fill a gap in the US arsenal, until the smaller tactical nuclear weapons were ready for deployment. With the technology of the time, the large calibre was just sufficient to be able to use a reduced version of the 'Little Boy' bomb as an artillery shell.

The T-131 was transported by two independent tug units, one at each end. In 1952 that very large mobile artillery piece, designed in the United States, was ready. Because of the extremely high costs of construction only 20 T-131 cannons were produced, which remained in service until 1963. At the time the development of the atomic cannon was considered to be one of the high points of American weapons technology.[199]

Only a few years ago it became known[200] that the Rheinmetall Company had, as early as 15 September 1943, put forward a proposal for a quite similar long-range gun under the designation of DüKa, or *Düsenkanone*. It was to be transported suspended between two Panther gun carriages. The Hanomag Company was also involved in the project. Comparison of the DüKa drawing with the American model reveals amazing similarities. The main difference was the fact that the Rheinmetall Company wanted to use a lighter, more modern cannon instead of a conventional artillery gun.

The German plan was for the cannon to be lowered to the ground to fire, and after firing for it to be driven away again by the Panther gun carriages. The system was designated as the Panther 'timber principle' by analogy to vehicles used to transport timber. The gun, with a barrel length L/52, was to give the 350 kilogram 28 centimetre shell a velocity of 750 metres per second. Each one of such mobile guns carried 10 rounds of ammunition with it, and including armour and ammunition, weighed a total of 115 tonnes.

According to information from a British author, the proposal was not followed up, and was one of many ideas that were not developed any further. However, the most recent publications[201] indicate that, in reality, efforts were being made, right up to the end of the war, to develop that weapon. Thus, on 13 February 1945, the Rheinmetall Company reported that designs for the mobile parts of the 28 centimetre DüKa had been developed and that development work was proceeding on the internal ballistics. Because the firm, due to a shortage of design staff, was not able to work quickly enough on the DüKa, the British source says that the OKM involved the Skoda company in the project. They were to work on the production of the gun carriage and on the mobility of the vehicle. It goes on to suggest that after some of the designers were transferred from the Rheinmetall Company to Trebsen, they worked on the design under the direction of *Oberingenieur* Krumm.

Meanwhile, the weapon was designated as DKM 44 or *Düsenkanone Marine* 1944. In the last years of the war, the Skoda Company worked on the development of the most advanced secret weapons technology as an integral part of the so-called 'Kammler complex'. For the most part the precise details relating to that activity are still undisclosed in Allied archives. The question may be asked as to why work was going on at such a late stage, in various places, on such an expensive special project, but the similarity of the German DKM 44 project to the later American atomic cannon suggests obvious conclusions. Mention is also made, in another source, that at the end of the war Germany was working on long-range cannons for atomic artillery shells.[202]

One must ask why that particular weapon was so important for the *Kriegsmarine*. The answer could be found in the 'SKL, i.e. *Seekriegsleitung* Emergency Armaments Programme' of 24 October 1944. In it the prime task of the German *Kriegsmarine* is stated to be the 'defence of the Reich coasts against enemy landings'.[203] What the planners particularly feared were Allied landings in Holland, Denmark and Norway. After its failure during the invasions of 1944, the *Kriegsmarine* required new, decisive weapons to be provided quickly for its assigned task of coastal defence.

Because its design restricted its penetrative power, there would have been no question of using the mobile DKM 44 as classic coastal artillery against targets at sea.[204] But the use of the DüKa, with atomic or sub-atomic ammunition, could have nipped in the bud any enemy landing attempts. Of particular importance for the *Kriegsmarine* was probably the fact that, in coastal defence, atomic artillery was not susceptible to the effects of weather.

Reference is made in the section on the Stadtilm uranium bombs, to the similarity of the American 28cm nuclear ammunition with that of German developments. At the end of the war, work on developing that miracle weapon had already been completed. It had even been possible to construct a prototype of the DKM 44, which was still undergoing tests at the end of the war. As with almost all the weapons that could be connected with Hitler's nuclear weapons plans, in that case too, all original photographs of the weapon, and the tanks used to transport it, are missing.

The preliminary investigations indicated that the 28cm DüKa could become a practicable weapon.[205] It was left to another time and another country to put the potential of the idea into practice.

2) The First Underwater Rockets in the World

In the last years of the war, there were plans to fire small rockets from U-boats submerged at a depth of 100 metres, to defend them against pursuing warships. A special version of these small rockets was also to serve as *Vergeltungswaffen*.

The background history begins as early as 4 July 1942. U-boat U-511 carried out the first underwater firing experiments, with Borsig powder rockets, near the island of Greifswalder Oie, close to Peenemünde. The rockets used in that experiment were so-called *Nebelwerferraketen* of 21-centimetre or 15-centimetre calibre. They were fired from a depth of 10 to 15 metres from a temporary launch pad. In those experiments it was possible to attain a range of 4 kilometres. 20 shots, in a salvo, were automatically fired from the U-boat without any problems. But the task of developing a practicable underwater rocket was not within the remit of Peenemünde. Developments there were carried out in two independent experimental establishments belonging respectively to the Army and the *Luftwaffe*, but under the central direction of the Army. The development of naval weapons did not come under that remit, and when no great urgency was assigned at that time to developing an underwater rocket, the improvised experiments were discontinued.

Only in 1943, when the situation in the Battle of the Atlantic changed, did that weapon again become a pressing issue. Project 'Ursel' was initiated. Within that framework the *Kriegsmarine* also had the Rheinmetall-Borsig Company develop larger rockets. Their planned dimensions were for length 1.8 metres, calibre 15 centimetres and weight 80 kilograms. It meant that two men could easily handle the rocket. The explosive charge was determined as 50 kilograms of high quality underwater explosive, by which a hole measuring approximately 5 cubic metres could be blown in the hull of the attacking destroyer.[206] Despite the above-mentioned experiments in the Greifswalder Oie, there were no documents or experimental results, relating to the underwater behaviour of rockets without guidance mechanisms. So the development of such a weapon still faced fundamental problems.

Therefore the CPVA, the Institute for Fluidics Research in Göttingen, the 'Graf Zeppelin' research establishment in Stuttgart Ruit, and the Departmental Group FEP in the OKM were commissioned to carry out an appropriate research and development programme. The scientific direction of the project was assigned to Dr Lindberg. In the late summer of 1944 the work was transferred from Kiel to the CPVA outstation on the Toplitzsee. There the rockets were lowered, by wire cables on a launch pad, into 100 metres of water and set off electrically. In that experiment they were targeted at the surrounding Austrian Alps. But it was soon realised that the principles of land-based rocket artillery no longer functioned in the case of underwater rockets, because the exterior ballistics of the underwater rockets are decisively determined by the high density of the water.

At the Toplitzsee[207] they discontinued the use of the Rheinmetall-Borsig stabilisation system. Instead, they tested rockets of various designs stabilised by means of tail fins. The body of the rocket was then streamlined, had a central jet engine in the tail, and possessed five different types of tail assembly. In such experiments, speeds of 60 nautical miles per hour, and ranges of some 200 metres were achieved with reasonable accuracy. The new rockets for Project 'Ursel' were produced by the Wasag Company in Wittenberg. They also carried out various tests there. The aim was both to solve the problem of underwater ballistics, and also to increase the range of the underwater rockets. Progress made in that connection, however, is still not clear.

While there is evidence of ranges of 200 metres, eyewitness accounts indicate that, in subsequent experiments, later rockets subsequently flew for many kilometres into the Tote Gebirge. That would have been sufficient range to hit cities such as New York that were based around a port. According to information from French agents, in 1944 small rockets of the V-2 type were also fired from a mini-submarine in the Toplitzsee.

There is no definitive evidence as to whether such rockets were being used in a test for the Laffarenz project, or whether they were test rockets connected with Project Ursel. Most probably it was a rocket based on the Peenemünde A-5, the successful predecessor of the V-2. The A-5, which was only one twelfth of the dimensions of the V-2, was extremely reliable. Earlier tests of that small rocket, included simulated drop launches from a He 111. There were another 30 proper launches with parachute recovery, from the establishment on the Greifswalder Oie in Peenemünde. There were no recorded failures. The experiments achieved a height of 9,260 metres, and a range of 18 kilometres on land, was achieved.[208]

Therefore Peenemünde offered the *Kriegsmarine* a modified A-5, which was given the designation A-7. Essentially the A-7 was an A-5 fitted with tail fins, and with control surfaces that were to give an increased thrust of 1,800 kp (A-5: 1,500kp). But the design, although it promised to be so successful, was not accepted by the *Kriegsmarine*. It appeared to be too large for the *Kriegsmarine*'s U-boat purposes. Instead, the *Kriegsmarine* demanded a further reduction in size.[209] Was it the reduced-size A-5 that was referred to in the reports of the French agents in 1944? There may have been another underwater rocket project about which we still know nothing.

At the beginning of 1945 the underwater rockets of Project 'Ursel' had reached a stage where it was possible to carry out test launches from an actual U-boat. During two dives near Bornholm, rockets without explosive were successfully launched from a Type VIIC test submarine. It is said that there was not time to complete the tests because of the rapidly deteriorating war situation.[210]

There is no doubt that Project 'Ursel' was planned as an underwater defensive weapon against warships. But it is very probable that rockets from the 'Ursel' Project were also intended to be used for retribution attacks. There were rumours at the Toplitzsee that never entirely went away. These reported that New York was to be attacked with the underwater rockets that were being tested there. SS *Hauptsturmführer* Otto Skorzeny confirmed the rumours, in the summer of 1947, in an interrogation while he was a prisoner of war. Skorzeny raised the sort of panic that was created by a radio play, by Orson Welles, about a supposed landing of Martians in America. He said: 'What would happen if a few such rockets crashed down now on Manhattan?' It is probable that Skorzeny was scaremongering. After all, he had nothing to lose.

People like to counter such statements from a leading SS official, from a technical point of view. They point out that the underwater rockets of the 'Ursel' Project were not designed for such a task at all. With the supposed payload of 15 kilograms per rocket no great damage could have been caused, in a city the size of New York, with a population of millions.

But it is perhaps the case that, with such a retribution attack, the underwater rockets would have returned to their original purpose, as envisaged in 1942. The refined underwater offensive weapon of 1944/45 could have been a sort of 'scale model' of a V-2 based on an A-5. Each of the small rockets could have contained a warhead consisting of one or two small radiological bombs, each coupled to a normal explosive as a detonator.[211] The rate of ballistic descent of the rockets could have been slowed by a parachute. Then an approach detonator would explode the warhead, at a predetermined height, to achieve optimal dispersion of the radiological substances. The idea of dispersing the small but dangerous rockets either individually, or in salvoes, over a port such as New York or San Francisco seems, in the light of the successful preparatory work at the Toplitzsee, to be a technically and financially interesting alternative to the gigantic A-9/A-10 project. With a radiological warhead the small payload of the 'Ursel' Project rockets would not have mattered too much. The technical arguments then come full circle.

The 'miniature' *Vergeltungsraketen* may have been developed further, as is being admitted today. The director of the CPVA at the Toplitzsee, Dr Lindberg, states that, as early as February 1945, he had inspected a modern U-boat onto which mechanisms for launching rockets were to be installed. But there was no time to complete the work before the end of the war. That may have been a stroke of luck for the coastal cities of the USA. It can be regarded as probable that the rocket launch mechanism, that could not be completed in spring 1945, was to be used, not for a defensive rocket against warships, but as a *Vergeltungswaffe*.

The normal 'Ursel' rockets designed for use against warships were not installed on the upper deck but were located in launch tubes in the stern of the XXI U-boats. The rockets seen by Dr Lindberg must have been for attacking targets on land. The advantages of launching them from the exterior of the U-boat, was that they could attain a greater range by means of a steeper launch angle. Possibly too they would provide greater radiation protection for the U-boat crew. In addition, rockets carried on the exterior of the U-boats could be bigger. To date, no pictures or plans of the final versions, nor of the launch mechanisms of the 'Ursel' Project, have been published.

The German underwater rockets in an Austrian alpine lake could have been predecessors of the later American and Russian underwater atomic missiles. Today, there are those who believe such missiles hold our world in a 'balance of terror'.

3) U-Boat VI against America

As early as May 1943 preliminary investigations were carried out as to whether the Fieseler Fi 103, the V-1, was suitable for launching from a U-boat. At that time it was mainly planned to use large Type XIV supply U-boats. By the summer of 1943, *Generalfeldmarschall* Milch was still expressing his scepticism about the idea. However, there was a meeting in November 1944, in the headquarters of the *Reichsführer-SS*, Heinrich Himmler, near Hohenlychen.[212] It was decided that SS *Hauptsturmführer* Otto Skorzeny should put all his efforts into making the U-boat V-1 a reality. Moreover, Himmler wanted to discuss the matter immediately with Adolf Hitler and *Grossadmiral* Dönitz.

It is not known what lay behind that change of mind. As always the Americans were well informed by means of ENIGMA and informers. However, from the autumn of 1944, they feared an attack on the USA by V-1 flying bombs launched from U-boats.[213] They assumed that there would be no problem in carrying up to four V-1s in a small U-boat hangar. Using a launching ramp, the Americans thought the V-1s could then be launched within a few minutes. It could be done by night or in hazy weather, some 300km from the US coast. Then the U-boats could quickly dive again.

But there continued to be a whole series of problems that stood in the way of putting the project into practice. In the first instance, at that time all the Type XIV U-boats, which it was planned to use to launch the V-1s, had already been sunk. From 1943, using decoded ENIGMA, all German U-boat supply missions were known to the Allies. They even knew the map co-ordinates at which they would meet at sea.

However, it was not planned to build any more new submarines of that type. The long-range Type X and IX D/2 U-boats, and also the new type XXI, could have been considered as alternatives. In the light of the massive surveillance by Allied air and naval forces of the Eastern coast of America, and of an area extending far into the Atlantic, only the revolutionary Type XXI would have had any chance of coming through such a mission intact. It is also true that the Type XXI U-boats were not then ready to be used in action.

Another problem was the target accuracy of the unguided V-1.[214] Its poor accuracy could well have been exacerbated by the rocking movements of the U-boat when launching the rockets. Consideration had also to be given to the difficulty of establishing an accurate location at night, to hazy weather conditions, and even the huge extent of New York. Experts at the time were not sure whether the target area could be hit at all.

But, according to Skorzeny, developments were already under way to improve the target accuracy of the V-1, and those appeared promising. Firstly, work was being carried out to build a guidance mechanism housed in the nose of the V-1. That would make it possible to regulate and influence the direction of the bomb, even during flight. To achieve that, there would need to be an additional radio station, close to the location of the launch, to provide radio guidance, e.g. a second Type XXI U-boat.

Secondly, another development was already well advanced. A small transmitter was to operate the guidance system in the nose of the V-1. It had to be set up in the immediate area of the target, and operated for a short time in co-ordination with the launch procedure. The target-seeking device in the V-1 could have been a version of the ZSG *Radieschen*, which had been available in small numbers as early as 1944. In experiments, the target-seeking equipment weighing 15 kilograms, had succeeded in automatically guiding experimental flying bombs to previously set up radio transmitters.

A similar procedure was also being planned for the A-9/A-10 America rocket. (see following volume). There was still a technical problem relating to the solution in the small amounts of energy that were available. In addition, a further difficulty had to be overcome. The small guidance transmitter had to be brought by agents to the right place, at the right time. The secret service chief, Dr Schellenberg, who was present at the same conference, may well have been invited in order to advise on the question concerning agents. He must have listed many problems and difficulties, quite apart from all the preparations that would need to be made. At the end of the conference it was proposed to wait until more suitable guidance devices had been developed.

The OKL therefore commissioned the DFS to develop remote-control guidance procedures. They resulted in the

'Ewald II' radio direction procedure and the 'Sauerskirche II' radio guidance system. A small production run of them had already been produced by April 1945. But because of the war situation it was no longer possible to conduct flight trials.[215] Events may have turned out very differently if that work had been carried out in May 1943 and not, presumably, only after Skorzeny had pushed the matter in the autumn of 1944.

The radio direction transmitters, needed to guide a flying bomb to its target, had been available before the end of the war. The devices of the *Wespe* [wasp], *Biene* [bee] and *Glühwürmchen* [glow-worm] types, were also called 'impulse repeaters', or 'impulse target guidance beacons'. They had a maximum range of 150 kilometres, with batteries allowing them to be operated for three-and-a-half hours. There were versions in a wooden box with folding aerial or even in a waterproof casing, for use by frogmen or U-boats. Consideration was even given to using them as transmitters for agents. They would have been of interest mainly in the case of deploying miracle weapons.

After initial trials in November 1944 the radio transmitters were in operational use from February/March 1945. They were principally used to enable dropping zones to be precisely marked for supply flights. According to a secret American report of 7 November 1944,[216] development of the special version of the V-1, to be used to attack the United States, had already been completed. That could probably have been one reason why the meeting was called at Hohenlychen.

Post-war Allied reports actually confirmed the existence of V-1 models that were painted in the naval camouflage colours RLM 72 or RLM 73, instead of the usual camouflage scheme. German *Luftwaffe* maritime aircraft and seaplanes also bore that type of camouflage from 1939 to 1945. It may have been planned to use those sea-green flying bombs in the North Atlantic. For normal operations against Britain their camouflage would not have been effective as they only spent a relatively short time in flight over the North Sea.

Although there are no documents relating to tests, work was continuing on the U-boat version of the flying bombs, called the Fieseler Fi-103, right up to the time when Peenemünde was evacuated.[217]

An attempt may actually have been made to use the V-1 against the USA. In the US National Archive there are documents which state that U-boats had set off to bombard New York, but had been sunk as they made their approach.[218] It would mean that older type U-boats were converted to transport V-1s. Perhaps their mission was betrayed.

Although the concentrated V-1 bombardment of London, from June 1944, had not turned the course of the war, the U-boat V-1 must nevertheless have been an extremely important development. Heinrich Himmler[219] said of the project: 'Here I can see a new, quite great possibility of bringing about a turn in the course of this war'. In saying that he quite clearly could not have meant the launch of a single conventional 1-tonne warhead against a major city such as New York. But it would have been possible to turn the course of the war by launching 'non-conventional' U-boat V-1s.

There may be indications that the German U-boat V-1 was intended to carry nuclear warheads. Such an indication is implied when one considers the corresponding post-war American developments. On 7 March 1948, the Americans succeeded in launching a remote-controlled flying bomb of the LTV-N-2 'Loon' type, from the submarine USS Cusk (SS 348). Three months later the submarine USS Carbonero (SS 337) was used as a guidance submarine for the 'Loon'.

The 'Loon' was a practically identical, Americanised version of the German V-1. It could be a coincidence that one of the directors of the 'Loon' project was the German scientist Dr Wilhelm Fiedler, one of the fathers of the V-1.[220] The 'Loon' was carried in a hangar behind the conning tower of the submarines. In several actions the USS Carbonero and the USS Cusk succeeded in carrying out simulated 'Loon' attacks on large cities, such as San Diego, in the face of the strongest anti-submarine defensive measures. Later the 'Loon' was replaced by the 'Regulus 1'. The Americans officially regarded the 'Loon' only as a pure research project and have never given precise information concerning its warhead.

However, in the intervening period it has become known that there was certainly a so-called 'war reserve' of 'Loon' flying bombs. From May 1948 a nuclear warhead was also being developed for it under the name of TX-10.[221] It was to be a smaller, improved version of the Hiroshima bomb, similar to the nuclear warhead of the 28-centimetre artillery shell. The 28-centimetre weapons system also has many strong traces of German ancestry. It is not known where the original idea came from, for the TX-10 (see section about large uranium bombs). It is therefore very probable that the nuclear 'Loon' of the US *Kriegsmarine* was a concept from the years 1944–45, developed by German scientists and taken over by the Americans.

4) The U-Boat V-2: the Laffarenz Project

Another question is, why so much trouble was taken to make the temperamental V-2 rocket, with its 1-tonne warhead, suitable for use under water. As in the case of the flying bomb, there were serious plans to take the liquid-powered V-2, by U-boat, close to a distant target to significantly increase its range. The impetus for the plan, for an underwater launch of the V-2, was provided by Otto Laffarenz, a director of the German Labour Front. In the autumn of 1943 he met Walter Dornberger, the director of the Army research station, at Peenemünde, and discussed the idea with him. Laffarenz suggested to Dornberger that the A-4 (V-2) could be towed by U-boat in a submersible container. Close to the target, the container was to be brought to the vertical position required for launch, by flooding its water ballast tanks.[222]

In that way it would be possible to fire at any target that was no further than 300 kilometres from the coast of any given country. In the first instance the proposal was of course related to the coastal cities of the USA. In Peenemünde, *Direktor* Laffarenz's proposal was taken up with interest. Consequently, in 1944, trials of the project were carried out on the Austrian Toplitzsee. In the trials projectiles, similar to the V-2, were fired from a small submarine while it was submerged.[223]

The trials were successful. Researchers have argued that a small submarine would not have been able to launch a missile of the size of the V-2, i.e. length 14 metres. But it is likely that the trials involved a scaled-down model of the V-2. Trials of a similar kind, with scaled-down models of aircraft and rockets, were often undertaken by the Germans in the last year of the war. They needed to save important development time.

The Toplitzsee would have been well suited for rocket trials because of its geographical position. It was deep, cold, remote, and the Austrian Alps provided the target area for the rockets. From November 1942 there had been a *Kriegsmarine* research establishment in that area. It was the Chemical-Physical Research Establishment, *Chemische-Physische Versuchsanstalt: CPVA.* The mystery of the Toplitzsee, and the real or alleged treasures that were sunk there on the collapse of the Third Reich, has not been finally solved to this day.

However, after a series of mysterious accidents involving treasure-hunters, in 1963 a large-scale salvage operation was undertaken by the Austrian Ministry of the Interior. The operation was abruptly halted under remarkable circumstances. Since then there has been further speculation as to which secrets have still to come to light. Of course, since then private researchers have continued their research, more or less unofficially. In 1987, the biologist Dr Fricke reported that during his expeditions underwater he could make out what were very probably parts of a V-rocket. That would have been consistent with the preparatory work for the Laffarenz project mentioned above.

Three different codenames, '*Teststand* XII', '*Apparat* F' and '*Projekt Schwimmweste*', are mentioned in connection with the Laffarenz project. However, it is not exactly clear whether they all related to the same thing.[224] It is striking that the actual work on the Laffarenz project was only seriously begun during the final months of 1944. That too is consistent with numerous other instances of miracle weapons development. Probably, in that connection, clear priorities only emerged after the development of the relevant warheads had reached a stage that promised to be successful. Valuable time had been lost.

In the meantime, scientists in Peenemünde had already calculated that the new Type XXI U-boats would be able to tow three submersible containers under water. They would measure 30-32 metres in length and travel at a speed of 12 nautical miles per hour. Once they had arrived at the launch point, the containers were to be brought to an oblique position by filling a gas cell. They would be held in that position ready for launch by means of special stabilisers fitted to them. The submersible containers had a design similar to that of a rocket, with a circular cross section, and four fins at the stern. The nose was sealed by a removable cover.

Directly below was the A-4 missile on a gyroscopically stabilised platform, surrounded by water ballast tanks. The circular service platform and a similarly circular exhaust tunnel led into the opening in the upper cover. Behind, were the control area, the tanks with their rocket propellants, and finally another water ballast tank in the stern. Once close to the target, the tank was to be flooded and bring the submersible container into the vertical position from which it would launch the rocket. Then the rocket technicians would climb out of the U-boat and prepare the rocket for launch. After fuelling the rocket, it was planned that it could be launched by remote control. Finally, from the bridge of the U-boat, the rocket would be launched and guided to the target by means of radio waves, i.e. guide beams.

For the voyage across the Atlantic, at an underwater speed of twelve knots, it was calculated that it would take about 30 days to reach the planned target in the USA. During that time the rocket unit would be supplied by electricity from the U-boat. Propellants such as liquid oxygen and ethyl alcohol could have been carried in the submersible containers beside the rocket. Appropriately large fuel containers could have compensated for the loss of liquid oxygen on the voyage.

The project was to be developed jointly by the Stettin Vulkan shipyard and the Schichau shipyard in Elbing. For that reason, as early as 9 December 1944, a comprehensive discussion took place at Weapons Testing Section 10 (Rockets).

Research does not agree as to how the project then progressed.[225] On the one hand it was planned to conclude the preliminary investigations in Peenemünde by the end of March 1945, but Peenemünde had been evacuated in February 1945. By then, work may have already been completed. On the other hand, however, many researchers state that A-4 transport containers were produced by the Vulkan shipyard in Stettin, and the Schichau shipyard in Elbing. The number of completed launch containers, cited by them, ranges from 1 to 24.

At the end of 1944 and the beginning of 1945, the old U-boat U-1063 carried out underwater towing trials without any problems.[226] The adaptation of the Type XXI

U-boats, to carry A-4 rockets, was to be carried out by the Blohm & Voss Company in Hamburg, and Weser AG in Bremen. How far work progressed on implementing such special measures on the Type XXI U-boats is unknown. Large numbers of them were certainly awaiting final fitting in Hamburg and Bremen.

The rocket that it was planned to use on the U-boat was a special version of the V-2. It was suitable for a long sea voyage and was capable of being stored. Most likely it was not intended to use the conventional 1-tonne warhead usually fitted to the standard V-2. As with the U-boat V-1s, the Laffarenz project was also expected to have limited accuracy, despite all the measures taken to guide the missile. But, in the case of radiological and nuclear weapons, that would not have been so important. The similarity in timescale between the Laffarenz project, and other similar miracle weapons, is also certainly more than coincidental. The great probability that in actual fact it was intended to fit the V-2 with nuclear warheads will be discussed in the following volume.

Perhaps it would explain the purpose of that new kind of underwater towing system. It was an alternative to the technically risky A-9/A-10 intercontinental rocket. A Type XXI U-boat could carry three times as many warheads, as the latter, across the Atlantic and then attack several targets in succession. But it was not known how the temperamental A-4 rockets would withstand the voyage across the North Atlantic.

The Americans were very well informed about the German efforts, both by German informers and their own agents. That was to have tragic consequences for the U-boats of *Gruppe Seewolf*.[227] They were six ageing Type IXC U-boats, fitted with snorkels. In March 1945, they left their bases to resume the U-boat war in the mid-Atlantic. But that last large offensive by the older U-boats was foiled by Ultra. The Allies decoded the radio messages that were intended for the U-boats in *Gruppe Seewolf*. On their maps, the Americans followed the long voyage of the six U-boats across the ocean with great suspicion. Agents had reported that German U-boats had been fitted with equipment from which heavy rockets could be launched. Possibly the six U-boats of *Gruppe Seewolf* were towing those rockets to the American coast to launch them against New York.

In actual fact the *Seewolf* U-boats had no rockets on board. All the same, a wretched fate was in store for them. The Americans sent a total of four combat groups, with four aircraft carriers, and a total of 20 destroyers against the six U-boats. Across the ocean, in deep formation, and over a broad front, the American warships sealed off the route of the six U-boats. Within a very short time, U-1235, U-880, U-516 and U-546 were destroyed. Allied radio intelligence gave them no chance of survival. Only two U-boats, U-585 and U-805, remained in American waters until the German surrender.

However, in spite of the Americans holding the trump cards, the cracked code and obsolete technology, to the almost grotesque balance of power, two of the old U-boats slipped through the tightly woven net. If the *Seewolf* U-boats had actually been towing rockets, the surviving boats alone could have hit several cities with nuclear or radiological V-2s.

So, what now remains of the Laffarenz project? Whether development got as far as practical trials with the planned Type XXI U-boats, or trial launches, is not known. Certainly the evacuation of Peenemünde, in February 1945, prevented any further progress. If then, some rocket launch containers were produced, it raises the question as to where they are now. In any event the Allies claim that they captured none of the rocket containers. Thus it could be that even today, somewhere on the bottom of the North Atlantic or the North Sea, such containers, with or without their contents, are rusting away in seawater. It is precisely in connection with the German U-boats at the end of the war that there still remain incongruities that have not been explained.[228]

Thus, on 23 February 1945, *Grossadmiral* Dönitz still had at his command over 551 U-boats. If one counts all the U-boats that were subsequently sunk by the Allies, all those that were scuttled at the end of the war by their crews, and those that were captured intact, it only gives a total number of 404 U-boats. One might well ask what became of the remaining 147 U-boats. Even if one assumes that the fate of some individual U-boats can be explained, there still remain a considerable number of unexplained cases. Possibly the containers from the Laffarenz project were among them.

All those German ideas were further developed by the Allies. In the postwar period, the Americans carried out experiments with the aim of developing a capsule in which a ballistic V-2 rocket could be towed by a submarine.[229]

5) Alternative Plan: Underwater Atomic Bombs in New York Harbour

If one assumes that the German Reich could have succeeded in developing nuclear warheads in time, another problem arises. The question would be, how the weapons were to be taken to the desired target areas, for instance, to New York or Washington. The answer, as far as the means of transport for rockets was concerned, would be by intercontinental rockets, flying bombs, and rockets carried by U-boats, and by intercontinental aircraft.

In the event that none of those means of transport was ready for use in time, there was, according to information given by SS *Gruppenführer* Heinrich Müller, an alternative plan.[230] According to Müller, the Type XXI U-boat would be used to transport the weapons. Because of its superior capabilities, that U-boat could have easily reached the American coast under water, without being spotted by the anti-submarine defences. Then, according to Müller, '... up one of the large rivers, put the bomb into the water, fitted with a delayed-action detonator. It was quite simple. Which location would have been best suited for such an operation, Washington, or New York? The decision was not my responsibility, but I would have gone for Washington. It would have been best when the President was making a speech before the legislative assembly. That happens only once a year, as far as I know ...'

Was it probable that there was such a plan to use an 'atomic mine'? Was there the technical support, equipment and experience for such a bold undertaking?

In the first years of the war, the Italians had already been able to gain great experience in that type of conventional operation. For example, they succeeded with midget submarine attacks on ports such as Alexandria and Gibraltar. The unit created to carry out such special operations, *X a Flottiglia Mas*, had, as a further project, already planned an operation against the port of New York. It was to proceed via the so-called 'Kangaroo'. The mother submarine, Da Vinci, was to carry a specially designed Type 'C.A.' midget submarine, on the 'kangaroo principle', into the estuary of the Hudson River. From there the midget submarine could travel to the harbour under its own power. Once it had arrived, frogmen would then proceed to lay mines in the harbour. The date for carrying out that operation against New York was planned for December 1943. However, the armistice in Italy, on 8 September 1943, meant it was no longer possible to carry it out.

The 'C.A.' submarine, which was already at the Atlantic U-boat base of Bordeaux to carry out the mission, was taken over by the German *Kriegsmarine* after the armistice in September 1943. It was never used. When the submarine base was surrendered, in the spring of 1945, the submarine was found, and destroyed by the Allies. Why had the German *Kriegsmarine* kept that submarine right to the end at its Bordeaux base? The submarine 'C. A. 1', and also the further developed submarines 'C.A. 3' and 'C.A. 4', were scuttled by their own crews at La Spezia, at the time of the armistice in September 1943. Afterwards they were raised by the *X a Flottiglia Mas* of the Royal Italian Navy, which was allied to the Germans, and put back into service.

It is known that many more experiments were carried out there with those submarines. But it is not clear how long the submarines remained in La Spezia and which of them were transported from there to Germany. One of the two later submarines is said to have been used by the German *Kriegsmarine* as a study on which to base its own designs. Interestingly, despite the trials, the 'C.A.' submarines did not appear in any other operations during World War II. However, it is striking that, with the exception of the 'C.A. 2' which was captured by the Allies in Bordeaux after the end of the war, all the 'C.A.' submarines vanished 'without trace'.[231]

There are indications that there were plans for other German midget submarines to carry frogmen. Project *Grundhai* can also be seen in such a context.[232] It was a midget submarine, designed by *Versuchskommando* [Test Command] *456*, as a type of underwater work vehicle. Officially designated as a 'deep water salvage vehicle', *Grundhai* had on its bow three round searchlights, and was driven by electric motors on each side. On the deck, there was an underwater escape hatch for frogmen, and a swivel-mounted electro-magnetic claw that could be operated from inside the submarine. With the wheels and tracks fixed to the bottom of the submarine, it could also travel along the seabed. Apart from salvage work, *Grundhai* could also have been used for other operations. Breaking underwater oil pipelines, and deep-sea telephone cables, and laying underwater mines were possibilities. The midget submarine, which could dive to a maximum depth of 1000 metres, could have been called modern from its conception. But by the end of the war, development of it had only progressed to the stage of building a prototype, if available sources are to be believed.

What, then, would the German underwater atomic bomb of 1944/45 have looked like? Small uranium bombs, designed for the purpose, would very probably have been fixed directly to the sides of the midget submarine. Frogmen would later place them in groups, or individually, within the area of the target harbour. In the case of a classic atomic bomb of some 4 tonnes, one can assume that they used the principle of the towed mine. In actual fact, from the autumn of 1944, the Germans increased the number of experiments involving the towing of mines, or torpedoes, behind midget submarines.[233] Individually, the midget submarine would tow that type of underwater mine to the target location. Frogmen would then place the mine in an appropriate place and set it.

It may be that the German project from the period of the Second World War, gave the English best-selling author, Ian Fleming, the idea for the later James Bond film 'Fireball'.

The *Waffen-SS* gave responsibility for developing secret weapons to SS *Hauptsturmführer* Otto Skorzeny. He maintained close personal and professional contact with the Italian corvette captain, Prince Junio Valerio Borghese, the commander of *X a Flottiglia Mas*. Therefore, it is quite possible that the project for carrying out a nuclear attack on New York, or Washington, was developed with the assistance of the earlier Italian project and involved an alliance with the Royal Italian Navy. It is known that in 1944/45 the Royal Italian Navy made many equally revolutionary proposals for new small combat vehicles to the KdK, i.e. *Kommando der Kleinkampfmittel*. In the opinion of the Germans who evaluated the proposals, many could have been put into practice, if there had only been enough time. At the end of the war all the proposals and evaluations are said to have been sunk in a welded box in the Baltic.[234]

6) German Atomic U-Boats

A group of 75 members of the American Naval Technical Mission was detailed by ALSOS to investigate the German *Kriegsmarine* developments. They set off for Kiel even before the British troops arrived there, and before the city was formally handed over. It was believed there was a special prize to be won. For the most part, today the so-called Walther propulsion system is said to have been the main reason for the Allied interest. But there is much to suggest that in Kiel there were also many other treasures to be salvaged.[235]

In his memoirs, Albert Speer admits that from the autumn of 1942, work was being carried out by the Germans on the development of uranium engines. However, that is not as revolutionary as it first appears. The Americans, the British and the Japanese were also working during World War II on developing special atomic propulsion systems for submarines.

The rocket researcher, Krafft von Ehricke, reports that the propulsion specialist Dr Thiel had already passed some secret reports to him in November 1942. The documents, he said, also contained the design for a nuclear-powered steam turbine which Professors Heisenberg and Pose had sketched out and designed in Leipzig. In 1944, when Krafft von Ehricke spoke with Professor Heisenberg about the project, the physicist said that in his opinion the military use of a reactor, to provide propulsion systems for U-boats, should be considered as a matter of urgency.

Unfortunately we do not know how far work on that project had progressed by the end of the war. In 1945/46, the American Dr Abelson published the design for a first atomic submarine. It was based on the simple adaptation of a sodium graphite reactor plant. It is quite striking that for 'his' atomic submarine he did not use one of the usual American submarine types, such as the 'Fleet' submarine, as might have been expected. Instead, he chose for his design the advanced Type XXVI German U-boat. In fact it had not then been developed. One must ask the question whether that project was not developed with the help of captured German plans. The Naval technical mission had done an excellent job.

Even the 'teardrop' shape of the American atomic submarines had German parentage. As early as April 1944, a project was undertaken by the *Reichspost* research establishment at the HSVA[236] for a 36 metre-long U-boat that had a 'teardrop' shaped hull. The German *Reichspost* research establishment, under the direction of *Generalpostmeister* Dr Wilhelm Ohnesorge, was known to be engaged on nuclear projects such as nuclear propulsion systems for rockets. Therefore, it is quite possible that the advanced U-boat design was also intended to serve as a U-boat for nuclear research. But it was never built. However, one could speculate whether the German U-boats were perhaps the basis for the design of the American post-war nuclear submarines of the 'Scorpion' Class. There were definite plans for their development in later years.

The prize for the greatest progress in developing nuclear-powered submarines in World War II could go to the Japanese.[237] American researchers discovered four remarkable sets of original designs for large submarines, for the Imperial Japanese Navy. Unusually, the plans proposed the use of steam-powered electric propulsion systems, instead of the diesel-powered electric propulsion systems usual in Japanese submarines. In their opinion there is almost no doubt that the designs were intended as a basis for nuclear boilers, which were to be powered by uranium in heavy water. Three of them planned to use pure uranium metal, whereas the fourth, smaller propulsion system probably required slightly enriched uranium.

All the designs show a significant difference from later post-war nuclear reactor designs, with the exception of the original French project *La Gymnote*. The project did not succeed because, although the reactor did work, it was too heavy for the planned U-boat hull. In this context it would be interesting to know what the British World War II nuclear submarine design was to look like. Apparently it was developed at the same time as the first Japanese project.

The two earliest Japanese designs were intended to use Type I-400 and C submarine hulls. In reference books the Type C propulsion plant is usually marked 'unknown'. There are indications that the Japanese began work on building their first nuclear submarines as early as 1944. Perhaps the Japanese, with German help, won the race for building the first nuclear submarine.

There might also have been other revolutionary submarine developments in the Third Reich. Again and again reports emerge, claiming that in addition to the Walther cycle and nuclear propulsion systems, other 'advanced' U-boat propulsion systems had been designed. Details concerning them are very scanty. They range from a system that perfected the Walther propulsion system, the so-called *Duellantriebslage*, through pure hydrogen propulsion plants to electromagnetic systems. The new types of propulsion system were intended to be used in Types XXXI and XXXII U-boats, among others.

An experimental U-boat of an old type, fitted with a *Duellantrieb*, is said to have attained the unheard-of speed of 75 knots, in tests run under water.[238] Even much higher speeds, and extreme ranges of up to 45,000 kilometres, were envisaged during the last months of the war.[239] The Glückauf engineering office itself had designs for a 'flying U-boat' on its drawing boards.[240] A bold project of that kind, even today, has not been realised, despite individual, perhaps copied, post-war designs from American aircraft companies. It is therefore no surprise that this former German project, like all the others, perhaps with the exception of the nuclear U-boat variants, remains 'forgotten', even today. There must be many relevant documents still to be found.

In World War II, as the Allies themselves admitted, Germany possessed revolutionary submarine designs that were many years in advance of their own.[241] The question is whether the full details will ever be found.

7) Kriegsmarine *1946: Super-Battleships with Nuclear Defences for the Post-war Period*

Why were plans still being drawn up for German battleships in 1944? On 26 August 1942, an interview took place between Adolf Hitler and *Grossadmiral* Raeder.[242] Their discussions recognised that the continuing construction of battleships depended upon the outcome of the naval war between the USA and Japan. The battleship would probably be obsolete within a short time even if it were to carry the heaviest guns. Although the armament situation at the time did not allow units to be constructed, Hitler nevertheless ordered investigations to be made into the construction of very heavy naval guns of 45.5 to 53.0cm calibre by the Krupp Company. According to Hitler, such guns were intended for battleships that would be the biggest built to that date. They would fulfil every imaginable technical and tactical requirement.

But the further course of the war drove developments in an entirely different direction. As a result there was no more talk of large-scale fleet construction. But it is striking that, on the basis of Hitler's August 1942 directive, further battleship designs were developed right up to the end of the war. At that time Hitler still gave great importance to battleships. In fact, by special request of the Fuhrer, the German naval attaché in Tokyo, Admiral Wernecker, was allowed to carry out a short inspection of one of the super-battleships of the 'Yamato' Class. On the basis of that visit to the shipyard, the observant Admiral was able to cable to Berlin a detailed description of the type. On 22 August 1943 Erich Gröner, one of the leading naval experts at the time, was shown Admiral Wernecker's Yamato report at Führer headquarters. Under the greatest secrecy he was to produce an exact drawing of the ship based on that report.

One must remember that it all happened at a time when German large-scale ship construction had officially been long since discontinued.[243] The work on German super-battleships may only have involved design studies, as is maintained today, or perhaps it involved much more.

In the preliminary designs of 1941, H-41 was a type with a displacement of 80,000 tonnes that had already been achieved.[244] In the post-war period, tonnage of that kind was only achieved in 1961, with the production of the American nuclear aircraft carrier 'Enterprise'. It had a displacement of 76,000 tonnes. The 'Battleship Design 1943', H-43, showed a ship 330 metres in length and an envisaged displacement of 111,000 tonnes. In addition, it was to be equipped with naval artillery with a principal calibre of 50.8 centimetres.

The high point was reached with 'Battleship Design 1944', H-44, which once again increased the size of the previous design and further increased the ship's defences by maintaining the armament. Even the power plant, in comparison with the previous design, remained unchanged. It comprised a mixed diesel turbine propulsion system, providing a total of 28,000 WPS, giving the design a maximum speed of 30.1 knots. It is striking that the H-44 design, despite the fact that it represented an increase in size on the H-43 design, showed no increase in armour plating. The increase in weight compared with the previous design must therefore be based on additional internal defensive measures that are not shown on the plan of the ship.

Did marine construction planning, from 1944, involve investigations as to how such battleships could be protected against enemy atomic bombs? Perhaps it was hoped that such a giant ship would be able to emerge victorious from future sea battles by using atomic weapons. Conventional ships, such as aircraft carriers, would not then be used. Under pre-atomic circumstances, it was clear to the planners that by 1941 the era of the battleship was already over.

It is conceivable that the principal armament could have been atomic 50.8cm naval shells driven by the *Trommsdorf* ramjet propulsion system, and remote-controlled flying bombs such as the *Enzian*. Work was also carried out on designing a defensive version of the Bachem *Natter*.[245]

It should be noted that American post-war nuclear tests at Bikini Atoll showed battleships, even older battleships, were able to withstand the explosion of atomic bombs to a quite considerable extent.

Of course it is not being maintained here that the H-44 battleships were directly connected with the Third Reich's nuclear weapons planning programme. However, against the background of our knowledge of such weapons developments, it is always interesting to investigate whether apparently 'inexplicable' developments can perhaps be explained within the context of the nuclear plans.

Once built, the ships of the H-44 class were expected to put all previous developments in technology and fighting power in the shade. They were to be deployed with a massive radius of operations, largely independent of land bases. Because such large ships could not be accommodated in normal harbours, the largest wartime harbour of all time was to be built in Trondheim, on the Norwegian coast. There, it was planned to construct five huge basins for large ships such as battleships. It was planned that the huge naval bases would, in the post-war period, serve as the basis for naval command of the seas.[246]

Fortunately, the H-44 battleships never needed to show whether their defensive measures were sufficient. It is striking that, even in the time of the Third Reich's greatest affliction, obviously the weapons for the next but one conflict were already being planned.

PART III

The Miracle That Never Happened

Germany's Futile 'Fight for Time'

From the end of July 1944, Hitler subordinated all war operations to the overriding task of gaining enough time to allow the new German miracle weapons to be completed and deployed. Many *Wehrmacht* units were sacrificed at that time, as a result of Hitler's apparently senseless orders to stand and fight. The only aim was to gain a few more days to continue the war. In that context, *Reichsminister* Goebbels also said to his personal advisor, von Oven: 'Now we have to do everything, and neglect nothing that can damage the enemy and hold them up, anything that can give us more time for Fate to turn to our advantage'.

In actual fact, at the beginning of 1945, even after the failure of the German Ardennes offensive, in the highest American circles hopes for a quick victory had faded. The pessimism was such that even experienced commanders, such as US Air Force General Arnold, temporarily doubted their current strategy.[247] Yet after so many years of war, gradually the point had been reached at which all the capacity for improvisation, and all the reserves of the Third Reich were beginning to slacken. Losses in personnel could only be replaced by ever younger recruits, for whose training there was no time left.

The Allied fuel potential at the beginning of 1944 was 100 times that of Germany. As early as August 1944, the time allotted for test runs of new German propulsion systems, fresh from the factory, had to be reduced from two hours to half an hour. It is hard to imagine the conditions, in which the miracle weapons had to be produced under a ceaseless hail of bombs. One must even consider that, because of the prevailing shortages, inadequate tyres on military vehicles almost became the norm. From October 1944, rock salt had to be mixed with conventional explosives, to make them go further. Everything was just '*ersatz* material', even foodstuffs. Thus there was bread mixed with sawdust, sugar was produced from wood, and butter from coal.[248] But would sacrificing and forgoing all those things be enough to continue the war?

After the Upper Silesian industrial district was lost to the Russians, in January 1945, the conventional armament of the Third Reich received the *coup de grace* from Operation 'Clarion'. In that large-scale Allied operation, beginning on 22 February 1945, daily raids by more than 9,000 aircraft destroyed over 200 railway centres. In the area of Western Germany alone, the air raids by the Allied aircraft destroyed among other things, 10,111 locomotives, 112,181 railway wagons and 2,395 railway bridges. Thus the entire amount of material produced in the last two months of the war, intended to be sent to the Front, was either destroyed, or lay unused in long rows of railway wagons whose routes were blocked. An attempt was made to repair the crippled German transport system, but it failed. Collapse was imminent.

Operation 'Clarion' practically guaranteed the collapse of the German war machine. At the time Albert Speer, in a 'Secret Reich Report' for Hitler, estimated that a period of only four to eight weeks stood between the German economy and total collapse. Finally, the only remaining question was whether the reserves of men and material that Germany still possessed would last long enough for the miracle weapons to be deployed.

Generalfeldmarschall Kesselring had finally become the Supreme Commander in the West. According to him, in March 1945, Hitler was still unshakeable in his expectation of success from the defence of the Oder front in the East. Kesselring himself expected to be able to stabilise the Western front along a line extending through Weser - Werra - Main - Altmuhl - Lech. He believed the supreme German leadership would be able to exploit such a situation 'in a meaningful way'.[249] Whatever that may have meant.

Even that decisive final battle, in which so many soldiers and civilians had been sacrificed, was lost by the Third Reich in the face of Allied superiority. It is a miracle in itself that, after 'Clarion', it was possible to put up any resistance at all for another two-and-a-half months. Despite that, and in the face of everything we are told today, the outcome of the war must, in the opinion of some, have been a really close thing.

We know now that the weapons on which the leadership of the Third Reich had set their hopes really did exist. It is true that a series of some very promising developments were not then quite completed, nor were some even begun. In the case of the German atomic bombs, however, progress had reached such an advanced stage that it was possible to foresee that they could soon be deployed.

Could it have been intended to hurl those weapons into the battle, in order to bring about a favourable outcome of a war that, in conventional terms, had already been lost.

Some years later, Winston Churchill wrote that World War II really only came to an end at 'five minutes to midnight'. Dr Osenberg was the director of the planning office of the Reich Research Commission (RFR). By virtue of his office he was very closely informed of all German developments. After the war, in an Allied secret report of 17 May 1945, he stated his conviction that, 'if the war had lasted six months longer, the Germans would have been in a position to use most of their new developments against the Allies. They would have been able to turn the course of the war, because of their technological superiority'. Hermann Göring, after he was captured, said almost exactly the same to the Americans.

Did Hitler know about the 'Manhattan Project'?

The American Manhattan project, to produce atomic bombs, was one of the USA's most closely guarded secrets. For years, the security experts and the military assumed that no unauthorised person knew anything about it. Then, in 1950, it was revealed that a European émigré scientist by the name of Klaus Fuchs, who was himself involved in one of the first United States 'Black World' Projects, had given away important nuclear secrets to the Russians.[250] Something known to only a few, is that the Germans and Japanese also succeeded, during the war, in breaking the secret of the Manhattan project.

Thus, after the war, SS *Gruppenführer* Heinrich Müller, known as 'Gestapo' Müller, reported that the SS Main Security Office had succeeded in intercepting and decoding most of the radio messages which the Soviet spy ring around Klaus Fuchs had sent to Moscow, regarding atomic weapons.[251] Another Communist spy ring, in the Ottawa area of Canada, similarly provided Moscow with decisive information concerning the American nuclear secrets. It, too, was identified by the Germans. After the difficult code had been cracked, its messages were intercepted and decoded. For the express purpose of evaluating such data, in April 1944, Hans Ogilvie founded *Amt VI W:/T* in the RSHA (Reich Main Security Office) under Walter Schellenberg.[252]

The intelligence gained in that way was to have been used to inform the SS of the progress the Americans had been making in their atomic bomb project, and thus to save their own development capacity. All the data from that espionage was made available to the scientists of the SS nuclear weapons programme. According to *Gruppenführer* Muller, that would have drastically reduced the time required for his own team to carry out their experiments. Interestingly, however, the SS radio intelligence information was not made available to the other 'competing' atomic bomb research teams. Petty jealousies, or security considerations, may have been the deciding factor. Considering the incredible extent of treachery, especially in the field of secret weapons, the latter was only too likely.

Apart from radio intelligence, it was principally the Spanish super-spy, Alcazar de Velasco,[253] with his network of spies, who cracked the 'Manhattan' project for the Germans and the Japanese. The activities of his espionage network called TO, stretched from Canada, right down into South America. The network was only discovered in the spring of 1944. The FBI still possesses about 10,000 pages of documents concerning Alcazar de Velasco and his TO spy-ring. They are kept secret to this day. An American journalist, who wanted to see those papers concerning a question relating to the 'Freedom of Information Act', was only told by telephone that the papers contained 'real hot stuff'!

Nevertheless, as we now know, Alcazar de Velasco was able to provide the Germans and Japanese with a precise picture of the American work on the atomic bomb. For that reason, in June 1943, he even had a personal meeting with Adolf Hitler, to tell him the important results achieved by one of his spies, with the code name 'Sebastian'. At that meeting, Alcazar de Velasco informed Hitler about the current state of information. According to it, work on the American nuclear weapon had indeed made significant progress, but still had a long way to go. His comments even contained remarks on the planned detonator for an atomic bomb. The detonator, according to Alcazar, was similar to that which had already been used, as early as 1943, by the Germans. The remaining material principally concerned earlier US plans to produce an atomic bomb. In any event, the information must have been important enough for the Spaniard to risk the dangerous two-way mission, between America and Germany, in order to report personally to Hitler.

It appears that there was an attempt to prevent him from reaching his destination. His aircraft was shot down on the way to Berlin. However, only slightly wounded, having a parachute he was able to bail out. In fact Admiral Canaris, the chief of German military intelligence at that time, took him aside before the planned discussion, and warned him that Hitler would not like his report. Perhaps Canaris wanted to prevent him handing over the information. Alcazar de Velasco, however, reported that his interview with Hitler was in the presence of Himmler, and passed off quietly. Velasco said that at the end of his report Hitler nodded agreement, and said that it was true.

Until the beginning of 1944 Alcazar de Velasco's network continued working both for the Germans and for the Japanese. It is not known what conclusions the Germans drew from the results of his espionage. However, Japanese sources often remarked that the Japanese concluded from his reports that the United States had indeed made respectable progress in atomic bomb research. But it was known that the US was still a long way from bringing the 'project' to a conclusion. Despite that knowledge, when the atomic bombs began to be dropped on Japan, it is said that the Japanese were very surprised. That may be the reason why, until now, the documents relating to de Velasco and TO have been kept secret. Their publication may perhaps reveal that, without the infusion of German nuclear research material from April 1945, the 'Manhattan Project' would not have been completed so soon, or even at all.

After it was uncovered in the summer of 1944, the remaining members of the Alcazar de Velasco network ceased their work. It was then only with great difficulty that the Germans were able to obtain direct reports from agents concerning the American atomic bomb. One of the direct sources that still remained could have been the determined spy Alfred Meiler, alias Walter Kohler, alias Albert von Loop. Until recently it had been regarded as certain that Alfred Meiler defected to the Americans even before his planned mission in the USA. Therefore, it was as a double agent that he fed German military intelligence with disinformation from 1942 to 1945.

However, in the intervening period, it has been proved that, from the outset, Meiler was working as a 'triple agent' within the framework of a cover story, cleverly prepared by German military intelligence. In fact he was only playing the part of a double agent for the benefit of the FBI.[254] His espionage network operated 'with the involuntary approval' of the FBI, until the end of the war. Walter Schellenberg even considers him to have been one of the best German agents. It is not known if Meiler was also able to carry out espionage on American nuclear secrets. But it can be no coincidence that, before he was sent to America in 1942, he had been specially instructed, in Paris, concerning nuclear research, by the Reich Research Commission chemist Henry Albers. Thus, even if we do not know what results he achieved, nuclear espionage was one of the tasks of Schellenberg's 'best spy'.

In order to obtain further up-to-date reports, concerning the crucial events on the other side of the Atlantic, attempts were made to take agents directly to America by U-boat. Several such U-boat landings were subsequently made in the USA. Many of them were never discovered.[255] One of the known attempts[256] failed, on 20 August 1944, when U-1229 was sunk by an American aircraft. As a result, the special agent Oskar Mantel became a prisoner of war. The official line is that he had been ordered to find out details concerning the combat readiness of American jet aircraft. But, according to the results of the latest research, it is probable that in actual fact he also had the far more extensive task of providing information concerning the American atomic bomb. *Sonderführer* Mantel succeeded in concealing important facts from his American interrogators, concerning his career and his plans. Mantel, who survived the war, had previously had close contacts with the highest circles of the top German leadership. He had even been several times on the Obersalzberg with Adolf Hitler. That, too, illustrates how important the nuclear problem was to the Führer of the Third Reich, and that all assertions to the contrary cannot be made to agree with the actual facts.

The last known attempt, to take German agents to the American coast by U-boats, was the so-called Operation 'Elster'. U-1230 successfully landed agents Gimpel and Colepaugh on the coast, on 30 November 1944. Colepaugh proved to be a traitor and finally caused the joint mission to fail. But, by 25 December 1944, Gimpel succeeded in radioing decisive information to Berlin. From an American businessman, he found out that the American atomic bomb would be ready for use in five to six months. But it was thought that the Americans only had two to three bombs. Berlin is said to have confirmed his 8-10 minute radio message. The account is based on information given personally by Gimpel. It is clear that there are no official German documents in existence relating to the mission, because at the end of the war they would certainly have been destroyed.

The second part of the mission was to sabotage the 'Manhattan Project'. Gimpel was to form a group of assassins, who were to carry out attacks with explosives, on installations associated with the atomic bomb programme. Money and men had already been made available in South America for that purpose. Because of the betrayal of the mission by Colepaugh, however, that part of the mission was not carried out. Gimpel was arrested on 30 December 1944.

Operation 'Elster' was, as mentioned above, the last known U-boat operation against the USA. But that in no way excludes the possibility that there were later operations of the same kind which, until now, have been hushed up, or perhaps were never discovered. The importance of information gained in that way for the Third Reich leadership cannot be overestimated. On the one hand it helped them to shorten the time they themselves required for research. On the other hand, in connection with the German plans to deploy their own nuclear weapons, it was extremely important to obtain information concerning possible developments of enemy offensive or defensive measures.

In any event, in the short term, the subjective impression arises that the German leadership was not too concerned about the expected danger of American nuclear attacks on Germany. But, in the medium term, plans had been set in place to secure the most important underground installations of the 'Xaver Dorsch Organisation' against nuclear attack. Ingenious protection measures were devised for that purpose.

The assumption is that the Germans knew all about the expected effects of nuclear attacks. Without having the results of tests of their own nuclear weapons, however, this would not have been possible. Thus the German leadership succeeded in obtaining an almost precise picture of the stage reached by American plans for the atomic bomb, at least up to the end of 1944. The other information, obtained by radio intelligence, could well have extended far beyond that period.

Were there Training and Testing Units for Miracle Weapons?

It can be assumed, with a probability bordering on certainty, that there must have been special experimental and testing command centres for German nuclear weapons. Such training and testing command centres must, under the pressure of war and after the quickest action at the front, have been formed very early on. Therefore they must have been formed before the weapons testing had been finally completed, and the weapons were ready for front-line service. From the point of view of the testing stations, the tasks of the training and testing command centres were similar to those involved with other new types of weapon.

Tests needed to be carried out, with regard to the operation of the weapons by troops. Instructional material had to be prepared as to how the weapons should be handled. In addition, the technical conditions for their deployment needed to be studied. Experience, later gained in using them, also needed to be evaluated.

The first of the testing command centres could have been active as early as June 1944.[257] At that time, trials had already been carried out in launching empty nuclear weapons casings from aircraft, but they failed. Another idea that was tested was dropping the container from a great height by parachute.

Unfortunately, to date there has been no success in identifying the testing unit that carried out the trial drops. But one clue, in looking for the unit, is the fact that the training and testing command centres could not have been stationed very far from the place where the respective nuclear weapons were being produced. Otherwise necessary collaboration could not have been maintained under the traffic conditions prevailing during the war. As a result of the continuing war, which brought ever more pressing and narrower restrictions, that 'short distance requirement' had been implemented in relation to other weapons systems.[258] It could also have obtained in the case of the miracle weapons.

Thus, if one wishes to discover more details in that connection after so many years, one must look for the relevant units, for example, on airfields close to Peenemünde, Ohrdruf, Innsbruck and Melk, etc. Such secret command centres could well have been connected with the *Geschwader* KG 200, or KG 100, and linked with the KdE. (*Kommando der Erprobungseinheiten*, i.e. the Test Units Command) Probably they were equipped with a mixture of various types of aircraft such as the He 177, a drop aircraft, the Bf 109, a drop aircraft, the Ju 87, a drop aircraft, the He 111, an observation aircraft, or the Fi 156, a communications and observation aircraft.

In February 1945, *E. Kdo 41* was formed, and given *Feldpost* number 61405.[259] That may provide a clue. Perhaps that mysterious unit, together with the famous *E. Kdo 600*, the manned rocket *Natter*, was one of the last German *Luftwaffe* test units to be formed. It may have had something to do with nuclear weapons plans. If that was the case, it could also be the final proof that by then there was a plan to use the new weapon in action. Admittedly, the 'nuclear units' could have been completely new, special command centres, about which nothing is known today, because all information relating to them is either under lock and key, or has been destroyed.

It is even possible that, for security reasons, the SS was involved. Unfortunately, little is known about the aviation units that the SS actually had. There is, however, clear evidence of connections between the atomic bomb programme and 'Himmler's *Luftwaffe*'. He had to provide protection for the nuclear weapons programme. Thus, as early as 1943, Heinrich Himmler sent the VI Squadron of *SS-Fliegergruppe z.b.V. 7* to Norway, where its Fieseler Fi 156s operated out of an airstrip close to the Rjukan heavy water factory.[260] In February 1944, the various *SS-Fliegergruppen z.b.V. 7* were enlarged to form *SS-Fliegergeschwader z.b.V. 7*. Their activities during the war remain largely unknown. In November 1944, the *SS-Flieger-Korps*, which consisted of voluntary pilots only, was added to the other units. Their task was to prepare revolutionary jet, pulse and rocket aircraft for operational use.[261] It would be amazing if the SS had not had similar intentions for the planned deployment of the atomic bomb.

Other remarkable events occurred earlier on 15, 16 and 22 June 1944 when the SS, with the approval of the RLM, produced 12 Horten Ho III, and 10 Horten Ho IX aircraft for 'test purposes'. As if the purpose and location of that aircraft mission were not already quite mysterious, the same document states that, as agreed, of the 12 Ho III aircraft, two were to be placed at the disposal of the *Reichsführer-SS* as courier aircraft. But the Ho III was a single- or two-seater glider, whose suitability for use as a 'courier aircraft' appears extremely dubious. It is far more likely that the document was referring to a 'disguised' operation, the real purpose of which was concealed. Significantly, one of the personnel appointed to *SS-Führungsamt* 'Amt X' was a certain *Ingenieur* Schaller. In 1945 he was to play a decisive role in the formation of *Ekdo 600*, and the first use of the *Natter* manned rocket.

However, some questions remain unanswered. What did the SS want to test with those flying-wing aircraft? Were there any radar-deflecting 'Stealth' experiments? It is known that Horten was also experimenting with aircraft made of synthetic material. Were there preparations for the later 'America bomber' programme? Was there pilot training, or attack training?

Through *Obergruppenführer* Kammler, the entire secret weapons development programme had fallen into the hands of Himmler's people. Therefore it is probable that the SS would, at the very least, have some involvement in the planned bombing missions. But the search for such SS training and testing command units could be a very difficult undertaking. To date nothing is known of them.

Why were the Nuclear Weapons never used?

There is clear evidence that Hitler had grasped the importance of the effect of nuclear weapons on the course of the war. Post-war assertions to the contrary are wrong. On the basis of the available material it also seems clear that German nuclear weapons did in fact exist. From the summer of 1944, most of the Third Reich's efforts, in the field of armaments, were directed towards making operational use of those weapons. Radiological weapons and atomic bombs, as such, must be considered separately here, because they played different roles in Hitler's understanding of 'victory weapons'.

Germany's radiological isotope weapons were ready first, from November 1943/January 1944, then came the uranium bombs from the summer of 1944, and finally, only shortly before the end of the war, the plutonium bombs, from April 1945. In his book, *Meine Kommandounternehmen* ('My command operations') (pages 149/50, Universitas, 1993), Otto Skorzeny states that, in October 1944, the talk was mainly of 'another terrible weapon which was to be based on artificially produced radioactivity'.

Hitler's attitude to the radiological weapons was ambiguous. He only wanted to use them as first-strike weapons, after it had been possible to create defensive measures to protect the German population. But, at the end of the war, such protective measures against gamma radiation were not available, or not available in sufficient quantity.

However, on 6 July 1944, Churchill wanted to give the order for biological and chemical weapons to be used against the German civilian population. It was to be seen as retribution for German V-1 attacks on southern England. But it could then have caused German radiological weapons to be deployed as a 'response' to any British poison gas and biological attacks.[262] Hitler's temptation was to annihilate the entire population of London, and to irradiate wide areas of southern England as retribution. The temptation would have been too great not to use the isotope weapons.

The serious destruction of Britain's political infrastructure by such an attack, at a time when it was believed that the German enemy was collapsing, could well have meant that Britain ceased to take any further part in the war. The American government would also have been placed in a very difficult position if, after that, Hitler had made diplomatic overtures that were coupled with the threat of also using such weapons against American cities. In that context, it becomes clear why Eisenhower, and also Churchill's own staff, exercised pressure on the British Prime Minister to drop his intention of using gas and bacteria against Germany. Therefore, on 28 September 1944, after a long period of consideration, Churchill's idea was buried. There was obviously fear of what the public reaction would be in the event of a German retribution attack.

In that connection, it must not be forgotten that the Americans were best informed about the availability of the German isotope weapons. They had originally expected the weapons to be first used at the Normandy invasion, in June 1944.[263] But there too, for the reasons stated above, Hitler would not have permitted them to be used. Thus, because there were no protective measures for the German people, Germany's isotope bombs were never used by Hitler before the end of the war.

If the atomic bomb is considered separately, in July 1944 development work on the weapon had been completed. From the middle of October it was in full production. Although great efforts were made to create means of intercontinental transport for miracle weapons, it appears that the first priority was given to using them on the battlefield. That would have the advantage that no untested long-range carrier systems were necessary.

In addition, using atomic weapons on the frontline promised to provide better possibilities for negotiations after an attack. It would then be possible to increase the stakes to a threat, of 'bombarding capital cities with miracle weapons'. The disadvantages of tactical use were that, before they could be used with sufficient effect on a long front line, a large number of the weapons first needed to be produced.

Similarly, significantly larger numbers of personnel were needed than for individual attacks on enemy capitals. Also, most importantly, it would be necessary for a large number of people to be 'in the know' about the weapons. In fact that was certainly one of the reasons for the failure of Hitler's plans for miracle weapons.

Winter 1944/45: the Ardennes offensive

If the available sources are to be regarded as reliable, it was intended that the first use of atomic bombs would be made within the framework of the Ardennes offensive, which had the German code name *Wacht am Rhein*.[264] Preparations were made for it in such secrecy that the enemy, despite intensive espionage and the decoding advantages provided by Enigma, were taken completely by surprise. The German offensive initially threatened to become a terrible disaster for the Allies in the West. Hitler wanted to end the war in the West at a stroke. By means of a bold thrust, motorised forces were to advance from the Ardennes to Antwerp and thus cut off the Americans and the British from their supplies. If that had happened, the US troops would have suffered the heaviest defeat in their history. The most recent research even suggests that it was likely that the US Congress, in such an event, would have forced the US Army to be brought home. Field Marshal Montgomery, the British Supreme Commander on the Western front, subsequently said: 'If that German plan had succeeded, then no second 'miracle of Dunkirk' would have helped us, because Dunkirk was still in German hands'.[265]

For that battle Hitler unceasingly ordered fuel and ammunition to be made available. The Eastern Front was stripped of almost all its armoured troops and reserves in order, by that last throw of the dice, to be able to achieve one more victory in the West. In that decisive offensive operation, for which everything had been mapped out, it was also planned to use from 6 to 12 atomic bombs. Otto Skorzeny, in *'Meine Kommandounternehmen'* (page 150, Universitas, 1993), reports that in October 1944, Hitler assured him that, in the course of the offensive, new revolutionary weapons would be used that would take the enemy completely by surprise. He said that despite treason and mistakes, the German Army would be victorious

In the winter of 1944/45, when the Ardennes offensive was about to begin, the modern German miracle weapons' carriers were not yet ready for frontline service. The available, conventionally powered, German bombers and fighter-bombers would, in daylight, have been almost helpless against the Allied fighter defences. Possibly the large-scale *Luftwaffe* attack, designated Operation *Bodenplatte*, was intended to be launched at the beginning of the Ardennes offensive. It had to weaken the Allied fighters and their ground organisation. The success of that plan was necessary before the planned use of the German atomic bombers. They had also to ensure that the slow aircraft would be able to get through. Hitler had only just forced through Operation *Bodenplatte* against the strong resistance of high-ranking *Luftwaffe* generals, such as Adolf Galland, who did not understand the purpose of such an offensive.

Although the Ardennes offensive began on 16 December 1944, Operation *Bodenplatte* was repeatedly postponed and only began on 1 January 1945. At that time, many of the German forces which it was planned to use in the operation, had already been heavily decimated in the previous fighting. As is now known, the attack itself was wrongly implemented, by the *Luftwaffe* General Staff, at what were important moments. But with the pyrrhic victory, achieved through Operation *Bodenplatte*, it was possible to gain a pause of only one week, in the tactical air war. That week could have been exploited for the planned deployment of miracle weapons.

However, the supposedly 'planned' nuclear weapons attack during the Ardennes offensive, never took place. The reasons given were the poor atmospheric and weather conditions, i.e. unfavourable west winds prevailing in the initial stage of the operation. They would have led to German troops being put at risk. Then, when it was decided to use the bombs, they could not be found, because, as it turned out, they had already been moved into depots far to the rear. Hitler demanded, 'Where are my atomic bombs?' He also threatened a court-martial. The outcome is not known. It could have been a secret trial.[266]

From the tactical point of view, using atomic bombs in the Ardennes, especially during the first days of the offensive, could well have been decisive. But, from the second week of January 1945, such a measure no longer made any sense. The German offensive forces had already been largely exhausted by that time.

It remains unknown today who was to fly that operation, or which aircraft types were to be used with which weapons. Were operational and dropping tests carried out beforehand, or was such a practice operation never carried out because of the extreme secrecy associated with the Ardennes offensive? An attack with both heavy bombers, He 177s, and lighter aircraft, Bf 109s or Fw 190s, would have been conceivable. A possible clue was provided by *Sonderverband Einhorn*, i.e. the Special Unit Unicorn. It was planned that the unit would carry out individual suicide attacks against crucial Allied targets. The attacks were to involve Fw 190 aircraft carrying very heavy bombs.

It is known that *Sonderverband Einhorn* was also standing by for the Ardennes offensive. But nothing has ever become known of its activities in those critical days. There is even some question as to whether the unit was ever in action or was only standing in readiness. That is also the case with the 2/KG 100. It was specially equipped with 44 conventional Heinkel He 177 A-5 long-range bombers. The unit was also standing by in readiness for the Ardennes offensive, but remarkably, the specialist literature hardly ever mentions it in that context. In fact 2/KG 100 does not seem to have been in action in the Ardennes.[267] So there is plenty of material for further research. In addition to those two units, there is also the question of other secret

Sonderkommandos that remains unknown to this day. It would, however, be very difficult to trace them today.

The fact is that without the promised use of revolutionary weapons, the Ardennes offensive failed after great initial success. Basically, German troops did not get sufficient supplies of ammunition and fuel. Therefore the moment came when they were no longer able to put up opposition against the advancing American and British reserves. There is still discussion today, as to whether sabotage might not have been involved.

On the German side of the Rhine there were large supplies of ammunition and fuel, specially stored for that offensive. However, despite the bridges being intact, the supplies could not be brought to the troops involved on the left bank of the Rhine, before the start of the offensive. Then, when the German troops urgently needed supplies during the offensive, the transport routes and bridges over the Rhine were blocked by the massive Allied air raids which had then begun. Thus the armoured reserves, so painstakingly built up in the snowbound Ardennes, were lost. Two-thirds of German armoured casualties occurred during the retreat, when the vehicles came to a halt for lack of fuel. Whatever the real truth may be, recent works of military history reveal that the outcome of World War II, in actual fact, was only decided with the failure of the Ardennes offensive.[268]

Despite, or more precisely, because of the Ardennes offensive, the plans to deploy miracle weapons were pursued with undiminished vigour. Thus, on 24 February 1945, Adolf Hitler, in a proclamation to the NSDAP *Parteigründungstag*, stated that 'the historical turning point' in the war 'will happen this year'.

Above all it was a question of gaining the necessary time. Therefore, on 3 March 1945, Hitler, surprisingly, travelled in a column of vehicles to the headquarters of the IX Army in Bad Saarow. He had to give some motivation to General Busse and his staff for the imminent, conventional, defensive battle on the Oder. Subsequently Hitler also visited the command posts of two other divisions and returned to Berlin in the evening. However, what the published history does not say about this, is that Hitler implored Busse and his officers to hold up the Russian assault at least long enough to allow his new weapons to be ready.

In his book '*Meine Kommandounternehmen*' (pages 390-1, Universitas, 1993), Otto Skorzeny states that in mid-February 1945, he was present at a meeting at which Reich Armaments Minister Albert Speer, in Skorzeny's presence, promised Heinrich Himmler new aircraft and new bombs for the beginning of April. Skorzeny's words were: 'Nowadays, Speer assures us that at the time he considered all hope to be illusory. But on that February day I was able to talk with him for a moment. I wanted to know more about the famous 'secret weapons' about which they had been bending our ears since August 1944. He could have advised me to abandon all hope in that regard. But he contented himself with declaring that the decisive moment will 'soon come'. The following events, which remain mysterious even today, could be connected with what Speer told Skorzeny.

Western Front, end of March to beginning of April 1945

The second use by the Germans, of atomic or radiological bombs, could have been planned for the end of March or the beginning of April 1945. There are many indications pointing in that direction. The secret weapons specialist, and 'father' of the multi-chamber guns, i.e. the high-pressure pump, or HDP, was *Oberingenieur* August Coenders. He reported, in February 1945, that the new weapons that would decide the course of the war could not be deployed before April 1945.[269] Even the American General Groves, responsible for the US nuclear weapons programme, reckoned on the possibility of the German atomic bomb being used from that time.[270]

Thus, during the last days of March 1945, German leaflets were dropped over the Lower Rhine area telling the population to evacuate the planned target area. From the beginning of April, they had to expect weapons to be used against them that would decide the course of the war. Therefore a 50km-wide area had to be evacuated.[271] From a military point of view, the end of March 1945 would have been the last chance to stabilise the Western Front. It was reported that, near Münster, Bf 109s were being converted for decisive missions, carrying 250kg special bombs. Whether more units in other places were being similarly converted is, unfortunately, not known, but it is conceivable.

A contemporary eyewitness described that time of fear, and of waiting for the miracle weapons, by saying that it must have been like that in the Middle Ages when the 'dragon's breath' hung in the air at night.[272] They were then into Hitler's notorious 'all-round, five minutes to midnight defence'. With it he hoped to stabilise the collapsing fronts once more, while clearly being prepared to accept casualties among the German population.

But it appears that it was the SS who, as 'Grail Keeper' of the German secret weapons, prevented them being used by simply not releasing them to the fighting units. Perhaps political considerations were the deciding factor. It is known that from January to April 1945, Heinrich Himmler was increasingly putting out peace feelers in the direction of Britain. On 25 March 1945, he even went so far as to include the offer of an armistice. Was it intended to await the outcome of those negotiations before deploying the miracle weapons? According to, as yet, unconfirmed information, during the discussions the British were shown a photograph of a nuclear mushroom cloud from a German explosion, as proof that Germany still had powerful weapons that it could use. But the British are said to have replied that they already knew what Himmler was talking about.[273]

Other possibilities are, that at the end of March 1945 the planned deployment of atomic bombs was refused by members of the *Luftwaffe* themselves. Perhaps *Luftwaffe* personnel were responsible for not releasing the atomic bombs. Another connection may be that, on 31 March 1945, in addition to the German *General* Barber, a total of 202 members of the *Luftwaffe*, including 16 airfield commanders and 85 officers and pilots were shot for 'disobeying orders'. The question is whether those incidents were linked to what was going on in Munster and Amstetten.

Unfortunately, and unsurprisingly, remaining German original documents show gaps at precisely that point in time.[274] In the OKL, *Luftwaffe* War Diary, the period from 19 March to 30 March 1945 is missing. In the OKW, *Wehrmacht* War Diary, the documents from 1 March 1945 to 20 April 1945 have been lost. Before and after those periods, data in the diaries is more or less complete. The fact that the gaps in the war diaries, which were maintained by different people, happen to relate to the same period of preparations and discussions concerning the planned use of miracle weapons, gives food for thought. One is reminded here of the similarly 'missing' US documents concerning the American push into the Ohrdruf/Crawinkel area.[275] It could be coincidence.

At the beginning of April a plus point went to the Americans with the German loss of the secret factory there. The documents of the German leadership show how surprised they were by General Patton's sudden thrust into Thuringia and Bavaria. They had actually expected a direct American thrust to Berlin.[276] On the basis of statements known to have been made by General Patton, it seems that he knew very well why he ordered his troops to swing in that direction. The German units of the district around Stadtilm/Ohrdruf, put up a stubborn defence in an effort to seal off the secret installations. They covered up all traces and attempted to remove the weapons parts. However, the loss of the production bases still represented a decisive blow. At that time, Adolf Hitler is said to have told *General* Kammhuber that he knew himself that the war was lost.[277] That stands in striking contrast to statements he made in mid-March, in which he still assumed that 'the war would be won'.

On 3 April 1945, with his command train, *Generalfeldmarschall* Kesselring, who was the Supreme Commander on the Western Front, succeeded in leaving Ohrdruf only shortly before it fell. There were no supply reserves either for the *Wehrmacht* or the civilian population in the Harz region. On 8 April 1944 Hitler had declared the region a *Festung*. Kesselring, in agreement with four *Gauleiters* and leading Party officials, had decided not to carry out any further defence of the Harz.[278] However, despite the desperate, and to all intents and purposes hopeless war situation, there was a serious plan to retake the Harz region.[279] It may have been hoped by that operation to secure the secret weapons bases again.

From the very last conventional reserves of the Third Reich yet another new army had been formed. It was originally planned that this *Armee Wenck*, which was later given the crazy mission of relieving Hitler in Berlin, would execute a thrust into the Harz region. It is said that the aim was to cut off the Allied armies' supply lines. However, it is known that in reality different aims were planned for that operation. To ensure the success of the mission, *Oberst* Hans Ulrich Rudel was to take command of all the available jet fighters and with them to maintain clear air space over *Armee Wenck*. It was clear to the planners that a thrust into the Harz would only have a chance of succeeding if the air space could be kept clear of Allied aircraft. But *Oberst* Rudel refused the command because he was no longer convinced it could be carried out. Against twentyfold enemy air superiority even Germany's few turbine aircraft, which themselves had hardly any fuel, could only just manage to survive. Rudel's opinion was that it would only be possible to keep the air space clear for a few days. After that the jet fighters' combat capability would be nil and *Armee Wenck* would inevitably fail in the Harz, just as the 'Rundstedt Offensive' had failed earlier in the Ardennes.

Meanwhile, using his train that had been hidden in the forest, Kesselring left the Harz, to take command in the south of the Reich, as *Oberbefehlshaber Süd*. The time was imminent when the Reich would be split into a northern and a southern half. Before Kesselring took up that command, he was in the Führer Headquarters with Hitler on 12 April 1945 to get a picture of the overall situation and to learn of further plans. When Hitler left no doubt that he would never surrender, Kesselring openly voiced his own doubts as to whether there was any purpose in fighting on. Hitler then told him of a 'new, highly-explosive bomb' which would be ready for operational use 'very soon'.[280] Unfortunately, we do not know what proof or evidence Hitler presented to Kesselring that caused that experienced soldier, who was not easily fooled, to 'soldier on'. But it must have been something very convincing, because Kesselring carried out the duties of his new post with great commitment.

On 19 April 1945, after the collapse of the Oder front was announced, the advance to seize back the secret factories and their stored treasures was called off by Hitler personally. Nevertheless, after abandoning the plan, Hitler said these words to Rudel: '... Even now there are still negotiations in the air, but I do not believe that they will succeed. Therefore we must survive this war at all costs, so that decisive weapons will still be able to give us victory'. In saying that, Hitler gave Rudel to understand that, in addition to the weapons lost in Thuringia, he still believed he had more trump cards up his sleeve. Hitler's hope was not at all based on flights of fancy. His Upper Danube *Gauleiter*, Eigruber, had presented him with the prospect of a very special birthday present.

20 April 1945, Innsbruck

Another chance to use miracle weapons presented itself. On 20 April 1945, exactly on Hitler's birthday, the group around Professor Stetter, based near Innsbruck, after working without a break succeeded in completing their work on nuclear weapons.[281] Munich was just about to be taken by the Allies. Party officials, on hearing the news, enthusiastically dashed from house to house spreading the news that the German atomic bomb was ready.[282]

But at that late stage, tactical deployment of atomic bombs no longer made any sense. The area still under the control of the Third Reich had already shrunk to a rump that was too small. In the west and in the south, it was announced that the fronts were disintegrating, and on the Oder the final defensive battle was underway. The only hope remaining to the German leadership was to hold on to so-called 'islands of resistance' such as the planned *Alpenfestung*, or *Festung* Norway.

The fact that atomic bombs were once more available gave Hitler his last chance to make offensive plans. It is true that by then the only thing left to do was to attempt to strike at enemy capitals. Hitler, who had previously taken the decision to withdraw to Berchtesgaden, suddenly changed his mind and stayed in Berlin. He is said to have agreed with Hermann Göring that he would order the atomic bomb to be dropped on London, on his own responsibility. He would then commit suicide, in order to simplify Göring's negotiations with the enemy. In the event that Göring found that the Allies were not willing to sue for peace after the first bomb was dropped, he should, Hitler said, drop another atomic bomb on Moscow, one on New York, and one on Paris.

Consequently it can be assumed that, at that time, the Third Reich already had available suitable long-range transport, even if the existence of such transport is now denied. The same was also suggested by a report from the news agency AP that was published in the Washington Post of 29 June 1945.[283] According to that report, officers of the Royal Air Force had reported from the Headquarters of the XXI Corps, on 28 July 1945, that the Germans had almost completed preparations to bomb New York from a base at a 'colossal airfield' near Oslo. At the same airbase, it was said, 40 new-type Heinkel long-range bombers, each with a range of 7,000 miles, had been captured. It had been planned for them to carry bombs with a 'new kind of effect'. Therefore, it can be concluded that New York faced being bombed, and that it was only by a hairsbreadth that the USA escaped the greatest disaster in its history.

But Göring, as his statements after the war indicated, was not prepared to order such missions. Possibly he had also reflected on what the Allies might do, in revenge, to the areas of Germany already under their occupation. Even if the attacks on enemy capitals had been successful, it was uncertain if it would be those who favoured a negotiated settlement, or the merciless advocates of the *Morgenthau* Plan, who would prevail. Was this worth the incalculable risk of a nuclear strike? Perhaps we are ascribing to Göring far too noble motives here. Perhaps he just wanted to save his own skin. But apparently he said this to Hitler only after he had arrived at Berchtesgaden.[284]

Göring probably intended, as had Heinrich Himmler before him, to enter into negotiations with the Allies, and in doing so use Germany's atomic bombs as a 'dead' pledge. His plan was to fly on 24 April 1945 to the headquarters of the Allied armed forces in order to negotiate an armistice with General Eisenhower.[285] But the day before, doubtless because he had refused to use the atomic bombs, Hitler stripped him of all his offices, and he was arrested by the security service. Thus the *Reichsmarschall's* peace mission was stopped even before it had begun.

Then, on 26 April 1945, in the middle of the battle for Berlin, Adolf Hitler gave a directive to move north all the 'bombs' that had meanwhile been completed in Innsbruck. It is not hard to imagine how difficult the circumstances were for escorting that transport, since the German Reich was at the time only joined by a very thin strip, which people called 'the wasp waist'. During the attempt to transport the bombs, an act of sabotage rendered the detonators useless. The bombs were therefore taken back to Innsbruck and buried there in one of the underground caves.[286]

As a result, according to the Allies, the Germans were never able to load up the long-range bombers standing by in the far north. Even the bombs intended for Japan did not reach the waiting submarines. On the morning of 29 April 1945, when Hitler received that shattering news, he knew then that finally, it was too late. As one of his last official acts, he stopped all *Werwolf* partisan operations, installed *Grossadmiral* Dönitz as his successor and only then informed him of the existence of the Innsbruck bombs. After that, following the Russian capture of Berlin, Adolf Hitler vanished from world history, by suicide.

Grossadmiral Dönitz then had the scientific director of the Innsbruck nuclear laboratory brought to him, by a circuitous route. He asked how the Innsbruck atomic bombs could be brought to the North Sea. Dönitz 'happened' to be very near to Hamburg's zirconium factory.

Perhaps it was because he hoped soon to have available the Innsbruck atomic bombs, that the *Grossadmiral* did not move his headquarters to Prague, as General Schörner had already announced. But at that late stage it would have been impossible to move the atomic bombs, or use them, even if anyone had wanted to. Time had run out.

Dönitz ordered the director, who had travelled to see him, back to Innsbruck, saying that he would receive appropriate orders there. It is not known whether he managed to get back. The last purpose that Germany's nuclear weapons could still serve was as some sort of security. Finally, there were several parties interested in them. It is possible that, at the end of the war, an exchange of just that kind took place.[287]

On 7 May 1945, in Rheims, *Generaloberst* Jodl signed the German instrument of surrender in World War II. It is true that the situation then arose in which the Americans accepted the German surrender in the West, but that the German surrender to the Russians, on Eisenhower's instructions, had to be repeated on 9 May 1945 in Berlin. Until then, the Americans had not been troubled by what the Germans were doing on the Eastern Front. The benefit of 48 hours, between the surrender in the West and the surrender in the East, made it possible for large parts of the German army in the East, and many refugees, to move out of the Russians' grasp and into the American and British zones of occupation. Was the American procedure, involving two dates for surrender, just a coincidence?

On 10 May 1945, although the war had ended, by way of thanks for gaining that period of grace, *Generaloberst* Jodl received the Oak Leaf Cluster, to add to his Knight's Cross, from *Grossadmiral* Doenitz. It was one of the highest German decorations for bravery.[288]

For the Americans it was very important to know where the Austrian hiding places for the atomic weapons were. From April 1945 the Russians had been advancing into Austria, just as, at the same time the Americans had also been advancing into central Germany and the Czech area. But the Russians had come far beyond the lines of demarcation previously agreed among the Allies. Evidently the Russians also knew what they were looking for. In Austria there appears to have been an extraordinary kind of race, between the Americans and the Russians, in order to reach many Austrian locations. According to eyewitness reports, the race was even said to have degenerated into isolated fire-fights between the Allies.

According to American reports, the German *Kriegsmarine* was still trying to carry out an attack against New York, by U-boat V-1s, very probably with nuclear charges. But all that is still nebulous and mysterious. There were also said to be plans for using nuclear weapons on the Eastern Front, and even planned attacks using rocket-powered flying bombs, with nuclear warheads. Despite many announcements that it would happen, nuclear weapons never came to be used by the Germans.

This book tries to outline definitively the chronological sequence and circumstances surrounding the known attempts to deploy nuclear weapons. But it may not explain everything. It can be assumed, with some degree of certainty, that the final answers to the questions are still lying undiscovered in the obscurity of the Allied archives. Only after the archives are released, complete and unabridged, will there perhaps be conclusive evidence of what really went on in the *Götterdämmerung* of the doomed Third Reich.

Was there a Threat of Global Nuclear War?

The disturbing question is whether, in 1945, the world was standing on the brink of the catastrophe of a first global nuclear war. What would have happened if, with the available nuclear weapons, Germany had brought the battle on the fronts to a halt, or if rockets with nuclear warheads had fallen on cities such as New York?

In considering such questions, it must not be forgotten that the Japanese were also seeking for ways to strike the American homeland with their own nuclear weapons that had been produced with German help. Would the Allies have given up the war in such a case and been prepared to negotiate a settlement? Or, instead of that, would their answer have been to mount nuclear counter-attacks on targets in Germany, Austria, Norway and Japan? Such an exchange would certainly not have then led to the ending of World War II. However, it would have meant instead an escalation of the war into the first global nuclear war in world history.

Otto Skorzeny reports in his book '*Meine Kommandounternehmen*' (pages 150/1, Universitas, 1993), that Hitler had warned him, in October 1944, of just such a prospect. In doing so he had used the following words: 'Of course! Even if radioactivity from a controlled radiological bomb, and then nuclear fission from an atomic bomb weapon were used the effects would have been terrible. It would have been the Apocalypse. And how could such a secret be kept? Impossible! No! No country, no group of civilised human beings can deliberately take such responsibility. With strike, then counter-strike, humanity would inevitably have exterminated itself. Only tribes in the Amazon area and in the primeval forests of Sumatra would have had any certain chance of surviving'.

Did that danger really exist? On the basis of the documents currently available it is not possible to decide whether, 'when it came to the crunch', a peace party, prepared to negotiate, or the hard-liners of the *Morgenthau*

Plan would have gained the upper hand on the Allied side. There is also too little information concerning whether the Allied coalition would have disintegrated as the result of such attacks. But from the point of view of military technology the question must be asked whether the Allies were, at that time, actually in any position to mount such a counter-strike.

In the spring of 1945, the American Manhattan project was in a severe crisis. By that time, it had already expended $2 billion of taxpayers' money. Despite that, the *creme de la creme* of international research scientists had not succeeded in producing sufficient enriched uranium, nor in developing a detonator for the plutonium bomb. According to the American author, Carter Hydrick, the Manhattan project was even on the brink of failure. The American Senator, James F. Byrnes, in a letter to the American President Roosevelt on 3 March 1945, threatened to conduct a merciless inquiry in the event that the programme turned out to be a failure. For that reason, he demanded an interim enquiry by scientists who were 'not associated with' the 'Manhattan project' as to whether the results, obtained to that date, justified continuing the nuclear programme at all.[289]

Thus the Americans, according to their own information, at the time that we are considering, were not in a position to respond to a threatened use of German nuclear weapons with similar weapons. But the fact is that after the events of April 1945 there was suddenly very great and very rapid progress on the American atomic bomb project. In the interim period, Stadtilm had been taken, on 12 April 1945, and Haigerloch on 21 April 1945. Only four days later, on 25 April 1945, the American President Truman was in a position to announce that the American atomic bomb 'will be completed within the next four months'.[290]

A short time later the case of Innsbruck, on 4 May 1945, and the surrender of U-234 in an American port, on 19 May 1945, came as further 'nuclear developmental aid'. One could therefore ask the unthinkable question as to whether the American Manhattan project would have succeeded at all without the captured German nuclear material?

That brings us back to our evaluation of the danger of a nuclear counter-attack by the Allies. The answer could be left to an American scientist who must have actually known. Wendell Radics, one of the closest colleagues of Robert K. Oppenheimer, stated quite clearly:[291] 'The heavy blow which we struck on Hiroshima and Nagasaki has stopped the world in its tracks. People think us to be the new gods who are in possession of this overwhelming power. But in actual fact we do not possess this power at all and, what is far worse, we refuse to discover it. In May 1948, the first usable atomic bombs, which were actually of American design, were dropped on Enivetok'.

However, the American 'Bikini bomb', only had the effect of 11,000 tonnes of TNT, as against the 20,000 tonnes of the captured German bomb. The American scientist Edward Teller said at the 'birth of the bomb' at Bikini: 'It's a girl'.

The 'Japanese Connection': the Germany-Japan Nuclear Transfer

On 15 April 1945, the ALSOS mission was plundering Germany's secret nuclear laboratories in Stadtilm and Ohrdruf. At the same time the large transport U-boat U-234 was leaving for the port of Kristiansand in Norway. The Type XB U-boat under the command of *Kapitän* Fehler was one of the largest German U-boats. It was to take 240 tonnes of documents and war matériel to Japan. According to the official complement list of U-234, in addition to German *Luftwaffe* personnel and two officers from the Imperial Japanese Navy, there were also German civilian personnel on board. Among them, were jet and rocket specialists from Messerschmitt and EMW/Peenemünde. According to more recent American documents there were possibly also German nuclear physicists concealed among the passengers.[292]

In May 1945, after the German surrender, the tragic voyage of U-234 led directly into the American port of Portsmouth in New Hampshire. The captain of the boat showed little inclination for continuing his route to Japan, as he had originally been ordered. Even today it is not known precisely what was on board the German submarine at that time. Members of the crew vanished without trace in American captivity, and even now the lading list is shrouded in mystery.

All possible storage areas in the boat had been used for the transport of the cargo. Some of it was even used as ballast in the keel of the boat. In addition to blueprints, microfilms and many different kinds of secret weapons parts, there were also items which were described in the official German list as 'confidential', and which have never subsequently been identified.

There is evidence that there was uranium on board, in 10 metal containers, with an overall weight of 560 kilograms, i.e. containers plus their contents. According to the crew member Wolfgang Hirschfeld, the containers looked like modern isotope containers.[293] As additional anti-radiation protection they were wrapped in gold foil. On one of those mysterious containers there were also the inscriptions 'U-235', and 'For the Japanese Army'.

Although today there are detailed descriptions of the most modern American post-war nuclear weapons, it has still not been made known what was in the uranium containers on board U-234 in 1945. Recently, it has even been contested that there was any uranium at all on board

U-234. However, it had already been admitted that there was. Knowledge of the exact composition of the uranium cargo must therefore involve something more important.

Possibly we have here one of the tangible proofs of the existence of Germany's nuclear weapons programme. Because Germany supposedly did not possess any kind of functioning nuclear reactors, or other equipment to enrich uranium, such as cyclotrons or linear accelerators, there should never have been any enriched uranium on board U-boat U-234. Perhaps today that is the reason for the silence. What, then, could have been the cargo of material captured on U-234?

The following options are conceivable, taking account of the possibilities available to the Germans in the spring of 1945.[294]

- **Uranium 233**: enriched uranium produced from thorium. (see section concerning the thorium bomb)
- **Uranium 235**: the inscription which the Japanese officers wrote on at least one container. But uranium 235, suitable for the production of uranium bombs, should never have been in Germany, at least according to the official line. But we know that the Japanese too had planned a bomb similar to the 'Little Boy' concept (see section concerning the large uranium bomb).
- **Plutonium**: Charge for plutonium bombs ('Nagasaki' type). There are in existence statements by Japanese scientists that a delivery of plutonium was expected from Germany (see section on the plutonium bomb).
- **Radiological isotopes**: It is known that Germany was working on radiological weapons, and the uranium cargo on U-234 could have been uranium which was not weapons-grade, but which was enriched by radiological isotopes. They could have been considered as a component in mixed charges for radiological weapons (see section concerning the radiological 1- tonne bomb).

Possibly there were also various other nuclear materials on board U-234.

From 1941, Japan had two atomic bomb programmes, independent of each other, under the respective auspices of the Army Air Force (NI Programme) and the Imperial Navy (F-go-Programme). But because of the war situation, Japan did not get hold of the secret cargo of U-234.

It appears that the other material did arrive. Thus, on the 7 July 1943, uranium pitchblende was ordered by the Imperial Army, from Joachimstal in Bohemia, and Moravia. Despite the fact that one of the U-boats assigned to transport the material was sunk, some of it was delivered to Japan.

In the opinion of American researchers, there are indications that another 500 kilograms of 'uranium oxide' did actually reach Japan on another U-boat. That U-boat most probably set sail for Japan before U-234. There is very little information relating to that, instead, the secrecy is noteworthy.

Transport by air was also planned as an alternative for carrying important documents and vital war material between Germany and Japan. One known attempt to make a courier flight, with a Tachikawa Ki 77, failed in July 1943. It was on the way from Singapore to Berlin over the Indian Ocean, and came under the fire of British fighters. In 1944 Tachikawa converted the fourth prototype of the Ki 74 aircraft type, a high-altitude bomber, to carry out non-stop flights between Germany and Japan. But the Third Reich surrendered before the first planned flights could be made.[295] The Ki 74 could also have been used to transport parts of atomic bombs. Perhaps that was the reason why it was precisely that aircraft type that was selected. The Ki 74 possessed a large bomb bay. In it the important working parts of the 'containers' could easily have been accommodated and brought by the quickest route to Japan.

On the German side there were attempts to fly the route to Japan with a long-range Junkers Ju 290 aircraft. But according to current understanding, such flights with the Ju 290 were never carried out. But is that true? There are certainly grounds to doubt it. Thus there exists a secret telegram, decoded by ULTRA, dated 30 June 1944, from the army and naval attaché at the Japanese embassy in Berlin.[296] The secret recipients of the telegram were the deputy minister and deputy Chief of the General staff of the Air Force and Navy in Japan. The English text reads *verbatim*: '... also, as the aircraft to be used, they could assign the one that was got ready last time for the Asia-Europe service'. It would seem to prove that by then there had been at least one flight to Japan and back.

The next attempt to transfer material could have been a co-ordinated operation, involving air and sea transport to Japan, which was to start at the end of March 1945. It looks very likely that the Ju 390 V-2 was to be used for that mission. The aircraft subsequently disappeared without trace (see relevant section). Did that flight take place?

On 24 April 1945, four British Hawker 'Typhoon' fighter-bombers may possibly have stopped a planned attempt to transport V-weapons. For weeks previously, groups of Allied aircraft had systematically combed the inland lakes between Lübeck and Hamburg, without success.[297] Their efforts were directed towards finding the large six-engined Blohm & Voss BV 238 V.1 flying boat. After its successful flight trials, the one existing prototype of that aircraft was, from the summer of 1944, hidden under camouflage netting on the Schaalsee, near Ratzeburg. There it remained under constant guard, in order to be ready to carry out very long-distance flights, requiring a range of 6,600 kilometres.[298] The changing vegetation in the spring of 1945 then led to the camouflage being spotted from the air and to the subsequent sinking of the BV 238.

They searched for weeks for the prototype. However, it is not known how the Allies had found out about it. In the post-war period it is curious that it was never made known which pilots had sunk what was, at the time, the heaviest aircraft in the world. On the contrary, they repeatedly cited the wrong pilots, the wrong aircraft types and the wrong air force! Probably the discovery of the real identity of the pilots would have explained why the Allies were searching for the BV 238 V.1. The reason for this could have been that the aircraft was to play a part in the German *Vergeltungswaffen* programme.

That is the explanation also maintained by a British post-war source of 30 June 1945.[299] But the fact that the BV 238 V.1 was an unarmed transport flying boat only allowed one possible role for it. The large aircraft's 20-tonne payload allowed the Third Reich to transport to Japan extremely important, heavy components, such as V-weapons, i.e. atomic bombs and rockets. That possibility, which had somehow become known to the Allies, could have been the real reason for the desperate aerial search for the single BV 238 V.1.

But there was another mysterious attempt, announced on 30 April 1945, in a telegram intercepted by ULTRA, from Berlin to the Japanese. That date is interesting, too, because at the time the Russians had already occupied the whole of Berlin, and Hitler had 'disappeared from history'.

The telegram[300] was probably the last known telegram to be sent by the Imperial Japanese Embassy in Berlin, to the Japanese homeland. The fact that it announced another flight to Japan illustrates the extreme importance of that operation. In addition to transferring key personnel, the operation involved passing on 'lessons learnt from the latest new weapons'. One must ask what important 'lessons' those could have been. In any event, it is certain that the Ju 290 was not able to carry heavy payloads to Japan.

The *Luftwaffe Generalmajor* Wild and a 'second person' were to accompany the flight to Japan. But that was never mentioned in the Japanese telegram. Research shows that the second person could have been the capable *Gruppenführer* Heinz Führer. After Saur and Geist, he was one of the leading people in the armaments ministry. Curiously, however, Heinz Führer disappeared without trace at the end of April 1945.

The Ju 290 flight to Japan, like the flight of the Ju 390, was to take the polar route from Bardufoss, in northern Norway. The route led from the Bering Strait, over the Kamchatka peninsula, to the island of Pamuschiro in the Japanese area of control. The distance to be covered was 7,700 kilometres. As the transport aircraft, a Ju 290 with increased performance was to be used. It had a range of 9,000 kilometres at a service ceiling of 6,000 metres. By allowing for 14.4% additional range, a wide safety margin was allowed for that secret flight. In addition to *Generalmajor* Wild and *Gruppenführer* Geist, there were to be one pilot, one navigator, one flight engineer and one wireless operator on board.

The flight was ordered for 8 May 1945, the day on which Germany surrendered. The flight was never made and *Generalmajor* Wild was taken prisoner by the British. It would be interesting to find out where he was captured by the British, and what documents he had with him. Was he already waiting in Norway for the flight to depart, and also waiting for Heinz Führer?

To date, with the exception of telegrams that have been published, neither the Americans nor the Japanese have ever said what really happened in 1944/45, in the Germany to Japan transfer. What can be the reason for this silence?

Perhaps *'Genzai Bakudan'*, the Japanese atomic bomb, was also developed in Germany. It does not seem impossible. One has only to think of the reports of 'Japanese guests' in the secret factories in Ohrdruf. Unfortunately, to date we do not even know the names of the Japanese scientists who were working in Germany. Despite that, from all the information it can be concluded that the Axis Powers' uranium bomb was jointly developed by the Germans and the Japanese. Many things point in that direction. It would also explain why details of experience gained, and also materials, were being sent to Japan.

The English author Philip Henshall[301] reports that on the list of German materials that it was planned to transfer to Japan in March 1945 there were also large quantities of beryllium. At that time, beryllium, in the context of nuclear reactors and special nuclear weapons, was almost as important as uranium U 235. Germany and the USA had known of its usefulness since 1943. Therefore it is clear that in 1945 Germany wanted to send a large quantity of it to Japan. Was that a coincidence? Is that not further evidence, that in 1945 the work carried out on nuclear weapons by Germany and Japan had already reached a very advanced stage.

It must be clarified whether the German-Japanese 'Joint Co-operation Programme' also applied to the competing NI (Army) and F-Go- (Navy) nuclear programmes. In 1945 the Japanese discontinued the NI Programme in favour of the F-Go- Programme. By the end of the war, great progress had been made in that programme, details of which are not known today, especially in Europe.

On 12 August 1945, six days after the explosion of the atomic bomb in Hiroshima and only three days before the Japanese surrender, Japanese Navy researchers carried out a successful atomic bomb test of the F-go weapon on the Konan peninsula in Korea. In that test, the atomic bomb, on board a remote-controlled boat, was steered into a makeshift collection of old ships, and detonated with devastating success. Probably the aim was to test a scheme for defence against an American landing fleet.

But the successful A-explosion was no longer of any use to Japan. The Japanese were then in a similar situation to that of the Germans in April 1945, in Ohrdruf. Only that time it was not the Americans, but the Russians who were advancing. All 'incriminating' material was to be burnt and blown up. According to available reports, however, most of the scientists were taken prisoner by the Russians.

A Japanese naval general managed to escape with vital papers. When in the postwar period he tried to sell his knowledge to the Russians, along with the F-go secret plans which he had saved, the American OSS secret service, the predecessor of the CIA, was able to prevent it in time. In that way the Americans gained possession of the documents relating to the Japanese uranium bomb. Sources agree in stating that it was said to have been largely similar to the 'Little Boy' bomb from Stadtilm/Ohrdruf.

Conclusion

This book could give the impression at its conclusion that at the end of the war, the last military chance of the Third Reich was well and truly thrown away. The logical consequence was total defeat in which everything became welcome booty for the victors. Germany had ample potential to win the race for the atomic bomb and thus to win the war. Therefore the question, even if it appears absurd today, is why the chance was thrown away, even though the potential of weapons was fully recognised by the leaders of the Third Reich.

It is striking how many German research groups were working in widely scattered locations, on parallel, but also partly competing, nuclear projects. For reasons of security, those groups often knew little or nothing of the other groups. There were also bitter antagonisms among the researchers themselves.

But those circumstances, which could almost be called chaotic, are not peculiar to the German nuclear weapons programme alone, but resemble the problems that were evident in the entire armaments economy of the Third Reich. There is no doubt that that caused considerable time to be lost. But time was one of the commodities the Third Reich had in only short supply.

Therefore, it is incomprehensible, in a state such as the Third Reich, completely directed towards total war, how it could happen that the uranium bomb was probably ready, in prototype form as early as July 1944, but never came to be used. One of the reasons could be because the Germans failed to provide suitable carrier systems in time. From the summer of 1944, the aircraft, rockets and U-boats, developed with the greatest haste, were certainly revolutionary. However they came too late.

Despite all those adversities, we know of several attempts that were made to deploy the nuclear miracle weapons. In the interests of a chance for a turn in the fortunes of war, in favour of the Germans, as was promised by their leaders, the German frontline soldiers held out to the last. They kept their positions against an enemy who had complete material superiority. All their hopes and sacrifices, however, were to be bitterly disappointed. Contradictory orders, confusion about areas of responsibility, indecision and sabotage from within and without, are the most likely reasons for the failure of Hitler's nuclear bomb plans.

The motives of the protagonists, in the evident attempts to prevent a possible use of the German atomic bomb, are still unknown, even today. Were they heroism, humanity and a spirit of resistance, or were they treachery and weakness? Was there perhaps a financial background? In any event, in 1946 Herman Göring claimed to have prevented the use of such a 'world destroying' weapon. However, it is not possible to check the veracity of his claim. Perhaps some light may be shed on the mystery if it were known what became of *SS-Obergruppenführer* Dr Kammler after the war. He knew everything concerning the developments of the miracle weapons.

Today, the dropping of atomic bombs on Hiroshima and Nagasaki rightly remain symbols of endless human suffering. We can therefore say, that in 1945 it was a matter of great good fortune that the world was spared further nuclear strikes. We can only hope that, despite the continually increasing number of states that have their own nuclear weapons, this will continue to be the case in the future.

Epilogue

On being arrested on 7 May 1945, when Hermann Göring spoke the words quoted at the beginning of this book, he was doubtless firmly convinced that he had saved the world from annihilation by an 'artificial sun' created by atomic bombs. Obviously, the arguments of the 'reasonable scientist' who warned him, had been able to impress him for a longer period than had Hitler. Perhaps he may even have believed that because of it he would have been welcomed with open arms by the Allies, as a hero.

However, he was mistaken.

APPENDIX I

Japan's Nuclear Bombers

The nuclear bomb projects of Germany and Japan began completely independently of each other. But during the last years of the war there were so many parallels and overlaps that it seems appropriate to cast a glance at the projects on the Japanese side (see section on atomic transfer).

On the basis of available material,[302] it seems that the nuclear weapons planned by the Japanese were a bomb weighing 850 kilograms and a larger bomb of the 4-tonne class. It is also conceivable that they were planning an isotope bomb weighing 250 kilograms. The 850-kilogram bomb was to serve as the main offensive weapon of the Aichi A6A1 *Seiran* special bomber, and the Nakajima *Kikka* jet powered *kamikaze* aircraft, both of which were to be carried by submarine.

It was planned that the Aichi A6A1 *Seiran* would be carried on the huge vessels of the hyper-submarine Class I-400. With an operational radius of 41,575 nautical miles they were to be in a position to sail to any port in the world and back. The I-400 submarines were fitted with a special crane that could lift a weight of 3.5 tonnes, an aircraft launcher, and a huge waterproof hangar with electrically powered doors. 18 such submarines were to be built. But at the end of the war, in practical terms, only three were completed. Each one of the boats could carry three M6A1s. Since the construction of the large I-400 submarine took longer than expected, another four large Class I-13 submarines were converted to carry aircraft, with each of the submarines being able to carry two M6A1s. Two more I-13 converted submarines were completed before the end of the war.

The M6A1 *Seiran* had first flown in November 1943 and was powered by a 1400hp Aichi 'Atsuta' engine, built on licence from Daimler-Benz. Only 28 would be built by the end of the war. The version of the two-seater aircraft, without floats, was to carry an 850-kilogram bomb under the fuselage. The version with floats was to carry a 250-kilogram bomb. The range of the aircraft with floats was 1,146 kilometres, without floats it was 1,532 kilometres. It can be considered relatively certain that an attack, using the aircraft without floats, would have involved a take-off using a catapult arrangement. After carrying out the mission, the crew would return into the vicinity of the U-boat and be picked up there. The M6A1 was brilliantly designed, so that despite the cramped conditions in a submarine, the aircraft could be prepared for take-off in less than seven minutes. In order to facilitate assembly at night, all the important parts of the aircraft were painted with fluorescent paint.

From the outset, the planned purpose of the M6A1 was to make surprise attacks on cities on the West Coast of the USA, or on the Panama Canal. For such attacks the 'First Submarine Flotilla' was formed. It consisted of two submarines of the I-400 Class and two of the I-13 Class. It was finally decided to carry out an attack on the locks of the Panama Canal. Such an attack would strike the most serious possible blow at American supplies for the planned invasion of Japan. Using models of the Canal Zone, the crews were thoroughly trained for a surprise attack planned for the end of August 1945. The training exercises took place in Nanao Bay. Since Nanao Bay is more like San Francisco Bay than the Bay of Panama, there are ongoing arguments as to whether in fact an alternative attack on San Francisco was planned. The argument has not yet been definitively resolved.[303]

The exercises of the 'First Submarine Flotilla' continued until 12 June 1945. From that date there was a sudden and significant change of plan. Instead of an attack on the Panama Canal, or even alternatively San Francisco, it was planned to carry out a considerably less ambitious attack on 17 August 1945, on units of the US Fleet at Ulithi Atoll. It is not known what led to that abrupt change of target. Recent knowledge strongly suggests the cause was the non-arrival of the German U-boat U-234, which was expected at the time in Singapore. U-boat U-234 had long since fallen into American hands. To test the soundness of that theory, which is also confirmed by Japanese sources, it would be extremely important to know exactly what kind of uranium cargo was being carried on the U-234. Did the surrender of U-234 save America from a Japanese nuclear attack? Despite the fact that further German material did not arrive, the Japanese continued their nuclear weapons programme.

Nakajima 'Kikka'

As early as the summer of 1944, the special Nakajima *Kikka* suicide aircraft was designed for defence against an enemy invasion. That was within the context of a new weapons programme to prevent the defeat of Japan. The *Kikka* looked like a smaller version of the Messerschmitt Me 262. Many parts of the aircraft were replacement or improvised parts from other aircraft. It had a wingspan of 9.76 metres, a length of 9.46 metres and was to be powered by two NE-20 jet engines each providing 472 hp. Despite frequent air raids, the first prototype was finally completed on 25 June 1945, and made its first flight on 7 August 1945. Although there was further development of the aircraft as a fighter, a training and reconnaissance version were also planned. The main purpose of the *Kikka* was to carry out a *kamikaze* attack with nuclear weapons, against the American invasion fleet. The effectiveness of such a bomb against shipping, was tested in August 1945 in Korea.[304] When Japan surrendered, the second prototype was almost ready to fly. At that time, there were further prototypes and production aircraft in various stages of construction.

Nakajima G8N1 'Renzan'

The same factory in which the Nakajima *Kikka* was produced, also produced the four-engined land-based Nakajima G8N1 *Renzan* bomber, codenamed Rita. The aircraft had been planned since September 1944. With a 4-tonne bomb load it was to achieve a range of 6,500 kilometres at a maximum speed of 603 kilometres per hour. But in that instance too, it must be noted that, officially, exactly as on the German side, there was no Japanese 4-tonne bomb. The Navy's commission for 48 G8N1s was also much too small, for any credible use, in normal conventional operations. It might be possible that the G8N1 was to have a similar purpose as the German miracle weapons' carriers.

The Japanese plans envisaged that all the aircraft would be completed by September 1945. The first flight of the first prototype took place in October 1944. The second prototype, however, only completed its first flight on 12 April 1945. The first test flight of the third aircraft took place even later, in June 1945. But the same month, after the fourth aircraft was completed, production was halted. The flight trials of the G 8N1 were constantly interrupted by enemy air raids. The third prototype was destroyed on the ground by aircraft of the US Navy. It should be noted that one of the remaining G8N1s was taken to the USA immediately after the Japanese surrender. But there are no records available of American assessments of that machine. It may be that something was to be concealed. Or again, it may be a coincidence.

Nakajima G10N1 'Fugaku', Project 'Z'

An even more mysterious project than the Nakajima G8N1 was the Nakajima G10N1 'Fugaku', or Mount Fuji. It was a design project begun by Nakajima, in April 1943, as Project 'Z'. Chaired by the company president, Chikuhei Nakajima, it was conceived by a special planning committee, to which the entire factory technical staff belonged. After an intensive three-month study, the committee put forward the proposal for the Z-Plan, which included the following technical data.

The wingspan would be 65.02m, the wing surface area 349.95 square metres, the airborne weight 160 tonnes, and its maximum speed 679 km/h with a bomb load of 20 tonnes. For that bomber, the HA-54 was proposed. It was an air-cooled, inline 36-cylinder engine providing 5,000hp, created by coupling together 2 HA 44 18-cylinder double radial engines which each provided 2,500hp. The large counter-rotating 3-bladed propellers on the HA 54 engines had a diameter of 4.79m. The necessary design drawings were almost ready in the autumn of 1943, and work on developing the HA 54 engine was well under way.

A little later, aviation experts from the Army and Navy, and also from other institutions, joined the Nakajima staff. They had to speed up the design and construction of the new experimental bomber. The special aim of the joint project was to attack the US homeland from Japanese bases.

But because it was expected that the HA 54 engines would only be ready at some later date, the HA 44 2,500hp engine had to be used. Therefore expectations from the project design had to be scaled down. The planned overall performance of the aircraft was reduced by almost half. Even so, in that form the G10N1 was still able to retain an operational ceiling of over 10,000m and a speed of 680 km/h.

The planned bomb load for targets in the USA 'happened' to be 5 tonnes. Therefore it is very probable that no 'conventional' bomb was to be loaded on board the 'Fugaku'. At the end of the war the aircraft was still being developed. A huge assembly plant, being specially built for the aircraft, remained incomplete.

All documents relating to the 'Project Z' plan were burned when Japan surrendered.

APPENDIX II

Supplementary Information

The following important information only came to hand shortly before this book went to press. The author and publishers have decided to publish it in the form of a supplement.

Russian Booty

The Nuclear Research Centres on the Baltic

In June 1945, before the Trinity bomb was exploded in New Mexico, prisoners from Buchenwald reported that the Russians had found two German atomic bombs 'on an island in the Baltic'.[305]

That report is interesting for two reasons. The first is that during World War II, prisoners of the Buchenwald concentration camp carried out work in the field of nuclear armament. There, according to an available report, they produced cadmium/paraffin protective shields that were an important part of nuclear reactors at that time. Secondly, it is also known that near to the Buchenwald concentration camp some secret underground passages remain unopened to this day. It is suspected that they contain gold, jewellery and other art treasures.[306] Perhaps they also hide something that is interesting from a technological point of view.

It could be that the statements, concerning the atomic bombs found by the Russians, came from inmates of the Buchenwald concentration camp who were taken there by Soviet troops after the German surrender. Perhaps there were people among them, from the military or civilian leadership of the Third Reich, who were well informed about Hitler's former nuclear weapons programme. In any event, the Baltic coast and the islands in that area warrant closer scrutiny.

Peenemünde, on the Usedom peninsula, is well known for the development and testing of V-weapons, and for various other secret weapons developments. There are indications that at least until the large-scale British air raid on 17 August 1943, the place also played an important part in the development of the German atomic bomb. Possibly, it was not the development of the V-1 and V-2 that was the main reason for the RAF bombing of Peenemünde, but rather the military nuclear research that was being carried out there.

Later, the long-serving American secret service chief, Allen W. Dulles, worked during the war in the OSS head offices in Zurich. On 19 July 1943 he sent a significant telegram to his chief, Bill Donovan, in Washington. His telegram stated that heavy water was being brought from Norway to Peenemünde, and that a German atomic bomb laboratory had been discovered there. That alarming news was immediately passed on to the British secret service chief, David Bruce, in London. The direct consequence, it is said, was the British air raid on Peenemünde on the night of 17 August 1943. When in the post-war period the cloak of secrecy was thrown over the German atomic bomb project, Dulles too had to tone down the telegram he sent at the time. But, when questioned, he confirmed that he had 'sent some telegram or other about German rockets or heavy water'.[307]

The direct connection between Peenemünde and the atomic bomb project was also confirmed in the early post-war period. The British newspapers, the *Daily Telegraph* and the *Daily Express*, printed similar reports[308] on 9 August 1945, to the effect that the RAF had probably saved Great Britain from an atomic bomb attack. It could then be revealed, the reports stated, that the 'mastermind' behind German atomic bomb research, *General* Chalmier-Chysynaki, had been killed in the RAF attack on the Peenemünde research station in August 1943. If that had not been the case the Germans, who were expected to complete their atomic bomb by October 1945, could have completed it before the end of the war.

The investigations of a Spanish researcher[309] revealed that German documents contain no reference to the *General* von Chalmier-Chysynaki who was killed, on 17 August 1943, in an air raid on Peenemünde. It had, however, been discovered that there was a *Generalleutnant* von Chamier-Gliszinski, who is said to have lost his life on 12 August 1943, in an air crash in Croatia. Whether the surnames of the two generals had been confused or whether there is something else behind this has not, to date, been resolved.

Important events must also have taken place on the island of Bornholm. At the end of the war, Russian troops had surprisingly occupied the island. The British newspaper, the *Evening Standard*, and the Danish newspaper *Politiken*[310] connected that with a significant announcement from Washington. It said that during the war, German secret laboratories for the investigation of nuclear fission had been located on Bornholm, and that experiments with nuclear energy had been carried out there. The report said that it was also the true reason for the rapid 'liberation' of the island by the Russians. The majority of the scientists involved in the production of atomic bombs on Bornholm had immediately been taken to Moscow. Among them, it was said, had been a Yugoslavian scientist. All their equipment and notes had also been taken with them to Russia.

In any event, the German research activity on Bornholm must have been really important. According to a report in the *News Chronicle* of 15 October 1945, the leading French scientist of the time, Professor Paul Rivet, stated that with the assistance of the German research station captured on Bornholm, the Russians would be able to discover the secrets of the atomic bomb within six months.[311]

Did the Russians really find two atomic bombs, complete or incomplete, on Bornholm or Rügen? Possibly they were the small types of uranium bomb that it was planned to use with the Bf 109.

The Hamburg Nuclear Factory: Zirconium and U 235

Close to Hamburg there was a secret nuclear factory that served as an important supplier for the Innsbruck bomb project.[312] There, in huge installations covering hundreds of acres, zirconium and U 235 were produced. Zirconium is a material particularly used in the nuclear industry. It limits the chain reaction in nuclear reactors better than does heavy water or graphite. It turned out that the Federal Republic of Germany, even in the 1950s, was at that time the only country in the world that possessed the technical equipment to produce pure zirconium. The knowledge necessary for that could only have come from the period of World War II.

The procedure for producing zirconium goes back to the Luxemburg scientist Justin Kroll, and was developed at the beginning of the 1940s. On 16 January 1945 the Japanese Navy had also ordered 500 kilograms of metallic zirconium, with a purity of 99.5% or more, from Germany, for their own nuclear weapons programme. The material, probably also produced in Hamburg, was to be transferred to Japan by submarine.[313] Therefore it must have been an important factory within the German nuclear programme.

On 10 January 1952 the American freighter 'Flying Enterprise' sank in a heavy storm. Its sinking remained surrounded by secrecy for decades. The ship's crew had refused help from other ships that were in the area. It was only in 1987 that it became known that the 'Flying Enterprise' had six boxes of German produced zirconium on board that were destined for the nuclear reactor of the USS Nautilus. The Nautilus was the first nuclear submarine in the world.[314]

In addition to a reactor, 'containers with porous walls' to produce nuclear explosive, are also said to have been used in the Hamburg secret factories. In the middle of January, the factory was so severely damaged by Allied air raids that production had to be temporarily halted. The last delivery from Hamburg arrived in Innsbruck on 15 February 1945. There was enough to enable atomic bombs to be produced.

Shortly before the end of the war the installations fell into British hands. Within a few hours the vital secrets of the Nazi nuclear factory were brought to England by the British 'T-force', and a special team under the direction of Lord Cherwell.[315]

Important Nuclear Research Plant in the Far North?

In addition to the Norsk Hydro plants for the production of heavy water in Vermork, in all probability there were also other nuclear plants in Norway. The former Allied Supreme Commander in Europe and later US President, Dwight D. Eisenhower, discussed the German secret weapons in his war memoirs. But he only mentions two places by name, Peenemünde as the centre for rockets and flying bombs, and Trondheim in Norway, for 'Nazi nuclear research'.[316] While the importance of Peenemünde, for the development of V-weapons, is today known to almost everyone, we do not yet know what went on in Trondheim. What was Eisenhower hinting at?

20 July 1944 and the Bomb

After 20 July 1944, and before they were executed, 'conspirators' held in the Mauthausen concentration camp told other prisoners that the Third Reich was on the point of possessing the atomic bomb.[317] How did they know? In any event, it points to a possible connection between 20 July resistance circles, and German atomic bomb research. Important members of the HWA (Army Weapons Office), such as *Generaloberst* Fromm, were members of the resistance against Hitler. At the same time some were driving forces behind the German atomic bomb research programme. Many nuclear scientists, particularly those in the group around Dr Diebner in Stadtilm, seem to have had at least some contact with the resistance circle.

In that connection it is noteworthy that in 1944 *Oberst* Graf von Stauffenberg stopped at the Wachsenburg. The Wachsenburg was quite close to the Ohrdruf troop exercise area, and in the evening was a popular meeting place for officers and scientists who opposed Hitler. *Frau* Cläre Werner at that time was custodian at the Wachsenburg. To this day she still has a pair of binoculars that *Oberst* Graf von Stauffenberg left behind on his hasty departure. She speaks of him in the highest terms. What reasons might he have had to stop in that area?

Thus one can assume, at least as a starting point, that elements of the resistance of the 20 July 1944 had more than a chance interest in the development of the German atomic bomb. The thesis may sound rather bold, but there are statements that are consistent with it. The eyewitness Rundnagel confirmed what scientists working in Stadtilm had said shortly before the assassination attempt on Adolf Hitler. They said that 'news would soon arrive' that could decide whether the atomic weapons were used or not. According to Rundnagel, after the failed assassination attempt on Hitler in the *Wolfsschanze*, the same people told him that 'the war was lost', and that 'now it was too late for the weapon to be used'.[318] That surely meant that if the assassination attempt on Adolf Hitler had succeeded, German atomic bombs were possibly to have played an important part for the new government of the German Reich in pursuing their own interest.

We now know that long before the attempt on Hitler's life, the Allies had investigated what kind of peace conditions the German resistance would demand, if the assassination attempt were successful. They wanted to stave off the spectre of unconditional surrender. But, instead of being encouraged to carry out the assassination, they received no further concessions. The well known Soviet writer, and former ambassador in Berlin, Valentin Falin, in evaluating Russian secret archives, revealed that the German resistance, which reached into the highest military circles, made a significant contribution to the success of the Allied invasion in June 1944. By marshalling a great deal of data and facts, Falin developed a faultless argument that would be difficult to refute.[319]

If the assassination attempt on Hitler were successful, the German resistance would have a problem. What would they do if they had not been able to come to an agreement with the Western Allies, who were already in France, and who might hold fast to their maximum demands. After a successful *coup d'état*, it had to be assumed that, at least for a period, there would be some weakening of the Germans' preparedness for defence, and of their will to continue the war. In that event, the threatened use of atomic bombs against the Allies would have been the ultimate means of forcing a negotiated peace.

Possibly it had already been suggested to the Allies that the Germans possessed such weapons. There are post-war reports[320] suggesting that in August 1944 the British were almost certainly expecting nuclear attacks on London. To prepare for such attacks, a comprehensive plan was developed by the Ministry of Home Security to deal with the large-scale destruction that such attacks could cause. The details of the effects following a nuclear explosion were at the same time sent to the chiefs of Scotland Yard, the Chief Constables and the most senior civil defence officials. When, after several months, nothing happened, the preparations were halted again.

It seems conceivable that after the failure of the attempt on Adolf Hitler's life, there was, at least in Stadtilm/Ohrdruf, a temporary and deliberate attempt to delay the development of atomic bombs. Probably it is also no coincidence that the programme for conversion of the He 177 atomic bomber, which had been begun in the spring of 1944 in Prague, was also interrupted in August 1944.

Was Hitler afraid of using the 'Bomb'?

According to a scientist[321] who had worked on the atomic bomb project in Innsbruck, it was planned that the atomic bombs in Innsbruck would be completed by 30 January 1945. That was the twelfth anniversary of the seizure of power by the National Socialists. Research work had already progressed to such an extent that from the end of November 1944 it only remained to actually construct the bombs.

However, to the great surprise of all the scientists involved in the development programme, there suddenly came from Führer headquarters a completely unexpected order. It said that further work and research on the atomic bomb was to be halted.

What had happened? According to that witness, at the end of 1944 Hitler had received a very long report from a 'very senior scientific authority' in the Kaiser Wilhelm Institute in Berlin. The report set out, in the most detailed terms, the possible consequences of an atomic explosion. It said that it could represent a potential danger for the whole of mankind. The scientist maintained that the heat wave produced by the bomb could lead to hydrogen fusion, and could cause a similar phenomenon to that which occurs on the sun. That sun energy effect, which is achieved by hydrogen fission, could possibly set off a chain reaction that could spread over the entire surface of the earth. It would create an artificial sun that could obliterate the earth within a few seconds.

During a meal with Dr Goebbels, in early December 1944, Hitler is said to have told him, 'These *Profax* (this is what Hitler called the professors) have done it now. They have actually created a way to blow the whole planet sky high'. Around Christmas 1944, the scientists involved in work on the atomic programme were sent to Innsbruck on leave.

Perhaps it meant that at the same time as the Ardennes offensive was underway, and other statements say that 'atomic bombs' were to be deployed, in reality it was planned to drop radiological bombs. Such bombs could not have caused an atomic explosion, but would 'only' have caused radiation damage.

After the failure of the Ardennes offensive, and the successful beginning of the large scale Russian offensive operation on the Eastern Front on 12 January 1945, Hitler changed his mind again. On 19 January 1945, the order was issued to resume work as quickly as possible on the atomic bomb. But during the one-month break the situation had completely changed. An important supply factory in the Hamburg area had been severely affected by heavy air raids. Only on 15 February 1945 was it possible to provide a replacement supply. That meant a delay of some two months. The order to halt the programme could have contributed significantly to delaying the production of the Innsbruck bomb.

Who was the 'very senior scientific authority', from the Kaiser Wilhelm Institute in Berlin, who wanted to distract Hitler from the bomb? In reality, did this expert simply want to prevent the possible use of the German bomb?

A contemporary witness,[322] held at the end of the war in the Garmisch-Partenkirchen prisoner of war camp, said that there were two men among the prisoners who were from the German nuclear research programme. After two days they were recognised by the Americans and separated from the other inmates. Before that happened, the eyewitness says the two men told him, 'We would have completed the atomic bomb 'in time', if we hadn't been stopped by someone very high up'.

Was a 'Nuclear Aircraft' being Built?

A captured SS scientist[323] told British interrogators that there was already in existence, at the 'Mecklenburg Science Camp' (see following volume), a model of a small nuclear power plant for aircraft. It was 60 centimetres long and had a diameter of 20 centimetres. A performance of 2,000 hp had been achieved with it. The scientist said that the miniature nuclear jet engine was intended to be fitted to a Messerschmitt small fighter. Three different power systems were planned for that aircraft. It would have a wooden fuselage with a long skid, a BMW 003 jet engine, and the nuclear engine already mentioned. The 'nuclear version' of the small fighter was to achieve a speed of 2,000 kilometres per hour at a service ceiling of 18,000 metres.

The nuclear engine, together with the entire 'Mecklenburg Science Camp', was completely destroyed before the Allies marched in. The power plant mentioned in the BIOS report would, in any event, have had enormous weight and performance parameters for its time. It does not need to be pointed out again that, after the war, all information relating to the Messerschmitt fighter project also disappeared.

Notes on Sources

This book is the result of long years of investigation and research. Material gathered together during that time comes from the most diverse sources, both within Germany and abroad. Among other things, these include former official sources, secret documents, eyewitness accounts, evaluations in books and specialist periodicals, and also many other sources which, until now, have not been published. I have had information given to me personally, from pages torn out of books and sent to me, from television and radio broadcasts, and also from informants who wish to remain anonymous. Despite this great diversity of sources, I have tried to put together a bibliography which is as comprehensive as possible. But, in view of the diversity and the large amount of material, such a bibliography can never be complete.

All publications, relating to the *Luftwaffe* of the Third Reich, suffer from the fact that a large part of their original official documents were destroyed in Allied air raids, shortly before the end of the war. Often, in the chaos of the German collapse, technical documents were left completely intact in the laboratories, only to be irretrievably destroyed a short time later by plunderers and marauders, as what they regarded as 'worthless rubbish'.

Therefore today one is forced to have recourse to the scattered copies of such reports as are still available, in aviation companies and in Allied evaluations, with all the disadvantages that entails. A closer examination of those documents often left the impression that important pages were 'lost'. Often within them there are also statements which do not correspond in any way with the 'published' opinion. Those statements, then, for the most part stand alone, because the other sources to which they are linked have similarly disappeared without trace.

It is conceivable that vital documents relating to this subject still remain unrecognised, in private collections. Who is going to find them?

Notes

1. Franz Kurowski, *Von der bedingungslosen Kapitulation bis zur Mondorfer Erklärung* (From the unconditional surrender to the Mondorf Declaration) in GFP Congress minutes 1985, overcoming Yalta and Potsdam, page 18, Bassum 1985.
2. David Irving, *Der Traum von der deutschen Atombombe* (The Dream of the German Atomic Bomb) page 313, Sigbert Mohn, 1967.
3. David Irving, op. cit., page 8, Sigbert Mohn, 1967.
4. Frederik Winterbotham, *Aktion Ultra - Deutschlands Code-Maschine half den Allierten siegen* (Action Ultra - Germany's code machine helped the Allies win) Ullstein, 1976.
5. David Irving, op. cit., page 302.
6. Henry Picker, Hitlers *Tischgespräche im Führerhauptquartier*, Propylaen Taschenbuch, 1997.
7. David Irving, op. cit., page 302.
8. Translator's note: *Uranbrenner* (uranium burner) was the term originally used by German nuclear scientists for what was elsewhere called a nuclear reactor. The modern German term is *Kernreaktor*.
9. David Irving, op. cit., pages 108-115.
10. .
11. ibid., page 311.
12. ibid., pages 122-8.
13. Thomas Powers, *Heisenbergs Krieg - Die Geheimgeschichte der deutschen Atombombe* (Heisenberg's war - the secret history of the German atomic bomb) page 472, Hoffmann und Campe, 1993.
14. Edgar Meyer, *Die deutsche Atombombe und andere Wunderwaffen des Dritten Reiches. Das Ende der Hochtechnologie-Lüge* (The German atomic bomb and other miracle weapons of the Third Reich. The end of the high-technology lie); work in preparation (May 2001); Gerhardt Remdt/Günter Wermusch, Rätsel *Jonastal - Die Geschichte des letzten Führerhauptquartiers* (The Jonastal mystery - the history of the last Führer HQ), Christoph Links Verlag, Berlin 1992; David Irving, op. cit., pages 244-5.
15. Edgar Mayer, op. cit.
16. David Irving, op. cit., pages 244-245.
17. Hans J Ebert/Johann B Kaiser/Klaus Peters, *Willy Messerschmitt - Pioneer der Luftfahrt* (Pioneer of air travel) in: *Die deutsche Luftfahrt* (German air travel) Vol. 17, pages 212-220, Bernard & Graefe, 1992.
18. Horst Boog, *Baedecker-Angriffe und Fernstflugzeugprojekte 1942. Die strategische Ohnmacht der Luftwaffe'* (Baedecker attacks and very long range aircraft projects. The strategic weakness of the *Luftwaffe*) in: *MGFA Militärgeschichtliche Beiträge* (Articles on military history) No. 4, pages 93-109, E.S. Mittler, 1990.
19. Dan Johnson, Luft 46 WWII internet page Me 264, www.luft46.com; Tony Wood, Bill Gunston, *Hitler's Luftwaffe*, page 237, Salamander, 1978; Manfred Giehl and Joachim Dressel (German long-range Luftwaffe combat aircraft), *Waffen Arsenal*, Vol. 139, pages 39-41, Podzun Pallas, 1993; Sönke Neitzel, *Der Einsatz der deutschen Luftwaffe über dem Atlantik und der Nordsee* 1939-45 (Operations of the German Luftwaffe over the Atlantic and the North Sea 1939-45), pages 149, 160-1, 208-9, 228-9, Bermard & Graefe, 1995; William Green, *The Warplanes of the Third Reich*, pages 640-641, Macdonald, 1970; Werner Baumbach, *Zu spät? Aufstieg und Untergang der deutschen Luftwaffe* (Too late? The rise and fall of the German Luftwaffe) pages 157-161, 3rd edition, Motorbuch, 1977.
20. Fritz Hahn, *Deutsche Geheimwaffen 1939-45, Flugzeugbewaffnungen* (German secret weapons 1939-45, aircraft armaments) pages 398-409, Erich Hoffmann Verlag, 1963.
21. David Irving, op. cit., page 244.
22. ibid; Harald Fäth, *Thüringens Manhattan Project* (Thuringia's Manhattan Project) 1st ed., pages 80-1, CTT-Verlag, Suhl, 1998.
23. Dieter Herwig, Heinz Rode, *Geheimprojekte der Luftwaffe 1933-45* (Luftwaffe secret projects 1933-45) Vol. *Strategische Bomber*, pages 76-7, Motorbuch, 1999.
24. Heinz J. Nowarra, *Die deutsche Luftrüstung 1933-45* (German air armament 1933-45) Vol. 3, page 130, Bernard & Graefe, 1996.
25. Karl Kössler, Günther Ott, *Die grossen Dessauer* (The great Dessau designs) - Junkers Ju 89, Ju 90, Ju 290, Ju 390, pages 102-5, Aviatic, 1993; Nowarra, op. cit., page 130.
26. Karl Kössler. Günther Ott, op. cit., pages 102-5.
27. Wolfgang Wagner; *Hugo Junkers, Pionier der Luftfahrt - seine Flugzeuge* (Hugo Junkers, pioneer of air travel - his aircraft) pages 500-1, Bernard & Graefe, 1996.
28. *The Washington Post* of 29.06.1945, Were Ready to Bomb NY (AP).
29. Robert K. Wilcox, *Japan's Secret War*, Marlowe & Company, 1995.
30. ibid.
31. Schabel Rolf, *Die Illusion der Wunderwaffen* (the miracle weapons illusion) pages 236-50, Oldenbourg Verlag, 1994.
32. Dan Johnson, Luft 46 WWII internet page Ju 488, www.Luft46.com; Wolfgang Wagner, op. cit., pages 471-472.
33. Alwyn T. Lloyd, *B-29 Superfortress in detail & scale, Part 2 derivatives*, pages 10-14 Arms & Armour (1987).
34. *Waffenrevue* (Weapons Review) Vol. 113, page 85, Journal-Verlag Schwend GmbH, 1999.
35. Dieter Herwig, Heinz Rode, *Geheimprojekte der Luftwaffe* (Luftwaffe Secret Projects) Vol. II: *Strategische Bomber* 1933-45, pages 29 and 220, Motorbuch, 1999.
36. Ian V. Hogg, *German Secret Weapons of the Second World War. The Missiles, Rockets, Weapons and New Technology of the Third Reich*, page 213, Greenhill, 1999; Edgar Mayer, op. cit.
37. Wilhelm Landig, *Wolfszeit um Thule*, page 152, Volkstum Verlag, 1980; Edgar Mayer, op. cit.
38. Manfred Griehl, Joachim Dressel, *Heinkel He 177, 277, 274 - eine luftfahrtgeschichtliche Dokumentation* (Documentation in the context of aviation history) pages 27, 97-101, 157-9, 160-1, 205, 2171, Motorbuch, 1998.
39. ibid.; Ferenc A. Vajda, Peter Dancey, *German aircraft industry and production 1933-45*, page 274, Airlife, 1998; Heinz J. Nowarra, *Junkers Grossflugzeuge* (Large Junkers aircraft) page 123, Motorbuch, 1988.
40. Vajda/Dancey, op. cit.
41. Ralf Schabel, *Die Illusion der Wunderwaffen, Düsenflugzeuge und Flugabweherraketen in der Rüstungspolitik des Dritten*

Reiches (The illusion of miracle weapons, jet aircraft and anti-aircraft rockets in the armaments policy of the Third Reich) page 282, Oldenbourg, 1994.
42. Thomas H. Hitchcock, *Junkers Ju 287*, page 27, Monogram, 1974.
43. Wolfgang Wagner, op. cit., pages 521-7.
44. Schabel, op. cit.
45. Wolfgang Wagner, *Die ersten Strahlflugzeuge der Welt* (the first jet aircraft in the world) *Die deutsche Luftfahrt* (German Aviation), Vol. 14, pages 206-11, Bernard & Graefe, 1989.
46. Dr David Myhra, *The Horten Brothers*, pages 23-24, Schiffer, 1998.
47. Dieter Herwig, op. cit., page 84.
48. Dan Johnson, Luft 46 WWII internet page Ho XVIII, www.Luft46.com.
49. Tony Wood, Bill Gunston, *Hitler's Luftwaffe*, page 237, Salamander, 1978.
50. Dan Johnson, op. cit.
51. Ian V. Hogg, *German Secret Weapons of the Second World War*, pages 213-4, Greenhill Books, 1999.
52. Edgar Mayer, op. cit.
53. Dr David Myhra, op. cit., pages 217-226.
54. Klaus W. Müller, Willy Schilling, *Deckname Lachs* (Codename *Lachs*) Heinrich-Jung-Verlagsgesellschaft mbH Zella-Mehlis, 1999.
55. *The Washington Post* of 29.6.1945, Were Ready to Bomb NY. (AP).
56. Dieter Herwig, Heinz Rode, op. cit., pages 92-4.
57. Ulrich Saft, *Das bittere Ende der Luftwaffe* (The bitter end of the Luftwaffe). *Wilde Sau - Sturmjäger* (Assault fighter aircraft) - *Rammjäger* (*Kamikaze* fighter aircraft) - Bienenstock, Verlag Saft, 1992; Arno Rose, *Radikaler Luftkampf. Die Geschichte deutscher Rammjäger* (Radical aerial warfare. The history of German *Rammjäger*), pages 34-62, Motorbuch, 1977.
58. Manfred Griehl, personal communication, 27.3.2000.
59. Edgar Mayer, op. cit.
60. ibid.
61. Ales Janda, Tomas Porhba, *Messerschmitt Bf 109 K*, page 88, Japo, 1997.
62. Janusz Ledwoch, *BF 109 K*, page 21, Wydamictwo Militaria, 1997.
63. Chuck Hansen, *US Nuclear Weapons - The Secret History*, page 139, Aerofax, 1998.
64. Wilhelm Landig, op. cit.; Edgar Mayer, op. cit.
65. Arno Rose, op. cit., page 243.
66. Ales Janda, Tomas Porhba, op. cit.
67. Harald Fäth, op. cit., page 171.
68. Richard Smith, Eddie J. Creek, *Arado Ar 234 Blitz*, pages 103-4, Monogram, 1992.
69. Heinz J. Nowarra, op. cit., pages 177-8.
70. Manfred Griehl, op. cit., page 100; Rose Arno, *Mistel - die Geschichte der Huckepack Flugzeuge* (*Mistel* - the story of the piggy-back aircraft), pages 153-6, 272, Motorbuch, 1981.
71. Rose Arno, op. cit.
72. ibid., page 181.
73. Richard Smith, Eddie J. Creek, *Me 262*, Vol. 2, pages 348-51, Classic publications, 1999.
74. Fritz Hahn, *Waffen und Geheimwaffen des deutschen Heeres* (Weapons and secret weapons of the German Army) 1939-1945, Vol. 1, pages 348-51, Classic publications, 1999.
75. David Irving, *Die Geheimwaffen des 3. Reiches* (The secret weapons of the 3rd Reich) page 66, Mohn, 1967; Ian V. Hogg, *German Secret Weapons of the Second World War - The missiles, rockets, weapons and new technology of the Third Reich*, page 210, Greenhill Books, 1999.
76. Arno Rose, op. cit., page 154.
77. Beale, Nick, D'Amico-Ferdinando, Valentini, Gabrielli, *Air War Italy 1944-45*, pages 169-170, Airlife, 1996.
78. David Irving, *Geheimwaffen*, op. cit.
79. William Green, *The Warplanes of the Third Reich*, page 655, Macdonald, 1970; Tony Wood, Bill Gunston, op. cit., page 239.
80. DM, Deutsches Museum Munich-Penfiles.
81. William Green, op. cit.
82. Kurt W. Streit, John W.R. Taylor, *Geschichte der Luftfahrt* (History of aviation) page 338, Faunus, 1975.
83. Heinz J. Nowarra, op. cit., pages 233-4.
84. Tom Agoston, *Teufel oder Technokrat? Hitler's graue Eminence* (Devil or technocrat? Hitler's *eminence gris*), pages 725-9, E.S. Mittler & Sohn, 1993.
85. Jay Miller, *The X-Planes*, pages 68-73, Aerofax, 1998.
86. Dieter Herwig, Heinz Rode, op. cit., pages 84-92; Dan Johnson, Luft46 WWII internet page Ar 555, www.luft46.com.
87. Revell Deutschland, internet page, 1999.
88. Dieter Herwig, Heinz Rode, op. cit., pages 84-92.
89. David Myhra, *Secret aircraft designs of the Third Reich*, page 258, Schiffer, 1999.
90. Dieter Herwig, Heinz Rode, op. cit., pages 128-31.
91. Wolfgang Wagner, *Die ersten Strahlflugzeuge der Welt* (The first jet aircraft in the world) pages 206-11, Bernard & Graefe, 1989.
92. Dieter Herwig, Heinz Rode, op. cit., pages 206-11.
93. Dieter Herwig, Heinz Rode, op. cit., pages 144-5; Dan Johnson, op. cit., internet page Ju EF 132.
94. Dan Johnson, op. cit., internet page EF 140; David Myhra, op. cit., pages 258-260.
95. *Luftfahrt International*, No.24, pages 3797-3820, Publ. Archiv Pawlas, 1977; Dieter Herwig, Heinz Rode, op. cit., pages 102-7; Heinz J. Nowarra, op. cit., pages 156-158.
96. Luftfahrt International, op. cit.
97. Dieter Herwig, Heinz Rode, op. cit., pages 102-7.
98. David Masters, *German Jet Genesis*, page 42, Janes, 1982.
99. All photographs of captured G-10 aircraft published to date have only been of *Mistel 3* conversions.
100. File PH/Int./Adm. NO XXXI-3, Alsos Dr Salant.
101. Mark Walker, *Die Uranmaschine - Mythos und Wirklichkeit der deutschen Atombombe* (The uranium reactor - the myth and reality of the German atomic bomb) pages 178-82, Siedler, 1990.
102. Michel Bar-Zohar, *Die Jagd auf die deutschen Wissenschaftler* (The hunt for the German scientists) (1944-1960) pages 195-7, Ullstein, 1996.
103. Chuck Hansen, *US Nuclear Weapons, The Secret History*, page 140, Aerofax, 1988.
104. Geoffrey Brooks, *Hitler's Nuclear Weapons*, pages 35, 69, Leo Cooper, 1992; Philip Henshall, *Vengeance. Hitler's nuclear weapon - Fact or Fiction?*, pages 146, 147, Alan Sutton, 1995.
105. ibid., page 142.
106. Geoffrey Brooks, op. cit., page 122.
107. ibid.
108. ibid., page 36.
109. ibid., page 45.
110. ibid., pages 122-3.
111. ibid., page 69.
112. ibid., page 69.
113. ibid., page 131.
114. ibid., page 135.
115. Sidney Trevethan, personal letter to Philip Henshall.
116. Sidney Trevethan, *The Controversial Cargo of U 234*, Revision 9, 1998.
117. Henry Picker, *Hitlers Tischgespräche im Führerhauptquartier*, pages 42, 188, 493, 531, 683, 443, 585, 531.
118. Information given personally by Markus Schmitzberger, 26.3.2000.
119. USS Report A-44, 136/5985 of 7.11.1944.
120. Edgar Mayer, op. cit.; Thomas Mehner, letter to the author

dated 26.1.1999.
121. David Irving, *Die Geheimwaffen des Dritten Reiches*, page 95; Wilhelm Landig, op. cit.
122. Edgar Mayer, op. cit.
123. Henry Picker, op. cit.
124. Edgar Mayer, op. cit.
125. The majority of German casualties in Operation *Bodenplatte* were caused by German flak units, who had not been previously informed of the attack. Was it the chaos that prevailed on the German side at the time that was responsible for this, or was sabotage at work here too?.
126. David Irving, *Der Traum von der deutschen Atombombe*, page 324.
127. Information given personally to the author by Thomas Mehner: Speer indicated that in Spring 1945 he had plans to get rid of Hitler, if Hitler was about to use a certain weapon at the risk of endangering the German population.
128. Edgar Mayer, op. cit.
129. Markus Schmitzberger, op. cit.
130. Incom. Cable 20.4.1945, USS National Archives, Washington DC, RG 260 Entry 121, Box 136, 1985.
131. Markus Schmitzberger, op. cit.
132. David Myhra, *The Horten bothers and their all wing aircraft*, pages 226 and 227, Schiffer, 1998.
133. Philip Henshall, personal letter.
134. *Stadtverwaltung* (municipal administration) Haigerloch, Atom-Museum Haigerloch, pages 134, 135, Eigenverlag, 1990.
135. Thomas Powers, op. cit., page 557.
136. John V.H. Dippel, *Two against Hitler: Stealing the Nazis' best-kept secrets*, pages 87-91, Praeger Publications, 1993.
137. *Luftfahrt International*, No. 24, page 3816, publications archive Karl R. Pawlas, 1977.
138. David Irving, *Der Traum von der deutschen Atombombe*, page 251.
139. A.P.W./U (Ninth Air Force) 96/1945, 373.2 of 19 August 1945, Investigation, Research, Developments and Practical Use of the German Atomic Bomb, Pkts Nos 47 to 53, published by COMNAVEU, 1946.
140. Ernst Peter, *Der Weg ins All - Meilensteine zur bemannten Raumfahrt* (The way into space - milestones on the road to manned space travel), pages 123-8, Motorbuch, 1988.
141. David Irving, *Der Traum von der deutschen Atombombe*, page 251.
142. Harald Fäth, *Thüringens Manhattan Project*, CTT-Verlag, Suhl, 1998; Harald Fäth, *Geheime Kommandosache - S III Jonastal und die Siegeswaffenproduktion* (The secret command affair - S III Jonastal and the production of miracle weapons) CTT-Verlag, Suhl, 1999; Edgar Mayer, op. cit.
143. Here we should recall the leading role played by the later opponent of Hitler, *Generaloberst* Fromm, in the German atomic bomb programme. Even Heisenberg took part in meetings of the so-called *Mittwochsgesellschaft* (Wednesday Club), among whose members were prominent conspirators. According to eyewitnesses from Stadtilm, scientists there linked the use of the atomic bomb indirectly with the success of the 20 July 1944 assassination attempt on Hitler. Did they want to use the bomb to force a peace deal?.
144. Edgar Mayer, op. cit.
145. Geoffrey Brooks, *Hirschfeld - The Story of a U-boat NCO as told by Wolfgang Hirschfeld*, pages 200, 216, US Naval Institute Press, 1996.
146. ibid.
147. ibid.
148. Thomas Mehner, information given to the author on 10.7.1999.
149. A.P.W./U. (Ninth Air Force) 96/1945, 373.2 of 19 August 1945, Investigation, Research, Developments and Practical Use of the German Atomic Bomb, Pkts Nos 47 to 53, published by COMNAVEU, 1946.
150. www. Geheimprojekte.at, World War internet page, 1999/2000.
151. Stefan Tiedke, information given to the author concerning US aerial photographs of the Kummersdorf training area taken in 1945 (16.2.2000).
152. Manfred Griehl, *Heinkel He 111 Kampfflugzeug, Torpedobomber, Transporter*, pages 278-279, Motorbuch, 1997.
153. www.Geheimprojekte.at, World War internet page, 1999/2000.
154. Thomas Mehner, information given personally to the author on 10.2.2000.
155. Harald Fäth, *Geheime Kommandosache*, op. cit., pages 81-84; Edgar Mayer, op. cit.
156. Theodor Benecke, Karl Heinz Hedwig, Joachim Herrmann, *Flugkörper und Lenkraketen* (Flying bombs and guided missiles) *Die deutsche Luftfahrt* (German aviation) Vol. 10, page 37, Bernard & Graefe, 1987.
157. Edgar Mayer, op. cit.
158. Thomas Mehner, letter to the author of 8.8.1998.
159. Chuck Hansen, *US Nuclear Weapons - The Secret History*, pages 172/173, 216, 221, Aerofax, 1998.
160. Harald Fäth, op. cit. (*Thüringens Manhattan Project and Geheime Kommandosache*).
161. Al Christman, *Target Hiroshima*, page 178, Naval Institute, 1998.
162. ibid.
163. David Irving, *Der Traum von der deutschen Atombombe*, op. cit., page 251.
164. Robert K. Wilcox, *Japan's Secret War. Japan's race against time to build its own atomic bomb*, Marlowe, 1995.
165. Harald Fäth, *Thüringens Manhattan Project*, op. cit., pages 156, 158.
166. Thomas Mehner, personal letter to the author of 8.8.2000.
167. Thomas B. Allen & Norman Polmar, *Codename Downfall, The secret plan to invade Japan*, pages 314-6, Headline Book publications, 1995.
168. Chuck Hansen, op. cit.
169. Markus Schmitzberger, information given personally on 26.3.2000.
170. Renato Vesco, *Intercept UFO*, page 105, Pinnacle, 1976.
171. Franz Kurowski, *Von der bedingungslosen Kapitulation bis zur Mondorfer Erklärung* (From the unconditional surrender to the Mondorf Declaration) in: GFP e.V. Congress Papers 1985 *Jalta und Potsdam überwunden* (Yalta and Potsdam overcome) pages 16-22, Bassum, 1985.
172. Wilhelm Landig, *Wolfszeit um Thule*, page 151, Volkstum, 1976.
173. Document Burgenland, 2000.
174. Leslie E. Simon, *Secret Weapons of the Third Reich*, page 26, W.E. Inc., 1971.
175. Franz Kurowski, op. cit.
176. ibid.
177. Diter Herweg, Heinz Rode, op. cit., page 94.
178. J. Miranda, P. Mercado, *Die geheimen Wunderwaffen des III Reiches. Die deutschen Raketen- und Raketenflugzeugprojekte* (The secret miracle weapons of the Third Reich. The German rocket and rocket-powered aircraft projects) 1934-1945, pages 48-9, Flugzeug Publikations GmbH, 1995.
179. Fritz Hahn, op. cit., page 265.
180. Leslie E. Simon, op. cit.
181. William Green, *The warplanes of the Third Reich*, page 655, MacDonald, 1970.
182. Hans-Peter Dabrowski, letter of 29.11.1998.
183. Despite the differing weight details, it could well have been the same bomb. This also happens in connection with other bomb projects: for instance, the weight of the 4-tonne Sänger bomb varies, according to which sources are used, between 3.6 and 3.8 tonnes, etc.
184. William Green, op. cit.

185. Fritz Hahn, op. cit.
186. Harald Fäth, *Thüringens Manhattan Project*, op. cit., pages 150-1/156-7.
187. Chuck Hansen, op. cit.
188. F.G. Houtermans, Gerard R. Kuiper, How to use thorium for nuclear energy from fission, letter of 3 September 1945 (ALSOS).
189. Philip Henshall, personal letter of 25.4.2000.
190. David Irving, *Der Traum von der deutschen Atombombe*, op. cit., pages 220-4.
191. Edgar Mayer, op. cit.
192. Wilhelm Landig, op. cit., page 149.
193. William R. Lyne, *Space Aliens from the Pentagon*, pages 38/9, 78/9, Creatopia, 1993.
194. ibid.
195. Karsten Porezag, *Geheime Kommandosache*, page 46, Wetzlardruck GmbH, 1996.
196. .
197. ibid.
198. Edgar Mayer, op. cit.
199. Larson, Georg A., "America's atomic cannon", *Journal of Military Ordnance*, Vol. 8, No. 2, 16-18, 1998; Chuck Hansen, *US Nuclear Weapons*, pages 171-3, Aerofax Inc., 1988.
200. Hilary Doyle, Tom Jentz, *Panther Variants 1942-45*, page 41, Osprey Publications, 1997.
201. *Waffen-Revue* (Weapons Review) No. 113, *Waffenentwicklungen im Jahr 1945* (weapons developments in 1945), pages 66, 83, Journal-Verlag Schwend, 1999.
202. Wilhelm Landig, *Wolfszeit um Thule*, page 150, Volkstum, 1980.
203. Guntram Schulze-Wegener, *Die deutsche Kriegsmarine-Rüstung 1942-45* (Armament of the German Navy 1942-45), page 201, Mittler, 1997.
204. Ian Hogg, *Deutsche Artilleriewaffen*, page 390, Motorbuch, 1978.
205. ibid.
206. Jürgen Michels, *Peenemünde und seine Erben in Ost und West - Entwicklung deutscher Geheimwaffen* (Peenemünde and its successors in East and West - the development of German secret weapons), page 127, Bernard & Graefe, 1997.
207. Markus Köberl, *Der Toplitzsee - Wo Geschichte und Sage zusammentreffen* (The Toplitzsee - where history meets legend) pages 75-84, OBV, 1990.
208. J. Miranda, P. Mercado, *Die geheimen Wunderwaffen des III. Reiches* (The secret miracle weapons of the Third Reich) page 66, Flugzeug Publications GmbH, 1995.
209. Fritz Hahn, *Waffen und Geheimwaffen des deutschen Heeres 1933-45* (Weapons and secret weapons of the German Army 1933-45) Vol. 2, pages 167-8, Bernard & Graefe, 1987.
210. Markus Köberl, op. cit.
211. Geoffrey Brooks, *Hitler's Nuclear Weapons*, pages 124-5, Leo Cooper, 1992.
212. Otto Skorzeny, *Wir kämpften, wir verloren* (We fought, we lost) pages 105-110, Helmut Cramer, 1973.
213. Wilhelm Hellmold, *Die V-1 - Eine Dokumentation* (The V-1 - a documentary account) Bechtle, 1988.
214. Otto Skorzeny, op. cit.
215. Botho Stüwe, *Peenemünde West - die Erprobungsstelle der Luftwaffe für geheime Fernlenkwaffen und deren Entwicklungsgeschichte* (Peenemünde West - the *Luftwaffe* testing station for secret remote-controlled weapons and the history of their development), pages 679-80, Bechtle, 1995.
216. OSS Report A-44 316, report 5985 of 7 November 1944.
217. Terry Gander, Peter Chamberlain, *Enzyklopädie deutscher Waffen*, page 320, Motorbuch, 1999.
218. Philip Henshall, *The nuclear Axis. Germany, Japan and the atom bomb race 1939-45*, Alan Sutton, 2000.
219. Otto Skorzeny, op. cit.
220. David K. Stumpf, *Regulus - the forgotten weapon*, pages 12-17, Turner, 1996.
221. Chuck Hansen, op. cit., pages 141-3, 203, 216, Aerofax, 1998.
222. Jürgen Michels, *Peenemünde und seine Erben in Ost und West* (Peenemünde and its successors in East and West) pages 75-6, Bernard & Graefe, 1997; Rudolf Lusar, *Die deutschen Waffen und Geheimwaffen des zweiten Weltkrieges und ihre Weiterentwicklung* (The German weapons and secret weapons of the Second World War and their further development) 6th edition, pages 205-6, J.F. Lehmanns Verlag, 1971; Dieter Hölsken, *V-Missiles of the Third Reich - The V-1 and V-2*, pages 261-2, Monogram Aviation Publications, 1994.
223. Markus Köberl, *Der Toplitzsee*, pages 87, 88, 170, front dust-jacket, OBV, 1990.
224. The name 'Teststand XII' or 'Prüfstand XII' is also mentioned in connection with an A-10 test pad in Peenemünde, from which the 'New York Rocket' was to be launched.
225. Jürgen Michels, op. cit.; Rudolf Lusar, op. cit.; Dieter Hölsken op. cit.; German Research Project, Rumored German Wonder Weapons, Report 3: *Fantastic German Submarines*, page 12, G.R.P. Gorman, self-published; J. Miranda, P. Mercado, op. cit.
226. Jürgen Michels, op. cit.
227. Günter Böddecker, *Die Boote im Netz* (The boats in the net) pages 356-60, Weltbild, 1993.
228. German Research Project, op. cit.
229. Robert Gardiner (ed.), *Conway's the World's Fighting Ships 1947-1982, Part 1: The Western Powers*, page 185, Conway, 1983.
230. Gregory Douglas, *Geheimakte Gestapo-Müller*, Vol. 2, pages 148-9, Druffel-Verlag, 1996.
231. Marco Spertini, Erminio Bagnasco, *I Mezzi d'Assalto della X a Flottiglia Mas* (The attack methods of *X a Flottiglia Mas*) pages 146-7/160-2, Ermano Albertelli; J.P. Mallmann-Showell, *U-Boote gegen England* (U-boats against England) pages 142-50, Motorbuch, 1974.
232. J.P. Mallmann-Showell, op. cit.
233. Harald Fock, *Marine-Kleinkampfmittel*, pages 42, 46, 80, 87, Köhler Verlag.
234. ibid.
235. Eberhard Rössler, *Vom Original zum Modell: Die grossen Walther U-Boote Typ XVIII und Typ XXVI* (From design to prototype: The great Walther Type XVIII and Type XXVI U-boats) pages 76, 86, Bernard & Graefe, 1998; Eberhard Rössler, *Geschichte des deutsche U-Bootbaus* (History of German U-boat construction) Vol. 2, page 454, Bernard & Graefe, 1987.
236. ibid.
237. Philip Henshall, personal letter, 1998; Joseph Mark Scalia, letter to (quoted by) Sidney Trevethan, Anchorage, 1998.
238. German Research Project, op. cit.
239. Siegfried Breyer, *Schlachtschiffe und Schlachtkreuzer 1905-1970* (Battleships and battle-cruisers 1905-1970) pages 333-42, J.F. Lehmanns, 1970.
240. Fritz Hahn, op. cit., page 10.
241. Axel Stoll, *Hochtechnologie im Dritten Reich* (High technology in the Third Reich) page 158, CTT-Verlag, 2000.
242. Siegfried Breyer, op. cit.
243. Hansgeorg Jentschura, Dieter Jung, Peter Mickel, *Warships of the Imperial Japanese Navy 1869-1945*, 4th edition, preface, United States Naval Institute, 1986.
244. Siegfried Breyer, op. cit.; Siegfried Breyer, *Der Z-Plan - Streben zur Weltmachtflotte* (The Z Plan - striving to develop the most powerful fleet in the world) Podzun Pallas, 1946.
245. Theodor Benecke, Karl-Heinz Hedwig, Joachim Hermann, *Flugkörper und Raketen* (Flying bombs and rockets) page 143, Bernard & Graefe, 1987 (for further discussion of non-conventional versions of the 'Enzian', see the following volume); Joachim Dressel, Manfred Griehl, *Die deutschen raketenflugzeuge 1935-45* (German rocket-powered aircraft 1935-45) page 55, Motorbuch, 1989.

246. Ralph Giordano, *Wenn Hitler den Krieg gewonnen hätte. Die Pläne der Nazis nach dem Endsieg* (If Hitler had won the war. Nazi plans for after the final victory) pages 63-4, Rasch und Röhring, 1989.
247. Arno Rose, *Radikaler Luftkampf, Die Geschichte deutscher Rammjäger*, pages 110, 112, 154, 193, 219, Motorbuch, 1977.
248. Ferenc A. Vajda & Peter Dancey, *German aircraft industry and production*, page 95, Airlife, 1998.
249. Arno Rose, op. cit.
250. Robert K. Wilcox, *Japan's Secret War. Japan's race against time to build its own atomic bomb*, pages 23, 28-34, 69-73, 80-85, 124-9, 134-5, Marlowe, 1995.
251. Gregory Douglas, *Geheimakte Gestapo Müller* (Gestapo Müller secret documents) Vol.2, pages 139-42, Druffel, 1996.
252. Thomas Powers, *Heisenbergs Krieg*, pages 473, 475, Hoffmann und Campe, 1993.
253. Robert K. Wilcox, op. cit.
254. David Alan Johnson, *Germany's Spies and Saboteurs*, pages 52-7, MBI, 1998.
255. ibid.
256. Günther W. Gellermann, *Der andere Auftrag - Agenteneinsätze deutscher U-Boote im zweiten Weltkrieg* (The other mission - Second World War German U-boat operations involving agents) pages 73-85 and 85-94, Bernard & Graefe, 1997.
257. Edgar Mayer, *Die deutsche Atombombe und andere Wunderwaffen des Dritten Reiches. Das Ende der Hochtechnologie-Lüge* (The German atomic bomb and other miracle weapons of the Third Reich. The end of the high-technology lie); work in preparation (May 2001).
258. Botho Stüwe, *Peenemünde West - Die Erprobungsstelle der Luftwaffe für geheime Fernlenkungswaffen und deren Entwicklungsgeschichte* (Peenemünde West - The *Luftwaffe* testing station for secret remote-controlled weapons and the history of their development) pages 402, 404, Bechtle, 1995.
259. Barry C. Rosch, *Luftwaffe Codes, Markings & Units 1939-45*, page 161, Schiffer, 1995.
260. David Irving, *Der Traum von der deutschen Atombombe*, page 212, Sigbert Mohn, 1967.
261. Renato Vesco, *Intercept UFO*, page 120, Pinnacle, 1976.
262. Geoffrey Brooks, *Hitler's Nuclear Weapons*, Leo Cooper, 1992.
263. Thomas Powers, *Heisenbergs Krieg - Die Geheimgeschichte der deutschen Atombombe* (Heisenberg's War - The Secret History of the German Atomic Bomb) page 485, Hoffmann und Campe, 1993.
264. Edgar Mayer, op. cit. Translator's note: *Die Wacht am Rhein* i.e. The Watch on the Rhine, the title of probably the best-known German patriotic song.
265. Hwrowe H. Saunders, *Die Wacht am Rhein - Hitlers letzte Schlacht in den Ardennen 1944-5 (Die Wacht am Rhein* - Hitler's last battle in the Ardennes) Vowinkel, 1984.
266. Edgar Mayer, op. cit.
267. Tony Wood, Bill Gunston, *Hitler's Luftwaffe*, page 114, Salamander, 1978.
268. Hwrowe H. Saunders, op. cit.
269. Karsten Porezag, Geheime Kommandosache. *Geschichte der 'V-Waffen' und der geheimen Militäraktionen des zweiten Weltkriegs an Lahn, Dill und im Westerwald*, page 46, Verlag Wetzlardruck, 1996.
270. David Irving, op. cit., page 302.
271. Karsten Porezag, op. cit.
272. Report *Dokument August.*
273. Edgar Meyer, op. cit.
274. Percy E. Schramm (ed.) *Kriegstagebuch des Oberkommandos der Wehrmacht* 1944-45 (OKW War Diary 1944-5) Vol. 2, page 1836, Pawlak, 1982.
275. Harald Fäth, *Thüringens Manhattan Project* (Thuringia's Manhattan Project) CTT-Verlag, Suhl 1998.
276. Arno Rose, op. cit.
277. Janusz Pielkalkiewicz, *Luftkrieg 1939-45*, page 414, Südwest, 1978.
278. Franz Kurowski, *Endkampf um das Reich 1944-5, Hitlers letzte Bastionen* (Final battle for the Reich 1944-45, Hitler's last bastions), pages 184-5, Podzun-Pallas, 1987.
279. Hans-Ulrich Rudel, *Trotzdem* (Nevertheless) pages 213-5, K.W. Schütz, 1966.
280. Franz Kurowski, op. cit.
281. ibid.
282. Tony Wood, Bill Gunston, op. cit.
283. *Washington Post* of 29.6.1945, 'Were Ready to Bomb NY'.
284. Franz Kurowski, op. cit.
285. ibid.
286. ibid.
287. ibid.; Valentin Kurowski, *Die zweite Front - Die Interessenkonflikte der Anti-Hitler Koalition* (The second front - the conflict of interests among the anti-Hitler coalition) pages 484-94, Knaur, 1997.
288. Wolfgang Paul, *Das Endkampf um Deutschland* (The final battle for Germany) pages 503, 505, Heyne, 1976.
289. Harald Fäth, op. cit., pages 39-53.
290. Officially, during World War II, the Americans exploded three atomic bombs: 'Trinity' (a plutonium bomb) in Alamogordo, 'Little Boy' (a uranium bomb) in Hiroshima and 'Fat Man' (a plutonium bomb) in Nagasaki. A fourth bomb was planned for Niigata, but - according to a statement made by President Truman - it was sunk on its way to Japan when the USS Indianapolis was torpedoed by the Japanese submarine I-58. 'Little Boy' alone contained 20kg *more* enriched uranium than the total of enriched uranium there could have been in the USA in Summer 1945, if the USA's own production indices are taken as a basis (see Harald Fäth, op. cit., page 47).
291. Franz Kurowski, op. cit., page 18.
292. Robert K. Wilcox, op. cit.
293. Geoffrey Brooks, *Hirschfeld*, Naval Institute Press, 1996.
294. ibid; Sidney Trevethan, op. cit.
295. Rene J. Francillon, *Japanese Aircraft of the Pacific War*, pages 259-64, Putnam & Company, 1979.
296. Ultra/ZIP/SJA792 of 30 June 1944.
297. Hans Amtmann, "Mistaken Identity", in *Aeroplane Monthly*, May 2000 issue, pages 38-42, IPC, 2000.
298. Dieter Herwig, Heinz Rode, op. cit., Vol. 2 *Strategische Bomber*, page 167, Motorbuch, 1999.
299. Hans Amtmann, op. cit.
300. Ultra/ZIP/SJA/792 of 30 April 1945.
301. Philip Henshall, personal letter of 27.10.1998.
302. Philip Henshall, *Vengeance. Hitler's Nuclear Weapon - Fact or Fiction?*, page 156 (Seiran/I-600) Alan Sutton, 1995.
303. ibid; Geoffrey Brooks, *Hitler's Nuclear Weapons*, Leo Cooper, 1992.
304. Robert J. Wilcox, *Japan's Secret War. Japan's race against time to build its own atomic bomb*, page 40, Marlowe, 1995.
305. Jacques Caval, *L'intransigeant*, Paris-Presse, 1955.
306. Wolfgang Schneider, *Die neue Spur des Bernsteinzimmers*, Kiepenhauer, Leipzig, 1994.
307. Thomas Powers, *Heisenbergs Krieg - Die Geheimgeschichte der deutschen Atombombe* (Heisenberg's war - the secret history of the German atomic bomb) pages 711-12, Hoffmann und Campe, 1993.
308. *The Daily Telegraph*, 9.8.1945, page 1, RAF killed Nazi Atom Scientist; *The Daily Express*, 9.8.1945, RAF killed Atom Chief.
309. Edgar Mayer, *Die Hochtechnologie-Lüge. Die deutsche Atombombe und andere Wunderwaffen des Dritten Reiches* (The high-technology lie. The German atomic bomb and other miracle weapons of the Third Reich) work in preparation (from Summer 2000). NOTE: This book appeared in print in May 2001 as the work of the two authors, Edgar Mayer and Thomas Mehner, under the title *Das Geheimnis der deutschen*

Atombombe - Gewannen Hitlers Wissenschaftler den nuklearen Wettlauf doch? Die Geheimprojekte bei Innsbruck, im Raum Jonastal bei Arnstadt und in Prag (The secret of the German atomic bomb - Did Hitler's scientists win the nuclear race after all? The secret projects in Innsbruck, in the Jonastal area near Arnstadt and in Prague) Kopp-Verlag, Rottenburg.

310. *Politiken*, page 2, 21.8.1945.
311. *News Chronicle*, 15 October 1945, page 1, 'Russia will have secret soon'; *Dagens Nyheter*, Stockholm, 5 December 1944.
312. Erwin K. Oppenheimer, *J'ai peur*, pages 32-41, Jean Froissart, 1955.
313. Philip Henshall, *The Nuclear Axis. Germany, Japan and the atom bomb race 1939-45*, pages 52-7, Alan Sutton, 2000.
314. German Press Agency report of 24.1.1987, "Taucher bargen geheime Fracht des See-Helden Kapitän Carlsen - Deutsches Zirkonium war für erstes Atom-U-Boot der Welt bestimmt" (Divers salvage secret cargo of maritime hero Captain Carlsen - German zirconium was destined for the first nuclear submarine in the world) (*Ruhr-Nachrichten*, Dortmund, on 24.1.1987).
315. *Evening Standard*, August 1945.
316. Dwight D. Eisenhower, *Crusade in Europe*, page 284, William Heinemann, 1949.
317. Jacques Caval, *L'intransigeant*, Paris-Presse, 1955.
318. Gerhard Remdt/Günter Wermusch: *Rätsel Jonastal. Die Geschichte des letzten Führehauptquartiers* (The Jonastal mystery. The story of the last Führer headquarters) pages 124-32, Christoph Links Verlag, 1992.
319. Valentin Falin, *Die zweite Front - Die Interessenkonflikte der Anti-Hitler Koalition* (The Second Front - the conflict of interests among the anti-Hitler coalition) Knaur, 1997.
320. *The Daily Telegraph*, page 5, 11 August 1945.
321. Erwin K. Oppenheimer, op. cit., pages 35-41.
322. Unpublished document *Zeuge Hugo* (Witness Hugo).
323. BIOS 412, page 8.